T

R A C E

F O R

U T O P I A

CW00501618

To the two Michaels S., Russell and Philip

BOOKS BY THE SAME AUTHOR

The Great Australian Stupor (1971, revised 1985)
Land of the Long Weekend (1978)
The End of Stupor? (1984)
Being Male (1985)
Conway's Way (1988)

THE
RAGE
FOR
UTOPIA

RONALD CONWAY

Allen & Unwin

First published in 1992

A Susan Haynes book
Allen & Unwin Pty Ltd
9 Atchison St, St Leonards NSW 2065, Australia

National Library of Australia
cataloguing-in-publication data:

Conway, Ronald, 1927–
The rage for utopia.

Includes index.
ISBN 1 86373 182 2.

1. Religion and civilization.   2. Religion and sociology.   3. Psychoanalysis and religion.   I. Title.

306

Set in 10/12pt Goudy by Graphicraft Typesetters Ltd., Hong Kong
Printed in Singapore by Chong Moh Offset Printing Pte Ltd.

CONTENTS

From the Occident: One of the first known official obsessive statements

I will make the City of the Horizon of the Aton, for Aton my father, in this place. I will not make the city south of it, north of it, west of it or east of it. I will not pass beyond the boundary stone to the south, neither will I pass beyond the northern boundary stone to make for Aton a City of the Horizons there, nor will I make for him a city on the western side. Nay I will make a city on the eastern side, the place for which my Father did enclose for his own self with cliffs, made a plain in the midst of it that I might sacrifice to him thereon. This is it.

(Found inscribed on the boundary markers for the vanished city of Akhetaton at Tel-El-Amarna built by the 'heretic' Egyptian Pharoah Akhnaton, c. 1370–68 BC)

From the Orient: A counter-statement

The Tao never *does*. Yet through it everything is done. If princes and dukes can keep the Tao, the world will of its own accord be reformed. When one is reformed and rising to act, let the world be then restrained by the Nameless pristine simplicity. The Nameless pristine simplicity is stripped of desire for contention. By the stripping of desire, a quiescence is achieved and the world arrives at peace of its own accord. . .In the way of Tao there is a principle. In the affairs of men, there is only a system.

(The Chinese sage Lao Tzu, c. 340 BC — translated Lin Yu-Tang)

THE ANATOMY OF AN ILLNESS

Now whether it be
Bestial oblivion, or some craven scruple
Of thinking too precisely on th' event —
A thought which, quartered, hath but one part wisdom
And ever three parts coward — I do not know
Why yet I live to say 'This thing's to do'. . .

(Shakespeare, *Hamlet*, Act IV, Scene 4)

It can hardly be chance that one of the greatest works ever conceived by a Western playwright is written around an obsessive hero: a tragedy of a man who could not make up his mind. Hamlet, Prince of Denmark, prefigures the modern person of intelligence in the post-Reformation scientific industrial culture, worshipping reason to the point of suffocation, only to find that the prompting of his heart must finally join with the phantom of a murdered father to reduce all his finely honed scruples to rubble. Hamlet likewise prefigures the dilemmas of human beings in an age in which healing ritual has declined and religious feeling has withered. This has produced creatures too narrowly educated to be properly wise, widely informed in the raw facts of the cosmos without the slightest comprehension of their own place in it.

Obsession is usually the disease of the person of sceptical intelligence, even as its mirror image, compulsion, is the malady of meaningless action. Both these linked dimensions of behaviour are cut off from the promptings of almost every strong emotion except a driving anxiety. The obsessive ideal thus portrays humans as predictable machines, the

rigor mortis of whose animated and well-serviced corpses often success-
fully counterfeits full-blooded spontaneous life.

As numerous clinical writers from Freud and Jung to contemporary
behavioural therapists have pointed out, most neuroses encountered in
the clinic are not so much special diseases but certain normal personality
traits inflated to the point where they overwhelm the balancing
contribution of others. Personality disorders of several kinds thus appear as a subtle to gross caricature of commonplace behaviour, different
in magnitude rather than in kind. In the case of obsessive-compulsive
neurosis, Sigmund Freud noted in 1913 that a predisposition to the
disorder was divided 'between these things which the individual brings
into life and these which life brings to him'. But always, society and
domestic culture provide the soil in which the peculiar rigidity and
persistence of obsessional behaviour is nourished and begins to flower.
True obsessive-compulsive neurosis is still relatively rare, occurring in
no more than 7 per cent of psychiatric patients. But obsessive traits
and compulsive routines, constantly fed by the practices and alluring
trinkets of the marketplace, can be seen among ordinary people
wherever one cares to look. Even our clinical and social concepts of
what is 'normal' tend to follow the over-defined categories of compulsion.

The first known application of the term 'obsessive' to clinical illness
was by the French physician M. Morel in 1866 but it was the more
famous psychiatrist Pierre Janet who first spelled out obsessive and
compulsive behaviour into a recognisable neurotic syndrome in 1903.
The recognition of severe obsessive traits as pathological thus came
relatively late in the history of psychiatry. The likely reason for this
is the highly structured nature of life and work in Western countries,
which has frequently enabled the sufferer to play a useful industrial and
social role for many years before his or her behaviour becomes disabling.
Western society benefits richly from its obsessive-compulsive neurotics.
The constant drive for order, security and certainty in accomplishment
which so torments the neurotic sufferer serves our prevailing world
view in empirical science, dogmatic religion and bureaucratic structures
all too well. All great social systems seem best served by those who
delight in efficient structures and who are otherwise filled with anxiety
or confusion where few formal structures are thought to be needed.

In the clinic the obsessed person usually presents with one or two or
an array of symptoms, all grouped around a single barely understood
objective, the banishing of unbearable anxiety or dread by seeking
absorption in a ruling distraction. Though painfully demanding in its
own right, this distraction is felt dimly to be preferable to facing an

awful primal dread. So arises the endless search for certainty and a final release from the ambiguity of existence itself which underpins all obsessive ponderings and compulsive rituals. One patient may suffer from repetitive, violent or hateful thoughts which parade ceaselessly through his mind. He knows these to be alien and disruptive to his civilised concept of himself. Yet such thoughts appear to have a life independent of his capacity to banish them. Another sufferer may be obsessed with a horror of infection and bacterial contamination. Surfaces are scrubbed and disinfected, doorknobs and handles constantly wiped, hands scrubbed to the point of bleeding, but the sense of being 'clean' lasts only briefly before the horror begins afresh.

In my own practice I can recall a religiously devout woman who felt that if she omitted her morning prayers she would insult Divine Providence. On the other hand, she believed, any wrongdoing during the day would make her morning offering to God a mockery in retrospect. To pray or not to pray? This simple dilemma took her two years to resolve. Then there was the case of a chartered accountant who took on the problems of one financially disordered business after another. Raging quietly at a duty imposed not by others but by his own deep compulsion to rescue 'lame ducks' and losing causes, he worked night and day until every part of his body burned with tension and fatigue. When his mind and body were on the point of complete collapse, he habitually fled not to his own home and bed, but to some remote overseas resort, where he would hibernate for a month or two, only to begin the same exhausting process over again. Full of exasperation and self-righteousness, my accountant patient could never decide whether he or 'the system' was at fault. In vain I pointed out that the issue for him was not one of praise or blame, guilt or innocence, but simply of cause and effect. He represented that paradox of the moralist who condemned and hated himself despite his scorn and anger toward social structures to which he was bound as surely as tormented Prometheus to the rock. His bondage was loathed and yet needed because of his hidden fear of what he might say or do or reveal in a moment of true emotional freedom. As long as he felt *intellectually* potent he was safe, though every organ in his deprived body argued the case for honest feeling. As Erich Fromm has observed, this sick 'fear of freedom' is not peculiar to individuals but can grip entire societies in time of political and economic danger.

Even ordinary people can practise simple but fluctuating obsessive or compulsive rituals for much of their lives. Many children's games, pious incantations and nursery rhymes have a ritualistic, compulsive quality which helps children impart a feeling of safety or formality to a world of change. By adulthood the realisation that we live and can survive in a world of paradox and randomness tends to make such games less relevant. Yet, the otherwise 'normal' housewife who needs to return home regularly to check whether the gas taps have been turned off; the otherwise staid bank manager who periodically has an urge to avoid stepping on the breaks in paving stones; the student who becomes uneasy or irascible if a toothpaste tube is not put back in its usual place — these are commonplaces of adult experience. They hark back to the magical world of childhood or primeval world of social barbarism when such rituals had a meaning in 'binding' the unpredictabilities of an often threatening natural world. Even the most tough-minded of obsessionals serves his or her secret superstitions.

THE RECOGNITION OF OBSESSION AND COMPULSION

There are two ways of studying any personality disorder: by epidemiological incidence in both the general and psychiatric populations, and from the accumulation of clinical records. Until the 1960s, obsessive-compulsive states were only rarely studied in large populations, if only for the previously stated reason that the distinction between industriousness and compulsion, obsession and usefully meticulous thinking tends to blur. The comic-ironic conjugation 'I am zealous, you are fussy, he/she is obsessed' has special significance here. The mean age of onset of the full-blown O-C neurosis has been estimated at somewhere between 20 and 25 years. The famous classifier of mental disorders, Emil Kraepelin, first noted in 1921 that obsessional patients tend to be of higher than average intelligence. Subsequent studies too have noted that the obsessional's ability to bear and rationalise his mental and physical rituals seems to require a higher than average IQ to sustain it.

Obsessive states and traits are believed to be more common among our middle classes, possibly because these groups are among those most driven by the old puritan-Protestant ethic. But such disorders cannot really correspond to a simple classification based upon social class without regard to family life, intelligence and ethical values. Though women seem slightly more disposed to obsessive-compulsive problems than men, males often show the worst examples of these disorders. The most significant variables involved in evoking such states of mind, seem to be (i) family background, (ii) ethical or ideological influences and (iii) capacity for emotional intimacy. Frequently in English-speaking societies there is a relationship between all three major variables. Furthermore, obsessive-compulsive personalities seem more likely to be single or even celibate, or at least involved in tepid friendships or unsatisfactory marriages. Since the obsessive condition and its signs usually antedate human coupling or intimate sex relationships, such limitations in human intimacy are likely to be produced by the obsessive lifestyle rather than coming from such coupling in itself.

Until the early 1970s there was little reliable data about the general spread of obsessive-compulsive neuroses and states through various societies. But latterly it has become clear that such clinical problems are more prevalent in Western European cultures and those American and British Commonwealth countries where the white Christian-scientific-libertarian world view has taken a strong hold. Far Eastern societies do assuredly show some obsessive traits. But even in China, Westernised and Christian Chinese are far more likely to display such characteristics than their Confucian or Buddhist fellow citizens. As for African or Pacific cultures, indications are that obsessional characteristics are again more likely to occur in urban centres where modern Western influence is strong, such as in business, technological occupations and in ethical outlook, than in areas where the old tribal norms and ritual traditions are still relatively intact. Commenting early in this century upon those Melanesian tribal societies which he knew well, anthropologist Bronislav Malinowski wrote 'I could not name a single man or woman who was hysterical or even neurasthenic. Nervous habits or obsessive ideas were not to be found'.[1]

A curious minor confirmation of the likely Western derivation of most obsessive-compulsive traits was presented to me recently when doing a random check on medical, science and engineering students of Chinese origin studying in several Australian tertiary institutions. Though the Christian, Westernised Chinese often achieved higher examination results than their 'pagan' counterparts, their success was often achieved at the cost of episodic emotional distress and decided limitations upon both spontaneity and recreational pleasure. Those from Buddhist-Confucian or neutral backgrounds were seen as being more relaxed and socially communicative. Similar reports concern Pakistani students studying in Britain compared with those completing their studies in Pakistan itself. Higher levels of excellence seemed to be attained in England at the same sort of emotional and social cost, obsessive traits often being found — even fostered — among British-based students. Though these surveys were informally conducted, I have little doubt of their significance.

What are the sort of individual backgrounds from which people with obsessive thoughts and compulsive action patterns are likely to come? Here cross-sectional research is ambiguous and accumulated case histories provide a clearer picture. More than in any comparable psychological difficulty, the obsessive or compulsive is tied strongly to his or her domestic environment. Patients rarely present in clinical settings without revealing a parent, grandparent or sibling with similar traits or problems. Even in cases where close relatives seem free in manner, confident, and lacking in rigidly fixed ideas or policies, one still finds a subtly demanding, guilt-evoking parental attitude experienced by subjects themselves in their childhood and adolescent years. 'You always felt you had to measure up and felt damned wretched about it if you didn't', was one patient's apt summary of his childhood situation. The worst cases of transferred obsessive habit-patterns are commonly linked to the kind of people troubled parents or significant mentors *are*. Yet what elders *demand* and *expect* holds an even greater potential for the creation of a childish compulsive superego.

The mention of superego brings us to the original Freudian formulation that neurotics with an obsessive or compulsive problem suffer from a savagely immature childish conscience which is never normally replaced by its better-managed, reality-based adult counterpart. Always the hellfire fears and guilts of childhood gnaw deeply at the freedom to live out one's own emotionally dictated adult wishes. Even today, when the 'hell' is no longer derived from the popular underworld of puritan Christianity, it lives on in secular forms of judgement and censorship, first from one's mentors and later more harshly from oneself. In such circumstances guilt breaks away from actual acts or deeds and becomes dread of existence itself, or perhaps even of ceasing to exist, except in further torment. As one of my haunted women clients remarked, with desperate irony, 'I'd kill myself to get free from my terrible thoughts and bloody-minded impulses if I dared. It's not physical death I fear, because an overdose of something would be easy enough. But suppose there *is* survival of the soul. I'd have to suffer some new guilt and there would be some new price to pay'. She added significantly after some thought: 'Perhaps it's better to suffer on the terms and in the ways that I know about, than to let some unknown horrible thing sweep me away'. Few obsessive patients articulate the *substitute* nature of their compulsions so well. To paraphrase again from *Hamlet*, the strange fearful pride of the intelligent obsessional makes him or her prefer those meaningless pains which are familiar, rather than confronting some abyss of madness, perilous freedom or danger that he or she 'knows not of'.

The characteristics of the obsessional state, whether neurotic or caused by situations, are well known. Let us examine three of the most important, bearing in mind that few people suffer the full cluster of obsessive symptoms at one time.

THE PATHOLOGY OF REASON

The obsessive sufferer is essentially a 'linear' cause-and-effect kind of thinker. He or she distrusts or fears most things that cannot be demonstrated in a concrete or logical way. 'Show me how it works' or 'prove to me that this is true' are the regularly ungratified pleas of the O-C person. These pleas are valid enough in the Cartesian-Newtonian world of applied science and technology, but a source of anguish when applied to the shifting nuances of daily intimate experience. 'The heart has reasons that the mind knows not of' is a proposition which distresses compulsive patients rather than consoles them. Order, tight structure, predictability, are the cravings of this threatened kind of consciousness. Rationalisation, *not* contemplation, feeling or instinct, is the lodestone to which their hopes for peace are tied. Unlike the concrete, ritualistic acts of fearful primitive people, which were designed to placate or harmonise with nature, modern obsessive traits are linked to rigid abstractions. Money, for example, becomes not merely a means of exchange or device to obtain goods or power but a self-existent reality; cleanliness is not merely functionally useful but an essential virtue in itself; religion is not merely an inspiring metaphor for the intellectually inscrutable ways of the Creator but a finite doctrinal 'truth' about what God 'wants' or how He 'works'. Reason thus ceases to be a sane testing principle for human experience and becomes a barbaric idol to which the obsessive sufferer must make constant sacrifice or be unhinged or destroyed. Logos (the symbolic world of 'the word') attempts to swallow up Eros (the domain of feeling, desire and instinct). To the degree to which our biological and emotional nature makes this aim impossible, obsessives often wear out their natural organism with their constant effort to gain complete intellectual control. 'Control', then, is one of the key concerns by which one is rendered safe in a universe of dangerous paradox.

THE ATROPHY OF FEELING

No person possessed of an *ideé fixe*, however rigidly constructed, can altogether abolish feeling. But it is the mark of the true obsessive style that most significant emotion is drained into the service of some concept or intellectual abstraction. Usually a moment of feeling is so charged with free-floating anxiety that it becomes either solemnly tense or feverish in its expression. Laughter, mirth, drollery, intellectual play-fulness are almost impossible because obsession is invariably *serious* in its unyielding aim. Obsessives do not, indeed *cannot*, become whim-sical about a thought or image so relentless that it will not let them go. Obsessive-compulsive personalities may impress the observer with their social loyalty and dedication, but this is usually undeviatingly dry and humourless. Emotion in its raw or lighter forms, helpless laughter, anger, erotic ecstasy or simple joy present some of the very dangers that the cerebral fixation itself is ceaselessly vigilant in avoiding. The 'gods' of the sufferer will punish him or her for anything not gravely considered and thrice-filtered of richer feeling. For those bound up in the weariness of compulsive, repetitive actions, pleasure (where it can be felt at all) is bound up in muscular movement and the sensate relief gained from the action itself. Here only physical exhaustion offers a temporary satisfaction. Like Sisyphus in the ancient Greek fable, the compulsive is condemned to labour without relief in order to dodge the vulnerabil-ity which might lurk behind one hour of rest or idleness. Joy in merely *being* is not only an alien notion, but a treason toward which any number of unknown gods and demons in the psyche might be vengeful.

AVERSION TO FANTASY AND IMAGINATION

The theme of obsessive 'control' drains the imaginative creativity of all but the most sublimely talented people. Freud and almost all depth psychologists ranging through Stekel and Ferenzci to Jung noted in analysis the automatic resistance of such patients to free-ranging fantasy. The instant urge to structure every set of images and passing sensations forbids easy access to the walled-off emotional world of the obsessive personality. Here we rarely see a truly creative or innovative spirit, but rather one who gives more ordered and 'corrected' form to the inven-tions of others. Many engineers, accountants, watchmakers, automotive mechanics, dietitians, even some neurosurgeons suit the obsessive style very well. Not for them the quantum leap of conception and inspiration which might quicken the pulse of a Mozart, a Neils Bohr, a Renoir or a Keats. Fantasy is at home with both light and darkness and embraces both good and evil, beauty and ugliness, as part of the basic stuff of experience.

For the obsessional there must always be a *moral* (or moralising) dimension. This forbids any openness towards the emotionally charged contents of fantasies which may encompass a woman as *either* madonna or whore, nature as *either* beneficent or terrible, a man as *either* debauchee or saint. The sufferer grimly attaches him or herself to some fixed polarity of 'good' and rampantly overdoes that attachment. Such obsessionals are most ingenious and tireless meddlers with the raw stuff of experience, convinced that they know better than to let native instinct and intuition speak to them *directly* before they are ready to *categorise* them. Assuredly, much of the reliability, order and even creature comforts of the economically developed world come to us from respecting such righteous categories. Most of the concrete marvels of modern Western endeavour come from this very determination to *polarise* existence and lay a tape measure across the firmament. But life tends to recede or wither when it is always approached in this way. The compulsive can never simply adore and let be.

These then are the three pillars on which obsessive illness or disaffection rest — (i) reason made unreasonable; (ii) complex emotions buried or evaded; and (iii) fantasy and imagination constantly bullied or suspected. All this is in the cause of a safely polarised world view from which troublesome alternatives and dichotomies are eliminated. But all neurosis implies *conflict*. In striving to remove uncertainty from the outer environment the obsessive-compulsive *internalises* a battle between the very polarities of choice and feeling he has sought to deny. Acute ambivalence, indecisiveness and doubt become part of daily experience as the illness advances. Efficiency disintegrates into meticulous nitpicking, prudence becomes a chronic hesitancy, dogmatic rigidity slides into a desperate obstinacy. Eventually there is an explosion into raw impulse, since not even the most stoical sufferer can long contain *all* feeling. A rare episode of doing next to nothing suddenly turns into doing too much or doing it badly. Stricken with new guilt, the unfortunate subject returns to rumination and tries to force his or her enfeebled spontaneity back into new containers of control.

THE CASE OF A PHANTOM CRIME

A patient whom I shall call Gregory typified some of these dilemmas. He was a foreman carpenter, greatly valued for the excellence of his work and his scrupulous attention to budget outlay. He presented with the fear that he might run over somebody in his service van. This soon became enlarged to a fear at night and on days of low visibility that he *might have* run over somebody. Despite his intellectual realisation of the absurdity of the fear he began scanning newspapers for reports of injuries or fatalities in his district. This further advanced to the point where even if he had *not* injured some person, he began to wonder if he had not *wished* to gratify such ideas of killing or injury, and began to torment himself with guilt on this score. In the recent history of his life as the elder son of a widowed mother was a longstanding memory of her gross partiality toward his younger brother. This left a legacy of resentment which the harshly implanted motherly superego could not permit Gregory to bear without anxiety. The wish to punish his mother through the agency of a fantasised removal of his brother was the real basis of this particular obsession. Alas, few conditions of compulsive guilt and dread are as easily traced to a single wish. Even in Gregory's case the general conditioning of guilt through punitively unjust moral censure (which the mother imposed but did not obey in her own conduct) was essential for his fixation to take hold and spread.

It can be seen at this point why the obsessive-compulsive syndrome can be the most agonising of all psychological illnesses. The ego of the obsessive is frequently too strong to permit him or her even the relief of a flight into a psychotic breakdown. And so the ever-fluctuating battlefield of fixation, doubt, guilt or compulsion often bears its clamour until the patient finally collapses into senility or dementia. It is also useful to see a continuum between severe obsession and some paranoid disorders. Many paranoid psychotics and paranoid schizophrenics represent a painful obsessive adjustment which has simply failed. In such circumstances Gregory would have crossed the border between fantasy and fact and presented himself to friends, family or police as his brother's murderer, or perhaps hallucinated the figure or voice of some phantom pedestrian he was convinced he had slaughtered. Having been held at bay for so long, malignant unconscious wishes finally take on the shape of a perceived reality.

Depression too frequently colours the obsessive world view, as the victim sometimes suffers such a sense of exhausted futility that a threat of constant failure or loss of worthiness becomes overwhelming. Such sufferers sink even deeper into a mire of self-hatred or self-accusation against which suicide becomes a real option. This differs from a severe depressive illness since the obsessive patient seems to suffer little of the frozen anger or rage which lies behind so much classical depression. This unfortunate has been too harrassed by his or her own demonic 'conscience' to permit much more than a melancholy wish for peaceful oblivion. But suicide too is often an unthinkable option for a depressed-obsessive personality. Death, when it occurs, is often brought about by some unconsciously dictated 'accident' or plausible misadventure. Thus the endless guilty sleights-of-hand of such a subject can remain busy even to the threshold of the tomb.

IS THERE A CURE?

The treatment of O-C disorders in the clinical setting is one of the greatest challenges of psychiatry. Only the more widespread and complex problems of various types of schizophrenia pose a more vexing problem. The boast of modern behaviour therapists that their methods hold out more hope for O-C disorders than previous analytic or reassuring counselling strategies has not been borne out by those surveys of improvement rates in English-speaking societies.

'Behaviour modification' has been used in the treatment of obsessions and compulsions since the mid 1960s. Coming from the basic argument that these conditions consist of faultily learned responses which in turn lead to abnormal sensitivity to social stimuli that most people can either surmount or ignore, behavioural treatments are concerned more with the removal of *symptoms* than with looking for causes. Despite the valid objection that symptoms must be *of* something, the patient is treated rather as a malfunctioning 'black box'. Yet most behaviour therapists would hotly reject the charge that they were neglecting human choice and individuality. They argue that both environmental conditions and the patient's anxious attempts to adapt to nonsensical propositions act as 'reinforcers' to his or her symptoms. These must therefore be restructured.

In the short term there is much to be said for the behavioural approach since it concentrates on strategies to remove reinforcing environmental factors rather than trying to break through the patient's stiff resistance to self-analysis. So far this method has been more successful in alleviating compulsive behaviour such as repetitive checking and other exhausting rituals than in helping the sufferer rid him or herself of obsessional thoughts and intellectual fixations. This is because the core of this neurosis, the *values* of the O-C subject and his or her desperately cramped interpretations of the world are put into the 'too hard' basket of treatment. The primitive stimulus-response theory which underpins behaviour therapies, with their facile aspirations to 'value-free science', rarely permit their committed apostles to see beyond the success or failure of *a technique*.

The percentage of adequate recoveries from O-C neuroses, using almost *all* approaches, has been disturbingly small — between 22 and 26 per cent at most. A key factor appears to be the reinforcing influence of most Western social environments. There is little doubt that countless sufferers, removed from the pressures of our clock-watching hyperkinetic culture and dropped inescapably into a tropical jungle or even a layabout hippie commune, would show a notable improvement. Alas, the very model of 'adjustment' favoured by modern clinical psychiatry and psychology itself shows an obsessively categorical approach to mental disturbance in general. Far from being a solution to the grossly over-systematised anxieties of this clinical group, therapeutic attitudes could well be part of the problem. I propose to say more about this in a later chapter.

In the 1950s and 1960s, surgical treatment techniques were infrequently tried by means of lobotomy or the more localised method of prefrontal leucotomy. Psychosurgery was most often used on more desperate older patients who had shown no satisfactory response to either medication or psychological approaches. This rather macho approach to the disorder was originally favoured by heroic materialists of whom there are undoubtedly too many in modern psychiatry. As one would expect from our pitifully small detailed knowledge of the role played by the frontal brain in thought and behaviour, the outcomes of surgery resembled a kind of lottery with successes and failures almost randomly distributed. In nearly half of all cases there was little behavioural change. This suggested very wide variations in frontal lobe function among individuals, partly confounding those who still insist that the brain–consciousness equation is reducible to the operations of a sort of super-computer. Not surprisingly, psychosurgery has markedly declined from favour over the past two decades.

Despite recent reports concerning the drug clomipramine, medication has had similarly disappointing results. Some unwanted side effects upon other behaviour are only a little less undesirable than those produced by surgery. Drugs usually only muffle awareness of, and blunt responses to, the worst of the ruminations, self-proddings and repetitions of the obsessional patient. The disorder is merely confined rather than quelled and usually flares up at full strength when drug administration is discontinued. Needless to say, the claims of many organically oriented psychiatrists that drugs rectify some metabolic imbalance which is allegedly responsible for severe personality disturbance are regularly refuted in detailed *individual* studies of the effects of medication upon such patients. In fact drugs hardly ever *cure* any neurotic disorder — a fact which some doctors and pharmaceutical manufacturers are not at all happy to concede.

The likely truth is that a simple adjustment/maladjustment model of obsessive-compulsive states is becoming less and less compatible with any serious study of the human personality interacting with a wider culture. Such disorders represent a chronic or acute narrowing of the sufferers' world views, greatly exaggerating the cognitive and emotional distance felt by patients between themselves and the outer world. Sufferers somehow feel torn out of the mental and behavioural pattern of the social environment, even as acute schizophrenics are swamped by their inner world and experience chaos. The obsessive's personal boundaries become like an enclosure of steel, and stiff transactions with others are as from an emotional stockade. While there is probably an inborn or inherited tendency to some types of schizophrenic disorder, no such tendency has been established for obsessional states.

Regardless of the clever behaviour models constructed by laboratory-oriented scientists (who often change the problem in the act of isolating it), it is the world and other people which drives most psychiatric patients mad. As Erich Fromm once noted: 'There is no medication or hormonal correction which can cure the ills of a rancorous family life or a moribund civilisation'. In a time of manic social change and the rapid dislocation by the mass media of so many useful customs and social values, it is the painfully faithful obsessives who still stand sentry at the leading edge of duty. Periodically loathing their personal obligations, such folk still feel guiltily compelled to offer the group and the community all they have. Sadly, this offering never seems to be enough.

'The gods have become diseases' — Carl Jung

Can there be any personal gain from neurosis, and obsessive-compulsive neuroses in particular? Ours is a hypochondriacal age surfeited with medicines, toiletries and creature comforts, where even the dead in funeral parlours may be treated to look more glamorous than their mourners. Accordingly, physical illness has become approximate to social sin. Those martyr heroes and heroines to its natural effects are a subject for the anxious fawnings and disgusting close-ups of the nightly television documentary. Far from being accepted as an inescapable burden or a vagary of the Divine Will as our flintier forefathers regarded it, chronic illness is now thought to be a moral and social aberration. It is an affront to our conviction that modern science ought not allow such things to be.

Mental illness, however, has a different status. Nobody wants to view senile prancings or listen to schizophrenic fantasies, much less to hear the tedious reiterations of the hapless obsessive on nationwide news hook-up. Psychosis and neurosis are felt to be a rebuff to our desire that everyday life should be as (paradoxically) controlled, untroubled and yet liberal as possible. Obsessive fixations are indulged as long as their connection with our own idiosyncrasies can be denied or buried in some fashionable social or political crusade. Fearful, yet fascinated, by bodily decay, we prefer to imagine by contrast that personality disorder is suffered by those weak-minded people who have nothing whatever to do with *us*. Depth psychologist Carl Jung expressed it succinctly: 'People will do anything, however absurd, to avoid facing their own souls'. And by 'soul' he also meant psyche.

A useful guide to obsessive versus 'normal' thinking and behaviour can be gained from Tables 1 and 2, which appear on pp. 15–17. Table 1 summarises the world view of the O-C personality in either greater or lesser degree. Table 2 poses the contrast between O-C sentiments and behaviour and those of the ideally adjusted person. Very few people, of course, will fully correspond to the elements of either polar position, but somewhere along this semantic differential most of us can be located, elements of the pathological and the ideal being culturally intermingled. The higher the tally of traits and concepts we can recognise in ourselves and others on the right-hand side of the two tables, the more pathological the personality is likely to be.

Carl Jung is also responsible for the arresting comment that far from being wholly an affliction, a neurosis is also trying usefully to remind the sufferer of something denied or waylaid in his or her own life. Jung noted:

> A neurosis has really come to an end when it has overcome a wrongly-oriented ego. The neurosis itself can heal us. The man is ill, but the illness is an attempt of nature to heal him. We can therefore learn a great deal for the good of our health from the illness itself. That which appears to the neurotic person as absolutely to be rejected is just the part of us which contains the true gold which we should otherwise never have found.[2]

Jung's observation has special force for the compulsive citizen who is forever trying to amputate unwanted portions of his or her own psyche because these distract from the compulsive's tunnel-viewed objectives. The compulsive dogmatic puritan who can hardly bear to go to bed with his or her spouse could do with a healing plunge into a little erotic frenzy; the compulsive libertine could likewise do with fewer calculating 'one-night stands' and attempt a deeper examination of his or her dread of emotional openness and vulnerability. Likewise, the obsessively careful accountant might be helped by the exercise of some daring bit of extravagance; the fastidious home owner could benefit from an occasional delve into some honest dirt.

Table 1: Comparison between Non-Obsessional and Obsessional worldviews

'Normal' cognitive and emotional outlook	*Obsessive-Compulsive outlook*
Person feels part of the environment and blends into it. Present-centred, here-and-now orientation. Past used as an occasional reference. Future expectations are flexible and adaptable, providing a hint of adventure.	Person feels apart from the environment and cannot feel natural within it. Dominated by fixations and ruminations about the past. Wants a *certain* 'gilt-edged' future. Unable to engage freely in present events to exclusion of 'what-if. . .' and 'what-will-happen-next' considerations.
Can accept ambiguity and recognises the paradoxical nature of reality — which can often be both 'this' *and* 'that'. Ready to revise a viewpoint when necessary. Prefers to 'bridge' polarities rather choosing their extremes.	Fearful or intolerant of ambiguity. Strives to exclude paradox in both the world and self. Reality seen as either 'this' *or* 'that'. Shows a determination to reduce all questions to a single answer.
Treats time-frameworks punctiliously, responsibly, but loosely. Rejects clock-watching, which interrupts the flow of behaviour. Trusts a personal sense of adequate time spent.	Haunted by time and its passing. Divides life into innumerable commitments which there never seems enough 'time' to fulfil. Much talk of 'time-wasting', with little insight into how the *inner* sense of time works.
Has good judgement of the match of personal capacity to tasks. Accepts reasonable limitations. Sets aside undue doubts in order to develop a chosen project to the full. Works steadily without applying unnecessary pressure, exceptions being in the case of genius.	Constantly overestimates or underestimates the match between capacity and task. Either becomes immobilised by doubts and frustrations or works frenetically to 'catch up'. Drives self and others to stressful yet counterproductive peaks of performance.

Table 1: **(Cont.)**

'Normal' cognitive and emotional outlook	Obsessive-Compulsive outlook
Treats body as a valuable servant for work, reflection and play. Cares properly for it and then leaves it to regulate itself. Keeps fit rather than tries to break records.	Hypochondriacal concern for health, alternating with stressful abuse of the organism by means of compulsive practices and abuse of substances. Obsession with winning.
Intellectual bent towards the satisfaction of curiosity and a care for quality and excellence. Enjoys reward of solutions and achievements but enjoys the *process* of doing just as much as what is actually done.	Intellectual bent towards 'performance'. Impatience and discomfort with exploratory processes. More impressed with quantitative achievement and concrete outcomes. Little real curiosity or wonder about problems for their own sake.

Indeed there can be great value in obsession, which is mostly a fanatical over-employment of a worthy thing. The world benefits from orderliness as long as it does not become regimentation, from economic parsimony as long as it does not topple into stinginess, from cleanliness as long as it does not become a morbid substitute for the 'cleansing' of one's moral self. The over-expression of otherwise worthy ponderings and acts only exasperates sufferers and those who must live with them, for these blot out so many other life-affirming alternatives. As the maxim has it: 'Nothing is more dangerous than a good idea, when it is the only idea we have'. Much of the pain of obsessionality comes from the inability of individual sufferers to accept the Janus-faced ambiguity of their own feelings and desires, so that they can really be immersed in their healing richness and variety.

Jung's celebrated but cryptic remark: 'The gods have become diseases' forms the bridge by which I propose to cross over from the individual anguish of the individual obsessive to the benefits and forfeits borne by a Western civilisation which has banished the caprices of the gods and the demonic terrors dreaded by ancient peoples, only to have them re-enter as morbid crazes through the back door of the modern psyche.[3]

Table 2: **Key words and concepts illustrating the behavioural differences between the 'Enlightened' and Obsessive-Compulsive styles**

Enlightened	Obsessive
Love	Power
Creativity	Achievement
Inclusive	Exclusive
Cooperation	Competition
Processes	Outcomes
Acting	Striving
Patience	Impatience
Awareness	Rumination
Trusting	Doubting
Calmness	Tension
Cause/Effect	Right/Wrong
Responsible	Guilt-prone
Remissive (*not* Permissive)	Moralistic/Guilt-evoking
Acceptance	Blame
Affectionate	Possessive
Detached	Over-involved
Spontaneous	Controlled
Erotically discriminating	Sexy or Puritanical
Joyful or ecstatic	Fixated or chaotic
Moderation	Excess
Satiation	Addiction
Satisfaction	Discontent
Assertive	Aggressive
Self-directed	Self-comparing
Quality/'Better'	Quantity/'More'

Note: This type of dichotomy can be converted to a graduated 5-point rating scale for evaluation purposes — either for self-appraisal or appraisal by others. The technique is similar to the 'Semantic Differential', a device developed by American psychologist Charles Osgood.

Thus Bacchus, robbed of his periodically regulated festal days of frenzy, turns into 'demon drink' and alcoholism; the noble Phoebus Apollo, god of light and intellectual harmony, dwindles within the brain of the modern technocrat to the nitpickings and reference-listings of some narrow academic prig; Dionysus, the divinity of passion, mourning and ritual abandonment, crumbles into the cocaine-maddened strummings and lewd caterwaulings of some moronic rock music band. Moreover, where the true gods still remain, contemporary intellectual obsessions make them over into convenient ideological effigies. Jesus Christ, Son of the eternal Father, has been converted by silly divines into Dr Jesus-Bar-Joseph, social worker and agitator for 'social justice'. Gautama the Buddha, Lao Tsu and Krishna, have had their lofty meditative teachings bent to the service of crash courses in relaxation, lowering blood pressure and buttock slimming. So far Islamic Allah has escaped treatment as a similar 'resource person', but probably not for long!

As I will later try to show, our liberation from the grandeurs and terrors acknowledged by ancient and medieval peoples, whose gods, saints and satyrs still walked the world with mighty steps, has marked a smaller spiritual and social advance than we care to realise: for every liberation from some capricious alien force 'out there' or 'up there', there seems to have been a growth of some new psychic devil *within*. This has made human beings the most menacing and destructive creatures known in our solar system. As George Steiner observed in *In Bluebeard's Castle*, having long denied the hell of the Christian Gospels and of Dante Alighieri we have learned, in the age of Himmler, Stalin, Ceaucescu and Pol Pot, how to build hell on earth. Even while proudly bearing the banners of modern applied science and shrewd economics, we continue to be a horror and an enigma to ourselves.

Seen against this cultural backdrop, the obsessive-compulsive neurotic becomes a caricature of the Western consciousness in microcosm. That microcosm contains so many good things shackled to one quite mad thing. It is the rage for perfection, for Utopia, in a universe which can only survive and flourish amid its own dynamically evolving imperfection. In striving for so much pragmatic finality and psychic certainty, we have abandoned wholeness of life.

ONE

THE TIME OF THE GODS

R eligious statements are the most improbable of all, yet they
have been maintained over thousands of years. . .The fact
their vitality so far exceeds what might be expected, points to the
existence of a potent cause, the scientific recognition of which has
as yet escaped the human mind.

Carl Jung

At the time when the gods still walked the earth and haunted the
consciousness of ancient peoples, what was the status of neurosis — of
madness or sanity? What was the shape of the human psyche and its
social expression in a world without modern doubt and scepticism?
The more obvious and conventional view is that we are well rid of the
caprices of the old gods who dwelt behind the lightning and tempest,
producing our fatalities and degradations along with a host of fairies,
demons and hobgoblins. Their menacing aspect is thought to be dispelled
under the benign searchlight of the modern science of anthropology.
It is assumed in dozens of antiseptic learned journals that science has
banished superstition and *reduced* our problems to simple rational for-
mulae of cause and effect. Yet our primordial shudderings still persist,
however plausibly they may be explained away as viruses or allergies,
or the result of work stresses or family power struggles. We still turn
secretly to the mysteries of astrology, divination, therapy or the more
respectable priestly comforts. We still need an outer stimulus for awe,
wonder and terror, as Aristotle observed, if only to make our minds
habitable and bearable. Science has not only found nothing to replace

both magic and the magi; it cannot even recognise that, 'real' or 'unreal', they once had a healing and harmonising function. By externalising so many human fears, ancient religion made it possible for people to live within their imaginative world without psychosis. It also usefully *personalised* the universe of abstract forces. The old pre-Copernican cosmos could be a savage place, but at least it was peopled with nameable beings one might invoke, anger or placate.

Assuredly the ancient world contained no real golden age to which a modern person might return for therapy. The gods of the ancient near east, Central America, India and Ancient China were frequently fickle, harsh and vengeful. Their priesthoods were eager to extract due tribute in coin, produce or even blood. In physical terms the price of remission from soul-dread ran high. Even human sacrifice might sometimes be required to appease gods who were jealous of the slightest presumption shown by their devotees. Many might die so that the harvest would not fail or monsters from the lower worlds would not strike at the social order. Yet most anxieties were external; life could be unreflectingly focused on the present and carefree when the gods relented or rested. The keeping of psychic meaning was in *their* hands and many a day before the onset of disease or death could be innocently blissful. Life seemed to have little portent beyond itself.

THE FERTILE CRESCENT AND
EARLY ANXIETIES

Civilisation may be argued to arise from two factors — the evolved ability of humans to reflect upon themselves and their needs, and the wish to build a haven against fearful or hostile things. The need for dignity and security, not trade, built the first town-fortresses and temples. Early economic activity was not possible without either.

The Fertile Crescent, swinging downward and westward from Mesopotamia to the Nile valley, cradled the world's first known high civilisations. Meanwhile most of Europe's lands lay under primeval forest and grassland, and even India and China were only fitfully stirring out of barbarism and shamanistic ritual. Almost the first fully elaborated theology and anthropology arose in the Egypt of the Memphite Old Kingdom. Supreme artisanship, artistry and high imagination, rather than political theorising or philosophy, prevailed in the Pyramid Age. The deed, rather than the ideal, ruled daily lives. A continuous, geographically enclosed civilisation made possible the development of a stable, humane and practical morality. Whilst Egyptians were prepared to enslave captives, kill ruthlessly in battle, have adulterous relationships and be economically exploitative, they were rarely prepared to murder or inflict suffering for a mere intellectual concept. This made them uncommonly cheerful and patient under the not unenlightened yoke of a demi-divine king and a priesthood whose control of knowledge and learning made it possible for the state to both inspire fear but remit sins in valid measure. Consuming obsessions were usually for the Pharaoh and his ministers alone. Only the Pharaoh heard the words of the gods and he alone was the mystical son of the solar deity Ra and the beloved of Hathor, goddess of love and fertility. Until contaminated by alien pessimism after the Persian and Ptolemic conquests, the documents of the ancient Egyptians show them to have been among the most happy and kindly of peoples. At the banquet of a king or a high noble, for example, it was commonplace by the time of the Fourth Dynasty for a miniature sarcophagus containing a mummiform effigy to be handed around among the guests with the first serving of the wine. Far from creating anxiety about the ending of life, this realistic reminder of death seems to have confirmed the resolve of the ancient Egyptians to seize upon the vivid pleasures of present life and health. The gods of Egypt, unlike those of Mesopotamia, Greece and even Yahweh of Israel, did not appear jealous of human fortunes and pleasures as long as life was lived observantly and justly under their sway. The Middle Kingdom scribe Onkshesonky wrote tersely: 'When you fare well do not be anxious lest you fare badly', a sentiment close enough to Christ's later teaching but contrary to much subsequent Christian mundane behaviour.

THE HIGHER LEGACY OF EGYPT

There has been a tendency to regard Egypt as a superstitious, polytheistic part-Mediterranean, part-African civilisation with a barbarous theological and moral system impressively masked by great works of architecture and art. But only the Judaeo-Christian world view, and the Mohammedan one which it influenced, taught that monotheism 'at the summit' was blasphemously incompatible with a 'lower storey' of lesser gods. Whilst nature under polytheism remained a continuously magical thing, an exclusively monotheistic outlook meant it came to be regarded as an inert, exploitable resource. This was to be an arrogant distinction of tremendous consequence for Western behaviour in later centuries. In fact the priesthoods of Egypt's temple schools were probably well aware that such gods as Anubis, god of the dead, Osiris, lord of the afterlife, and Isis the deeply wise divine Mother were merely sacred disguises, metaphors or aspects of that inscrutable One which the 'heretic' Pharaoh of Akhnaton was the first monarch to proclaim *exclusively* in about 1345 BC.

Contrary to the political desire of modern scholars to see Akhnaton's world view as superior to the 'barbarous' doctrines of the 'tyrannical' old order, the cult of the creator mummiform god Ptah of ancient Memphis soared above even the radiant teaching of the new sun god Aton and actually preceded the Pharaoh Akhnaton by at least a thousand years. The Memphite teaching not only surpassed in elegance and subtlety the crude solar monotheism of Akhnaton's period at Tel-El-Amarna, but partly anticipated the book of Genesis and the Indian Upanishads as well. Discovered by James H. Breasted in an obscure British Museum collection, there is a copy of the teaching of a Memphite priest of the temple of Ptah from the early Pyramid Age. This makes it clear that the spirit of God and that of man were originally a unity and that the 'creation' occurred when the One became 'two'. Human beings were thus the thought and spoken emanations of a Divine Unitary Deity which was seen under the mysterious outer guise of the god Ptah. The manuscript reads as follows:

> The Divine Word came into existence by the thought of the heart and the commandment of the tongue. When the eyes see, the ears hear, the nose breathes, they report to the heart. It is the heart which brings forth every issue and the tongue which repeats the thought of the heart. Thus (even before humans) were fashioned all the gods.[1]

Memphite text makes it clear that all the gods were *imaged* personifications of the various *aspects* of the One Divine Being. Mention of organs of the human body is, of course treated here psychologically and symbolically. In the words of Eduard Meyer:

> One can see how old the speculations of Egyptian wisdom really are. . .The myths can no longer be taken in their literal sense. They can be understood as a rendition of deeper thoughts striving to comprehend the world spiritually as a unit.[2]

Even so, the gods of Egypt persisted in their strange plurality, evidently in order to make the forces of life, death, time and nature close and comforting to the trusting children of the Nile. They could observe the cults of these lesser divinities, cherish their sacred animal totems and plough those haunted fields which were doubly blessed by the annual inundations of the Sacred River.

Through nearly twenty-nine dynasties to the Persian Conquest the Pharaoh ruled as a demi-divine mediator between these industrious people and the infinite. The Great Pyramid of Khufu at Gizeh seems less a work of stupendous royal arrogance when one realises that in this age, Egypt itself was the mystical extension of a god-king. Not until the Meiji Imperial Restoration of Japan in 1868 were one land, one people and one lord to be so symbiotically intertwined.

The quality of any culture, as both Plato and Confucius affirmed long ago, can be gleaned from its literature and music. The original music of Egypt has probably not been heard since the fall of Troy, but a rendering of the 12th Dynasty Harper's Song, found inscribed on the walls of a noble tomb, gives a hint of the poignant quality of both:

> Rejoice and let thy heart forget that day when they shall lay thee to rest.
> Cast all sorrow behind thee and think thee of joy until that day of reaching harbour in the land that loveth silence.
> Follow thy desire as long as thou livest. . .
> Set music and singing before thy face.
> Increase the delights which thou hast
> And let not thy heart grow faint. . .
> Do thy desires on earth and trouble not thine heart until that day of lamentation come to thee.
> Spend a happy season and weary not thereof.
> Lo, none may take his goods with him and none that have gone may come again.[3]

Was there ever a better testament to freedom from anxious rumination and obsession then in this bittersweet utterance of a long dead musician? This song is also a practical guide to life, which does not exclude those higher values not actually mentioned. For in the same epoch King Merikare said:

> Be not evil; it is good to be kindly. Cause thy monument to endure through people's love of thee. Then when men thank god on thine account, men will raise thy good and pray for thine health. Honour the great and prosper thy people for it is good to work for the future. But keep thine eyes open; he who is too solicitous or too trusting will become afflicted.

Art historian Kenneth Clark has called the Egyptians 'the most visual of peoples'. Amongst them the celebratory artistic, participatory mode of life and mind was paramount; the analysing, systematising mode was relatively rare outside the temple schools and the company of royal architects. Thus the people loved animals and plants and made them both emblematic and beloved of the gods. Even the physically handi-capped and the deformed were not rejected, and a singular affection was extended to dwarfs.

The mysterious hieratic stiffness of god-portraiture on the walls of the temples and tombs of the mighty was merely a solemn convention. Some of the most charming, and certainly the earliest, realistic domes-tic art also flourished in ancient Egypt. It depicted the life of a people living less in terms of praise and blame than of life and death, light and darkness, and of wrongdoing followed by direct punishment. Any *intrinsic* unworthiness felt by the wrongdoer seems to have been almost unknown.

The Cult of Akhnaton

The 18th Dynasty in Egypt, prior to the accession of Akhnaton (the first of the culture heroes of the modern liberal mind), is usually depicted as one dominated by the ruthless ecclesiastical power of the priesthood of the god Amon-Ra of Thebes. The vast temple complex at Karnak, with its rows of sphinxes and huge multiple columnar halls, has been described by Jewish writer Shalom Goldman and Philip Glass, composer of the opera *Akhnaton,* as showing the 'obsessive' mentality of the old Egyptian order. Their comments tritely reiterate the 'bad press' given to Pharaonic Egypt ever since the production of the Book of Exodus. Readers who have become accustomed to obsessional language might consider instead Akhnaton's numbingly pedantic dedication of the new city of Akhetaton which prefaces this book.

In truth Akhnaton, with his deformed body and dreamy aloofness, may have been history's first truly obsessive monarch. It would be absurd to claim that the overthrow of his monotheistic solar rule caused Egypt to return to the traditions of darkness and reaction, when we consider the brilliant achievements in the following epoch of the Ramesside Pharaohs. It is reforming visionaries who most commonly are obsessive, whereas traditions maintained by the 'old order' are usually too sedately entrenched to nurture much feverish anxiety.

Even so, the vengeful reaction to the fall of Akhnaton was the fiercest in Egyptian history. It was a measure of the damage his un-relenting drive to wipe out every cult save his own was seen to have done to mainstream Egyptian life. Far from lamenting their half-pious and half-hectoring new ruler's death, the common people must have been glad and relieved to support the priesthood of Amon in restoring the old ways. Religious or political leaders are easily invested with approval from the vantage point of 20th-century prejudices. Akhnaton's new 'glasnost' of sun-drenched simplicity and his entourage of 'flower persons' at Tel-El-Amarna seem very attractive nowadays when most establishments are being challenged and old icons torn down. However this quite disregards the Egyptian problems of long ago and the impact of Aton-worship on the common folk who always suffer most from official revolutions. It brought about the crumbling of the first Egyptian empire put together by Akhnaton's forefathers, disaffection amid a baffled army and civil service, and food and housing shortages. The gentle 'heretic' Pharaoh prefigured all the problems of the ruler visionary who refuses to govern amid political and social imperfections and who forces a reluctant populace to share in his own notion of absolute truth.

Meanwhile, the influence of Akhnaton was likely to be have been most significant amid a minority which probably migrated to Egypt of its own accord during the Hyksos period in Egypt when the native royal government had been temporarily overthrown. This minority comprised the Hebrew children of Abraham, Isaac and Jacob, the name being a corruption of their Egyptian name, 'habiru'. The 'steady-state' monotheism of Aton would have been rather more attractive to the Hebrew people in exile than the dynamic but elusive metaphysical concept of Ptah-Atum as the One God under many lesser manifestations. In their finished form, dating from no more than a few hundred years before Christ, the first five books of the Old Testament make unique claims about the Covenant of the sole Hebrew God, Yahweh, with Moses and his people. Yet it seems certain that Jewish monotheism did not receive its final shape until a millennium after the events on Mount Sinai, and that Moses was not the real author of the books of Genesis and Exodus.

A tradition has also persistently recurred since Hellenistic times that Moses was really a native Egyptian prince of the royal house and not a Hebrew changeling at all. Scandalising his fellow European Jews, Sigmund Freud even argued in Moses and Monotheism that Hebrew malcontents had probably murdered Moses, a claim not inconsistent with the social and economic problems of a frustrated, angry people in the wilderness. If Moses were indeed an Egyptian, this would strengthen the claims of Aton-style monotheism and its arbitrary outlawing of lesser divinities as having a decisive influence on the Hebrews in their captivity.

It is unlikely that the departure of the Hebrews for the Promised Land occurred before the time of Rameses I, who reigned a generation after Akhnaton. As a relatively obscure Semite group labouring in the region of the Nile Delta, the Hebrews would have received scant attention from the magnificent faraway court at Thebes, unless the recent discovery of the buried ruins of an early Ramesside city in the Nile Delta might explain Pharaoh's interest. Otherwise why would the Pharaoh himself be involved in the Hebrew departure at all? Such speculation of course is distasteful to Jewish orthodoxy since it suggests strongly that Yahweh is a god of partly foreign derivation. Nevertheless, the very close resemblance of Akhnaton's famous hymn to the sun god Aton to Psalm 104 in the Old Testament has been regularly noted by scholars. There can be no real monopoly of a great religious idea.

THE SEMITES AND PERSIAN INFLUENCES

Turning briefly to the religious and psychic life of those Semite peoples who lived in the Tigris-Euphrates valley, we hear a much harsher note than was usually sounded in Egypt. There is a Babylonian inscription from the time of King Nebuchadnezzar which reads as follows:

The sin I have sinned I do not know.
The offence I have committed I do not know.
The forbidden fruit I have eaten I do not know.
The uncleanness in which I have trodden I do not know.
Wash me clean God, from the sins I do not know.
Though my sins be seventy times seven.[4]

Here we have a very early expression of obsessively-reiterated guilt. Whereas shame is tied directly to a deed, guilt is often divorced from basic facts and generalised into a complex. Did the first guilt-evoking religion come from the near-eastern Semites? This seems difficult to prove but their sophistication in systematising guilt was both remarkable and potent. Perhaps trembling before an allegedly just God was better than trying to appease other terrible dieties for their own sake. Out of a guilt-prone style might come real law and order, whereas a sense of arbitrary imposed cruelty from above, in which the gods too lacked consistent virtue or restraint, sprang from much earlier worship. In this regard Yahweh was to be (on his better days!) rather an improvement on Marduk of Babylon, fiery Moloch of Carthage, Dagon of Philistia and the beautiful but deadly goddess Ishtar who slew men at the very moment of her embrace. Egypt alone appears to have avoided a widespread guilt mentality whilst still preserving the idea of a balanced divine justice, as shown in the elaborate weighing of hearts in the Theban Book of the Dead. The Pharaoh had taken upon himself the mantle of Egypt's responsibility; ordinary folk need only expect due penalities as they confronted their heart and confessed their deeds before Osiris, Lord of the Dead. Vengeance was not to fall capriciously on the ignorant and the knowing alike.

Both psychoanalytic theory and later clinical research have confirmed that if primitive guilt is intimately connected with obsessional behaviour, the source of this guilt can be historically traced to ancient taboos governing sex and aggression within family and tribal units. Despite the curious fact that something like 63 per cent of all murders in modern Western societies occur within family or blood-related groups, the social and psychological reprisals visited upon the family taboo-breaker remain grim indeed. The superstitious force or twisted worthiness we strive to attach even to bad or inadequate parents, siblings and relatives is so much more than we bother to offer our dearest friends or strangers. We even put on rose-coloured spectacles and utter guilt-prompted lies about our dead. The Chinese and Japanese cultures have coped with this problem by reducing the claims as well as the responsibilities of the individual ego. This used to be done by subordinating youth to elders, elders to the honourable clan and the nation and so on to one's interrelatedness with nature and the cosmos itself. The burden of ethical responsibility was thus shared and lightened as long as one obeyed the ethos of family and natural piety. The operations of the Sicilian mafia, with its garishly sentimental 'family' mystique contrasted with its remorselessly violent dealings with the outsider, show a very corrupt survival of this pattern in Western culture.

The Semites of the Mesopotamian region were the first people known to have prescribed a legal and moral code of such elaborate compulsion that the shame of wrongdoing and its public punishment gradually became absorbed into the psyche itself, as a potential reflexive capacity to feel general guilt. Lack of *permission* for a shameful deed was buttressed by an ever deeper threat of lack of *remission* (or forgiveness) for the sinner. The best known example of such a systematised legal and moral code was that of King Hammurabi which stood on an inscribed column in Babylon for 800 years after 751 BC. It had 282 articles, of which the greatest number, 68, dealt with family and sexual relationships: marriage, inheritance, adultery, incest, concubinage, divorce, desertion and adoption. No previous known code of ethics had given such emphasis to intimate behaviour. Its provisions exceeded in number even those concerning land ownership and tenancy which had existed since neolithic times. The Hebrews were later to push this emphasis on family and personal behaviour even further, with enormous social consequences for them and for Western civilisation.

The Babylonians and their Persian successors were not usually interested in the intimacies of private sexual behaviour unless these seriously threatened public order or basic family life. The less promiscuous sort of homosexuality was not frowned upon because it was appreciated better than today that this was a relatively harmless aberration which actually assisted in the control of an expanding imperial population. Furthermore, homoerotic sentiment promoted fraternal loyalties among soldiers on active service who might otherwise be distracted by absent wives or military concubines. An erroneous association of homosexuality with effeminacy and a lack of courage seems not to have occurred until well into the modern Western era. Belshazzar, the last of the Babylonian kings, had lovers of both sexes, a fact that would hardly have endeared him to his righteous captive, the prophet Daniel. Deviant activity was hardly frowned on up to the time of Alexander's conquest of the Persian Empire, since that actively virile conqueror was also bisexual.

As with all ancient peoples, including the Hebrews, the relative value of human life was chiefly defined in terms of 'us' and 'others'. A different nationality or class was never treated as equal to the ruling caste. Yet despite extensive concubinage, a sound core of monogamy was common throughout Mesopotamian societies and shame was attached to the abandonment of marriage without good reason. Marriage between brother and sister was generally taboo. Even in Egypt the occasional political custom of Pharaohs marrying their sister was not copied by the nobility and certainly did not exist among the common people. However, abortion and infanticide were common practices as a means of population control. This is in contrast to strict family compulsions imposed by the Jews who intended to flourish and multiply as a strong defence against their numerous neighbours. Such compulsions referred also to dealing with the Canaanites whose women and lands the Hebrews seized after a series of bizarre Yahweh-sanctioned wars. These led to brutal killings and displacements of population.

One of the strongest indications of the non-obsessive nature of the Persian Empire was its toleration of many races and religions and the granting of a large measure of equality to all of them under the royal law. Following the Median example, the Persians themselves had become largely Zoroastrian, a religion with a remarkable capacity to influence all others in the empire by contagion rather than conversion. The purest form of Zoroastrian religion celebrated only the earth, fire and water as sacred, whereas the popular form under the priests, or Magi, also permitted the worship of idols and their rites. A more restrictive and contagious doctrine was the Zoroastrians' definition of a dualistic universe where broadly equal powers of Light (led by Ahuramazda) and Darkness (led by Ahriman) battled for supremacy. This seems to have been extended into a recognisable after-death existence as well, and human souls on earth had to choose beforehand the domain in which they wanted to reside.

A dualistic universe had to lead to the idea of dual modes of after-death existence, and from this were to derive our first Occidental ideas of heaven and hell. The worship common in Egypt, India and Babylonia provided no such rigid polarity between good and evil. Hence the Zoroastrian insistence that one had to choose separate sides was to prove a powerful factor not only in promoting a guilty compulsion toward moral behaviour *but in promoting an epoch-making binary thought pattern about self, other persons and nature.* Ancient civilisations up to this time — especially the Chinese — made only passing temporal distinctions between the good and the evil thing; Persian dualism suggested their absolute *separateness* as well. Between the creative Good God and the destructive Evil God no real link existed other than the antithesis of conflict between them. So it was thought to be in the destiny of individuals. Therefore for the first time in a great imperial state, the moral demands of religion became equal with its spiritual and metaphysical promises.

The Great Kings of the Achaemenid Persian Empire comprised only a handful of men in a family of enormous talent which governed solely through a military caste. Ruling alternately from four capital cities — Susa, Ecbatana, Persepolis and Babylon — while permitting local languages and religions to flourish, they could not in C. D. Darlington's words, 'provide the moral framework, intellectual cement, or even the verbal formulas, to hold together a great society'. There is a warning here for all modern governments gripped by modern antiracist fervour in the wake of Nazi infamy. The true 'multicultural society' has always been a romantic dream rather than an attainable reality. Without some form of political or cultural hegemony imposed by *one* salient group, any great state, be it just or unjust, does not survive very long. It was the surrender of this confident and conscientious hegemony, coupled with postwar economic exhaustion and genetic wastage in two world wars, which brought about the reduction of Imperial Britain to 'little England' in the space of a single lifetime. This occurred when the British system had ironically evolved to the point of political and administrative enlightenment and was starting to greatly benefit most peoples of the old Empire.

THE DEVELOPMENT OF THE JEWISH STATE

Yet solutions other than the resolute policing of an empire can produce social unity. Freed from its Babylonian captivity, the Jewish community was given an honorable status and flourished as never before under Persian rule. The exile of the Jews in Babylon, like that suffered in Egypt long before, had strengthened their political resolve to retain and refine their religion, their moral code and identity with a tenacity unique up to that time. It was in Babylon in about 455 BC that Ezra the Scribe regularised the seven-day week, culminating with a Jewish day of rest and prayer. Far more importantly, it was his pen that gave the final shape to the books of Genesis, Exodus, Deuteronomy and Leviticus. The Persian Kings respected Jewish intellectuals and often called on them for advice on complex judicial matters. Even then the Jewish mind was noted both for its legal splendour and prickly compulsiveness in all matters of detailed observance. As the Old Testament itself makes clear, the children of Judah and Israel best found their sharpness of definition as the Chosen People whilst suffering dire adversity. When the tribes came together in one Jewish state, the obsessive irascibility of the Hebrew teachers all too often spent itself in bitter factional disputes and quarrels, whilst forever finding new prophetic ways to chasten the refractory faithful.

Was this compulsive aspect of the Jewish mentality a genetic curiosity, or was it favoured by historical circumstance? Certainly it had been evident from the Mosaic period. Even the most respectful interpretation of Exodus makes it clear that in many ways Moses and his immediate successors had to deal with an often barbaric, refractory and suspicious people who were quite capable of killing or deserting a prophet when too strongly provoked. The episode of the Golden Calf, which was fashioned by Aaron, co-leader of the Exodus, is one example. It showed that the forty years in the desert (itself an inexplicably lengthy period) throughout numerous apostasies and rebellions had not made the Hebrews either docile or humble. Little real religious sophistication or subtlety had been carried over from the time of Abraham, Isaac and Jacob. This had to wait as least until the time of the later prophets and judges. The final shape of the nation came when the prophet Samuel and later Zadok the priest confirmed David as King of Israel and Judah.

'Jewishness' of course was a slowly evolved identity frequently punctuated by intermarriage and heterogeneous intermingling by a robust

Semitic people with their neighbours, captives and even their conquerors. However the genetic core of Israel lay always with its priestly class, the Levites. These in time became the Sadducees who eventually governed the affairs of the great Temple in Jerusalem. This group practised deliberate genetic selection by marrying within their class and they were imitated by followers who obeyed and believed them. This was to help the survival of the Jews as a cultural group, through its rabbinical class, on into the Christian era. As for the majority of the people, the Mosaic tradition favoured not so much 'Jewish' blood lines as such but those who kept the Law and made sure that their children did likewise.

Possibly for the first time, this compulsion of a moral code and a religious idea produced a form of sexual selection where family continuity had nothing to do with the biological instinct or natural selection. Mating became a *psychological* compulsion which drove a people to ceaselessly define and redefine themselves, almost as a living Talmud, over so many centuries. Out of such a unique mental drive came the first systematised social system clearly based upon an obsessional motivation. This dogged motivation was intended to perpetuate the significance of Israel until the end of time. Thus, in the words of the historian Moscati, 'the Jews became the driving force of that history itself'. Most Jews came to find it impossible to entirely detach themselves from the historical experiment of Israel. Even if the Gentiles or *goyim* did not find them out, a guilt-ridden feeling of psychic alienation through being an apostate, if not the wrath of the Lord Yahweh, would deal out retribution.

Yet within the ever-tightening embrace of Israel *as an idea* there had to be some freedom if so many faithful followers were not to rebel or go mad. The *ad hoc* safety valve of the system was the periodical emergence of the prophets. Their often socially disruptive questioning of the Levite ordering of things provided the Jews with a window against psychic suffocation.

The prophets of later Israel, such as Elijah, Micah, Jeremiah and Isaiah, came from varied occupations and backgrounds but they assumed the poetic posture of pastoral shepherds who stood for fundamental truths. It was believed that the effete townspeople, with their lascivious pagan 'Canaanite' tendencies, had too often set such truths aside. Thus it took the prophet Nathan to denounce King David for conniving at the killing of Uriah the Hittite so that he might lie in fornication and make a marriage with Bathsheba. The prophets also provided a useful focus for resentment held by the common people against the ruling priestly class, even though Jeremiah and Ezekiel were themselves Levites. More emphatically, the prophets restated the perpetual claims of the Law and the primacy of the will of Yahweh in face of political expediency. Only one national leader was ever a match for these prophetic-poetic rebels in force, King Solomon, the Lion of Judah.

The extraordinary tension between two sources of authority, one prophetic and supposedly divinely inspired and the other politically and socially devised, more than once tore the Jewish state apart. Elijah broke up the alliance of Israel with Phoenicia only to have both nations lose their independence to foreigners. No wonder some prophets were actually put to death. Jeremiah was imprisoned for his savage attacks upon the state and the warnings of the political disaster his own demoralising power may actually have helped to bring about. In the end, religious fundamentalism always triumphed over political policy in a manner with no parallel in history.

The most tenacious claim of Judaism was that of the exclusive Covenant made between Yahweh and the children of Israel. All of human history was to be treated as its future proving ground. As George Steiner has noted, this is the most stunningly audacious statement in the entire history of religion and it could not have failed to arouse the enmity of the goyim of many nations.

Despite all the practical contradictions involved the Jewish religious leaders of ancient Israel constantly tried to have their policies both ways. Visionaries and zealots may quicken and even purify a public order but, once grown too powerful, they wreck it beyond repair. Noble and stirring as their utterances still lie upon the King James-inspired Biblical page, the later Jewish prophets seldom set much store by kindness, moderation or even common sense. As one scholar has wryly observed, nowhere amid the grand utterances of the Old Testament is there much evidence of laughter or wit. It certainly contains a glowing record of glory, wrath and measured compassion, yet the repetitive moral imperialism and aesthetically barren literal-mindedness of all its prophetic authors (save perhaps Ezekiel) cut a deep graft, not only into the Jewish psyche, but into larger Western consciousness itself. Even the Lord Yahweh himself seemed too often involved in social denunciation and manipulation to allow for much faith in the ability of honest men and women to uplift themselves on their own account. Such a jealous and minutely observant God seemed hardly qualified to assume the later role of Lord of the whole universe. No religion has ever imposed such comprehensive moral requirements upon its faithful as Judaism. Such a stifling ethical system contained the enduring elements of a guilt-driven obsession. As we shall see this was to provide all of later Western civilisation with a kind of permanent nagging impetus towards self-righteous public reformation, towards a recurrent longing for a New Jerusalem built on earth. This perfectionist hankering was to produce some of our grandest achievements as well as our most miserable follies.

THE GREEKS AND THE MORNING OF THE WEST

If the Jew was in some measure 'the spur and irritant of history', as Jacques Maritain called him, ancient Greek civilisation moved away from the moral and legal preoccupations of Israel by providing a *rational* foundation for man's appraisal of man. The ordinary student of history tends to think of ancient Greek history only in terms of its cultural zenith during the Periclean Age of Athens in the 5th century BC. But Greek life and thought gradually evolved from the time of Crete and Mycenae for more than fifteen hundred years until the fall of the Roman Empire in the West. In terms of mental outlook and emotional tendency, the Greeks gradually developed from the stark earth-bound fatalism of the Archaic Age, which Homer so eloquently records in the tales of the *Iliad* and the *Odyssey*, to the lofty mysticism of Plotinus and later Platonism in the 3rd century AD.

In the beginning the Greeks felt themselves to be no more than playthings of the gods. Thus in the *Iliad*, Agamemnon justifies his abduction of the mistress of Achilles because of his need to make up for the loss of his own woman: 'Not I was the cause of this act, but Zeus and daemon who walks in darkness. It was they who put wild *ate* in my understanding. . .so what could I do? Deity will always have its way'.

The concept of *ate* can described as a fixed tendency to succumb to a demonic portion of human nature through which the gods could prompt people to wrong or rash behaviour against their real inclination. This behavioural fatalism persisted for a very long time in Greek sentiment. It forms a central theme in the dramatic *Oedipus* trilogy of Sophocles and it is the foundation of most motivation in the earlier tragedies of Aeschylus. This sort of wild moral climate marks a far cry from the days centuries later when the Christian apologist Justin Martyr was to say in half-admiration and half-disapproval of later Greek Platonism: 'Its main aim is to see God face to face'.

Halfway across the millennium of antique Greek experience, the belief in the power of human reason gradually grew to produce the overemphasised aspect of the Greek way of life we admire today. The triumph of rational thought in mainland Greek society was mainly confined to a small educated class. It lasted for little more than 250 years from the defeat of Persia at the time of the battle of Salamis to the conquest of the Greek states by Philip of Macedon *circa* 330 BC. The glories of Greek philosophy, drama, science and liberal politics we celebrate today are chiefly of Aegean origin. The Ionian coastal cities of Asia Minor such as Miletus and Ephesus, the Greek islands and Athens produced the greatest early philosophers and thinkers of the Greek world. By contrast, the most powerful mainland state of Sparta remained a closely inbred introverted society, prodigious in war and the games but backward in politics, economics and family life. Sparta was to destroy the Athenian empire in the early 4th century BC and later succumb to exhaustion itself without producing much of a legacy beyond tribal harshness, athletic prowess and military heroism. As for the free Ionian cities at their best, these could hardly fail to be influenced by ideas from the older and larger states of western Asia. Yet the proud spirit of curiosity, independence in thought and a quarrelsome individuality seemed peculiar to the Ionians themselves.

The one great secret the Greeks might have learned from their imperial Persian adversaries in over four centuries of disastrous conflicts between tiny city-states was how to reconcile cultural and political differences for the common good of all. In their *hubris* and political restlessness the Hellenes all too frequently refused to confront the issue. Ironically, it was from a well-organised semibarbaric state to the north, Macedon, that the city-states had to be taught a final political lesson. Yet it is the pride of the Greeks in their common deposit of language and culture that has most enriched the Western mind, to say nothing of sowing the first seeds of some of our own endlessly compulsive search for novelty. The Greeks took the astronomy and mathematics of Babylon, the metaphysical speculation of Persia, the medical, mystical and architectural knowledge of Egypt and the critical philosophy of the native Ionian cities and married all of these to a new idea in the ancient world. This was the developing belief that right and useful behaviour in both domestic and public life should be arrived at through common social experience and rational inquiry. Such behaviour should not be merely derived from some godly demand or sanction from Olympus, Sinai or any other mountain top. God (or the gods) worked *through* the human spirit and not merely *upon* it from some force above or beyond mankind. This latter perception was a very potent idea which may have originally come from India, but it was only to survive very narrowly in the Christian ages to come.

THE SPIRITUAL OUTLOOK OF THE GREEKS

What of the religion of Hellas? Here we have to grapple with the seemingly contradictory character of the antique Greek mind, its wide alternations between hard-headed rationality and its emotional lapses into what the modern agnostic would dismiss as occult superstition. E. R. Dodds, in a searching analysis of this interplay between rational and irrational tendencies among the ancient Greeks, notes that the modern mind has seized upon the Apollonian/rational aspect of the Greek legacy while ignoring or slighting its balancing Dionysian/ecstatic side. Nothing better illustrates this seeming antithesis than the famous Oracle of Delphi, which not only held both states and rulers in thrall but indirectly led to the famous Games of Olympia. Even cynics who doubted that the god Apollo spoke through the 'cryptic' prophecies of the Pythian Priestess at Delphi found the Oracle invaluable as a sounding centre for all manner of projects and plots, and the Pythia became not only a voice of counsel and warning for all Hellas but a political listening post for most of the Mediterranean world.

Even at the height of the Periclean Age in Athens, the alternation of the Greek mind between the rational/investigative and the magical/esoteric is neatly illustrated by the entrance into the city of the sacred image of Asclepius the demi-divine physician in 420. At a time when most of the finest Hippocratic medical treatises were being published, the statue of the physician-extraordinaire was preceded by his Holy Snake, to which he and the populace freely attributed magical healing powers. 'Asclepius' was even housed for a time by the great dramatist Sophocles (whose views on holy reptiles were not disclosed). What Jacob Burkhardt remarked of 19th-century Christian religion — 'rationalism for the few and magic for the many' — was also true for Ionian Greece from about 400 BC onwards.

The Peloponnesian War of 431 to 404 BC was the longest and most destructive ever fought by Greek against Greek. The sense that the gods cared at all about the fate of humanity began to wane. After the Great Plague of 430, the historian Thucydides declared religion to be useless. Even pious folk recalled that both fallible gods and ordinary men had come originally from a common source in the Great Mother

of archaic legend. If the gods could not redeem men from such mis-
fortunes, they could probably not curse with much effect either, they
reasoned. Shame and guilty obligation could be confined to the affairs
of family and clan as they had been in the days of Homer. This return
of spiritual pessimism — the sense that people had nothing to look to
beyond their own fated limitations (*moira*), might have plunged a
rigidly monotheistic people like the Jews into cultural eclipse. For the
Ionian Greeks, it fuelled an intense desire to live more fully in the
present moment and plumb earthly experience to its depths. Any
communal sense of immortality before the time of Plato had been
weak. The Elysian Fields were only prepared for the souls of heroes;
whereas for other discarnate souls, the cold, shadowy half-world of
Hades beckoned with an attraction for nobody.

Yet a highly significant footnote to mainstream Greek thought at
this period was provided by the late Greek mystery cults of Orpheus
and Eleusis. These taught for the first time in European experience a
clear doctrine of the soul's full survival of death. The Orphic teachers
were the first to assert that the soul of man had 'fallen' into the material
world — 'An exile from God and a wanderer'. Before then, Soul was
thought of as merely a general spiritual category in which all human
beings partook with no allowance for individuality. Orphic teaching
was not far removed from the 'Wisdom' of some later mystic Jewish
teachers who saw the immortal soul on a long pilgrimage through time.
Yet, Jewish orthodoxy itself tended to be agnostic about the soul's
survival and indeed remains so today. Only after the time of the Prophet
Daniel was spiritual immortality seriously debated by the rabbis.
Following the destruction of Jerusalem by the forces of the Emperor
Titus in AD 70, the suffocating grip of the Temple authorities was
broken, and scattered Jewish intellectuals became significantly involved
in the speculative religious thought held by Greeks and Egyptians.
This was the case in the great cosmopolitan city of Alexandria,
where Jews and Greeks even rioted in the service of their respective
beliefs.

Later thinkers in the larger Greek cities began to look for a middle
term in the grammar of human existence — a raft of temporary bliss
between an unkind earth and a seemingly unattainable heaven. They
found it, as did no other ancient civilisation, in the twin cults of
Apollo and Eros — in the clear light of the reasoning intellect and in
the fullest celebration of human love. The inner life of the educated
Ionian Greeks between the defeat of Athens by Sparta and the
Macedonian conquest seesawed — sometimes harmoniously, often

awkwardly — between a cool rationality in public life and a frequent exaltation of human passion and personal feeling in private.

For the later Hellenic spirit, love and the worship of its most beautiful human objects were almost inseparable. Humanism in its most devout form was the basis of all art and aesthetic judgement. The celebration of Nature in her primal form, as the later Northern European romantics practised it, was absent from this sort of focus. (Indeed, to this day, most Mediterranean peoples have been indifferent towards natural conservation.) Such an outpouring of feeling in the service of earthly love made the later extreme rationalism of Greek thought relatively free from obsession as we know it. The passions and sexuality were never the tensely ambivalent sort of concern for most ancient peoples they have become for us. Nor was Eros diverted into the falsely sub-limated channels of industrial power and social dominance which mark modern Western communities. For the Hellenes, love and its un-ashamedly passionate component became a ticket-of-leave from the tight obligations of family and clan, from guilt and fate, and ultimately a provisional answer to death itself. So Eros and Thanatos (death) were balanced in a way hard to appreciate in the death-denying culture of the late 20th century.

Out of this balance between love and reason came an art and archi-tecture which were idealisations of humanity. The worship of love, allied with ideal beauty, was chiefly a creation of the Athenian and Ionian educated class but it struck a chord in all the mainland Greek cities. By Plato's time the distinctly homoerotic slant of Eros was made plain in literary works which embarrassed the prim Christian trans-lators of the 19th century. Even pederasty — the tutelary love of an older man for an adolescent or younger male — was not treated as the furtive or shameful thing it is today. Nor was it habitually associated with buggery, or even the molestation of pubescent children, as was so often the case in early Imperial Rome and in our sicker epoch. Indeed, Plato warned, via Socrates, in the *Symposium* that 'no-one should love the very young', and the sentiment was endorsed by his company. Later Aristotle wrote in the *Nicomachean Ethics* that while homoerotic love was noblest of all, sexual intercourse between males was un-natural and to be avoided. Plato too, who wrote more movingly of 'Greek love' in his *Phaedrus* than anyone, partly revised his views in *The Laws*, written in old age, declaring that physical love between men should be prohibited.

Under the long shadow of the early Christian Fathers we have anxiously averted our eyes from the liberal masculine loves of the

Greeks but conveniently overlooked men's frequent sexual abuse of women. Even contemporary unbelieving folk remain heirs to the absolute Hebraic moral reflexes of their Christian forebears. These reflexes gradually evolved, via the subordinate wife of the Calvinist and Jansenist Catholic ethic, into the overwhelmingly comprehensive bourgeois romanticising of married life in Victorian times. Meanwhile, homosexuality as 'the love that dare not speak its name' could still be punished until only recently by imprisonment with hard labour and lasting social ignominy. Only in their greater reverence for children were the Victorians more compassionate than the Greeks, who were not beyond permitting infanticide in times of economic hardship.

The subordinate role of women in Greek society was not greatly different from that of other highly civilised patriarchal cultures, but a good wife and children could still be greatly loved and cherished. Women were largely kept out of public life, as suggested by the opinion of the great Pericles in a funeral speech when he said to his female hearers: 'The greatest glory is to be least talked about by a man, whether they are praising or criticising you'. Such an attitude deprived women of the *moral* force they were to have in the Christian centuries. Yet the Christian epoch created the strained paradox of an intense male erotic obsession with the female, even while fearing, devaluing or scorning her. In ancient Greece women were never treated as a source of moral and sexual corruption. Some misogyny was certainly evident in Greek literature, but never to the degree that we find it in the Old Testament and in the writing of many of the early Christian Fathers. In Ionian Greece a truly devoted love for *either* sex was believed to transcend many sexual taboos.

Being thoroughly anticompulsive in sentiment, this attitude acted as a useful erotic counterpoise to the otherwise overheated intellectual fixations of an argumentative, perfection-seeking civilisation. The paradoxical modern treatment of the female as both the source of guilt and conscripted moral policewoman was happily absent from ancient Greek life. The omnipresent sexless Western 'mom' was, as yet, far off.

SOCRATES AND THE PLATONIC LEGACY

In the period from the Peloponnesian War to the Macedonian Conquest, the social philosophers of Ionian Greece can be fairly said to have fashioned the basic contours of the Western mind. The great playwright Euripides in *Medea* sounds a theme which came to be stressed by Socrates, Plato, and Aristotle and several others in the 4th and 3rd centuries BC — that it is the rational *intellect* which gives a person the loftiest attributes he or she possesses. *Feeling*, whether based upon passion or higher intuition, is a lesser faculty, to be suspected if not actually excluded. Such a view reached its ultimate form with Aristotle, who taught that intellect and rational thought made men virtually divine, while the rest of behaviour was linked merely to animal appetites. Any distinction here between mind and spirit became quite blurred.

So began a fundamental Western confusion between higher consciousness and dialectical thinking. Reason was enthroned above imagination and intuition and even above direct spiritual knowledge (*metanoia*). Only religious mystics were left to point out that people can be as blind and deluded in their logical calculations as in their baser feelings, and that only by transcending *both* hairsplitting rationalisations and passionate feeling could humans be reconnected with God and the Divine.

The subtle but deadly confusion between the claims of rational discussion and those of *direct* knowing through holistic experience has tormented the spiritual life of Westerners for centuries. It became the cause of many dilemmas suffered by the religiously rebellious or fanatically obsessed in later Christian centuries. Protestantism dealt with the problem by ignoring or denying *metanoia* almost totally, except in some naively excited sense of being 'saved'. Of course, such a problem is meaningless in an Oriental religion such as Buddhism which teaches that intellectual activity must exist on a much lower level than meditative awareness. This is why the regular containment and meditative quieting of active thought is required for the health of the spirit.

This compulsive divinisation of the faculty of reason was to be further promoted by Socrates — the archetypal subversive of what sociologist Philip Rieff has called 'sacred order' in public life. If indirect sources and his pupil Plato represent him rightly, Socrates originated the ego-justified habit of unbridled rational questioning and criticism. He taught that the basis of spiritual security and freedom lay in trusting no law, truth or tradition at its face value. These were views as daring as they are impractical, since no society or religious system which hopes to conduct its affairs effectively can afford to give them unlimited latitude. It was Socrates' bold disregard of the necessity for prudent statements and directions to youth which led to his condemnation to death — not without great regret — by an Athenian tribunal in 399 BC. Perhaps it is best to hear Socrates' own justification in the *Apologia* of Plato, a free paraphrase from memory of the philosopher's defence at his trial:

Throughout my life I have spoken my mind; I have poured scorn on the things that most people care for — the making of money, the management of their estates, participation in one of the political factions in the city. . .I went to you as individuals and tried to persuade each one of you to care about the perfecting of his wisdom and virtue, to think more of his inner self than any internal attributes. . .[5]

This is a basic position which even Christ would have endorsed. Yet, from a more prudent view of human frailty, there is something infuriating about even a good man — and Socrates was one of the best of any epoch — who does not wish to know when to hold his tongue.

Despite the hazards of their talkative rationalism, it is from Socrates and Plato that earliest Europe gained a firm philosophy of the soul and its survival of bodily death. In the *Phaedo*, Socrates is paraphrased by Plato as declaring:

If I did not believe that among the dead I shall meet better men than any alive on this earth, I would be justified in resenting death. . . I am confident that something awaits us after death, and that is why I trust a tradition that, whatever awaits us, it is something far better for a good man than for an evil one.[6]

The influence of the earlier Orphic teaching about the soul's spiritual survival is clear here. However, the notions of sin and punishment in the afterlife never played much part in the religion of Greece. It was to be otherwise with later Jewish and Christian teaching. Certainly the promise of the soul's survival *does* open out human existence and alleviate the frequent pessimism and anxiety of the agnostic. But when the harsh doctrine of an eternal punishment for temporal misdeeds — as in the Christian fundamentalist view of Hell — is added to the promise of immortality, anxiety returns in a new and even more oppressive guise. Glory and damnation each beckon to frail humanity out of a seemingly impossible ethical imperative. This is the very marrow from which obsession and soul-terror are formed.

PLATO AS A PIVOTAL INFLUENCE

Many historians rank Plato second only to Christ as the most influential teacher in Western civilisation. A list of the great philosopher's learned admirers extends from his most eminent personal pupil Aristotle to Sigmund Freud, Albert Einstein and Alfred North Whitehead in our own century.

His most remarkable achievement was to place the intellect below the spiritual summit of soul-life which culminates in the direct apprehension of the Godhead. Plato's method was to push reason to its farthest operational limits and then to step boldly beyond it to a rapt contemplation of an Infinite Mystery which included an acceptance of both the gods and God. This Mystery had to lie beyond the capacity of any rational mind to comprehend. Without the influence of Platonism, Christianity itself may well have remained no more than a baroque offshoot of Judaism, with Jesus of Nazareth wrongly presented as the last of the politically meddlesome prophets of Israel. But aided by Plato and his later Academy, St Paul, Origen, Clement of Alexandria and Augustine were able to clothe Christ's teachings in the rich vesture of a philosophy which rose far above the narrow Yahwism of the Levites in Jerusalem, whose fixations Jesus himself had both answered and transcended.

Plato was born to an aristocratic family in 427 BC. He served as a soldier for Athens in the Peloponnesian War and became a disciple of Socrates, travelling widely about the Mediterranean region. He spent some time at the court of the tyrant of Syracuse, and visited North Africa and possibly Egypt. His experience under several styles of government led him to the conviction that since mere public opinion could never amount to real knowledge, democratic rule was unworkable, frequently collapsing into autocracy. This occurred because most electors lacked wisdom and virtue themselves, and were rarely disposed to listen patiently to those who had such qualities. Notwithstanding Sir Karl Popper's withering criticism of Plato's politics in *The Open Society and Its Enemies*, Plato's argument that true democracy was only possible when the majority really embraced the good and the beautiful has never been convincingly refuted. For Plato, as for his successors, sufficient *self*-knowledge had to be the test of one's trustworthiness as either ruler or elector.

Plato's range as a metaphysician and sociologist was immense. But his insistence that the natural world of the senses was only a pale reflection of a higher supersensible Reality is central to his entire output of thirty-five known Dialogues. Popper has scorned his ideal ruler, the philosopher-king, but Plato took pains to make it clear that only what the Indian Vedantist doctrine would recognise as a spiritually Enlightened person could live up to such a lofty role. After all, at least five autocrats in Greece, Sicily and elsewhere tried out Plato's leader model and failed to measure up to it.

In discussing obsession-compulsion, perhaps the most important feature of Plato's teaching was that the ethical burdens of virtuous statecraft are too great for most ordinary people. Bearing too much responsibility from *without*, people too easily become distracted from their essential inner development. Plato argued that full democracy is rarely worth the spiritual energy expended upon it, since it stirs up ill-informed political passions in the majority instead of confining such preoccupations to those prepared and educated to handle power wisely. Far from being a blueprint for dictatorship, Plato's *Republic* supports a rule by a *spiritual* elite of guardians whose qualifications depend upon loftiness of soul-life rather than wealth, the power of a clan or a military clique. The difficulty is, of course, to identify, test and form such spiritual supermen and superwomen. Only Tibet's Dalai Lama has approximated to a serious replica of the sort of ruler Plato envisioned.

Regardless of its supreme idealism, Plato's teaching remains one of the greatest philosophical correctives to the fixated, compulsive life. Platonic virtue is rooted in spiritual awareness, not in the checking-off of a catalogue of virtues and sins under the ever-watchful eye of an anthropomorphic deity. Moreover, Plato was among the earliest exponents of the view that, far from curtailing any personal freedom which really mattered, the well-disciplined outer social order left far more scope for the cultivation of knowledge, love and beauty and the contemplation of goodness. The ruinous socio-economic upheavals of our century suggest that Plato may have been right. After all, how valuable is political freedom in a vaunted 'open' society when the general populace are a constant prey to anxieties, envies and guilts related to economic status, social approval, to material personal possessions or even concerning their next meal? As Plato queried, how 'free' is a person in bondage to all manner of tormenting personal appetites? A bachelor aged 81, Plato died at the wedding feast of a friend. His famous Academy at Athens endured for another 800 years until the Emperor Justinian confiscated its funds.

THE CONTRIBUTION OF THE NEO-PLATONISTS

Plotinus, the last great thinker hailing in spirit from the pre-Christian 'time of the gods', was actually not born until AD 204. He was the son of a Greco-Roman freedman resident in Egypt and he came to Rome in 244, where he remained most of his life. By the time of Plotinus, Christianity was firmly entrenched against its powerful heterodox rivals. The element of rigid Jewish monotheism at its base had partly triumphed over Gentile influences, rendering it characteristically intolerant of other religious perceptions. Thus, the founder of Neo-Platonism was able to weigh the claims of both orthodox and Gnostic Christianity together with other pagan philosophies such as Stoicism.

It was typical of the gentle, luminous soul of Plotinus that he was able to take what was valuable in many strains of belief while remaining faithful to 'the divine Plato', especially in his unswerving assertion that, while human qualities were worthy in themselves, it was the divine spirit in man which mattered. But Plotinus was deeply critical of the body-rejecting, world-denying aspects of Gnostic teaching, and found in many of its sects too much of oriental magic and occult mystification for his taste.

A garbled knowledge of Neo-Platonist works in earlier centuries first came to the West through Christian theologians such as Augustine, Anselm, Bonaventure and Aquinas, who took plentifully of what they favoured while dismissing the rest. For his part, Plotinus was coolly reserved toward orthodox early Christianity, doubtless detecting in its declarations a fanaticism too much linked with its long experience of official persecution. He preferred to correspond privately with such admiring Christian thinkers as the great Origen, who was ultimately to suffer discredit himself because of too fervent an acceptance of Neo-Platonic ideas. Porphyry, a distinguished disciple, has left a fascinating portrait of Plotinus, who was widely believed to be a saint during his lifetime. We are told of the patience, sweetness and beauty of the philosopher's nature. His face became radiant when teaching of spiritual things, he never spoke harshly of other opinions and always accepted well-argued dissent from his audiences. The health of Plotinus was never robust, but he lived simply with moderate frugality while warning his pupils against the violent excesses of asceticism.

Plotinus was the most brilliant eclectic thinker of the early centuries AD. He turned back to the lofty teaching of Plato on divine and earthly love while taking in something of Aristotle's observations on nature and ethics, and the mysticism of the Hermetic philosophers of Alexandria. To crown this synthesis with the genius of his own inner experience, Plotinus saw God as the intellectually unknowable Absolute, which is the transcendent non-material origin of all creation while still remaining at the core of every moment of human existence. Had Christianity embraced this concept instead of the anthropomorphic legends in the books of Genesis and Exodus, the early Church might have taken a far wiser and kinder course, truer to the spirit of Christ, than it subsequently did.

Meanwhile, if modern Western scientists accept any notion of a

Godhead at all, it is still to Plotinus they must turn. Those working at the frontier of physics would have little quarrel with his statement:

> Those who despise what is really so close to the spiritual in material things, show that they know nothing of the spiritual world, except in name. The world is worthy of its Author — complete, beautiful and harmonious. There is nothing Yonder which is not also Here.[7]

This astonishing visionary taught nearly 1700 years ago that the Universe had no beginning in time, nor any temporal end. However the Universe, while functioning *in* time, consists of a vast series of finite schemes which do have a beginning and an end. This is a cosmology quite consistent with the state of our empirical knowledge, and probably the only one held before our own century that can withstand scientific scepticism.

Most significantly, Plotinus opposed any moral or ethical system that was not grounded in a higher spiritual perspective, as well as any sanctions upon human conduct that did not take account of that spark of God which is in all human creatures. It is from him that Christianity received the final poetic perception that we are all made 'in the image and likeness of God,' though the notion was debased during the 18th century into a shallow political concept which has been used to prop up modern representative governments. Plotinus' vision was of a supreme One presiding over a hierarchical universe of plural intelligences all partaking of Divinity at different levels of consciousness and potency. This made him capable of an exquisite tolerance towards lesser deities, even those with morally ambiguous traits. Porphyry, his pupil, best expressed the Neo-Platonic view of the psychological usefulness of polytheism:

> Images and temples of the gods have been made from all antiquity for the sake of forming reminders to men. The object is to make those who draw near them think of aspects of God thereby, or to enable them. . .to address their prayers and vows to the seen representing the Unseen. When any person gets an image or picture of a friend, he certainly does not believe that the friend is to be found in the image. . .His idea is that the honour which he pays to his friend finds expression in the image. While the sacrifices offered to the gods do not bring them any honour, they are meant as a testimony to the goodwill and gratitude of the worshippers.[8]

This chapter has sought to examine the roots of the curiously obsessional slant of Western thought and civilisation. Though maligned by the

Hebrew-Canaanite theological system, much that was valuable in the Egyptian outlook — its humanely realistic anchorage in shame rather than guilt as a curb upon human behaviour and its perennial, if limited, faith in immortality — gradually filtered into Greek thought and practice, especially after the conquests of Alexander. The Janus-faced nature of the later Greek experience, moving precariously between the beauties of fleshly life and the contemplation of lofty spiritual things was, unfortunately, ruptured under the later Roman Empire. Through Aristotle, Greek rationalism was pressed into the service of Christian theology, while the Greek praise of Eros and earthly love was harshly rejected. Unbridled reason without the tempering influence of ordinary human love and delight is the stuff of which obsession and fanaticism are fashioned. Finally, we must notice the persistence in Christian attitudes of Jewish social and personal morality over a deeper Greek appreciation of human psychology, and its ambiguities. Out of this uneasy mix between Old Testament legal and moral coercion and New Testament spiritual liberation, much of the productive yet stormy social and political endeavour of the West was to emerge.

· TWO ·

CHRISTIANITY AND PERFECTIONISM

Any religion which does not recall people to the divine is use-less — both to persons and nations. And divinity is not in the skies, but within.

Jalaluddin Rumi

All orthodox bodies of religious faith stir uneasily from epoch to epoch against the danger of becoming the mere corpses of their inspired founders. Christianity, with its Jewish precursors, is no exception. Religious orthodoxies, no less than their modern counterparts in political ideology, are always foolishly concerned to insist upon the literal truth of their arguments and doctrines. By contrast, saintly religious visionaries, the great *experiencers* of divinity, are always disrupting the tendency to over-concretise and systematise religion because they are partakers of that 'living water' which can never flow past the earthly shore a second time. Without its mystics and their personal revelations of truth beyond the power of the rational intellect to demonstrate, any formal religion is either threatened with the prospect of drying up or preparing for its own death.

If Christianity has retained some of its fragrance down through the centuries, this is most likely due to its true saints and lovers rather than its theologians. Saint Francis of Assisi, Teresa of Avila, Meister Eckhart, William Law, Seraphim of Sarov and Bernadette of Lourdes have done more to hearten Christians than all the popes and bishops who have ever taught and decreed and all the contending theologians who have ever written. If a religious faith is to be finally justified in the breast of its adherents, this justification must come from the higher intuitions it inspires and the loving deeds it prompts, *not* from mere historical justification. Judaism and Christianity, more than any other world religions, have been obsessed with history. The Hebrew belief in a special Covenant between themselves and Yahweh promised fulfilment only after much chastisement and prophecy, and only at the end of time. Prophecy became linked with compulsively anticipating history; its original purpose in distant antiquity was probably to replace the here-and-now divinatory practices of pagan societies.

Alas, the burden of waiting for some far-off millennial redemption created conditions in which the most violent futuristic obsessions could be cultivated. Despite the efforts of St Paul to loosen ties with Jerusalem, the Christian Church incorporated this weighty burden of Hebrew history into its own tradition. Yet it is precisely on the literal historical record that Biblical claims are most vulnerable to being seriously doubted or scientifically disproved. Just as the neurotic-obsessive is haunted by time and the linear continuity between historical past and an uncertain future, so the obsession of scholars with the historical Jesus has often barred from their awareness the timeless *experience* of the Christ-Spirit which makes all historical justification, all canonical cursing and blessing, of little importance.

We shall probably never know much more of the actual historical person and motivation of Jesus of Nazareth than Scripture scholars and historians are able to tell us today. But we still know more about the life and times of Jesus than of the Buddha, whose teaching and Way always mattered far more to his followers than the shadowy historical figure of Prince Gautama — which is as it should be. The four Gospels in the form that we know them now probably date from no earlier than the start of the second century. Moreover, as St John's Gospel itself finally makes clear, the accounts embodied in the canonical Four are incomplete, suggesting that the record of not only the deeds of Jesus, but some of his teaching also, had not been fully preserved, except from memorised oral sources which were then already fading. Many Scripture scholars are now convinced that even the three synoptic Gospels may contain non-Apostolic interpolations and do contain evident passages of inconsistency, at times suggesting that *two* levels of Christly revelation have been collapsed into one.

After the Resurrection — whether considered as historical fact or spiritual truth shrouded in myth — Jesus' disciples were reluctant to surrender both their own Jewish credentials and the seeming claims of their Master to be the Redeemer and Messiah foretold in Jewish prophecy. There was, after all, only one religious structure they knew of, and Jesus even as its victim had seemingly not repudiated it. Peter, James, John and the rest were not rabbis or theologians, and they understood little of the wider Gentile world their Master had exhorted them to convert. Any wider vision they may have received on the first Pentecost evidently did not cut them off from their psychological roots in Israel. Finally, Jesus had observed the Commandments in the Torah and upheld their value, even while rebuking those fanatics who used them as a means of implanting moral compulsions. But rather than the Law, he stressed love.

If orthodox Jewish religion was somehow thought incomplete, to what was Jesus trying to convert his followers? Here the ambiguities begin. If Jesus were indeed the Messiah, he was empowered not only to 'fulfil' the law of the Prophets, but to supersede it and pass beyond its limitations. There is sufficient evidence in the Gospels themselves to suggest that this is exactly what Jesus was attempting, and it was this dangerous course that set him on the road to Golgotha. Jesus was, by every piece of convincing evidence, a spiritual radical bent upon transforming Yahwism into *something else*. The constant outbreaks of crude Jewish anthropomorphism and concretism in later Christian history suggest that Jesus eventually failed in this aim, except in the case of a mystic minority. But it is important to guess at what sort of widespread spiritual transformation he hoped for:

1. Everything Jesus taught points to his insistence upon the primacy of the *spiritual* essentials over the worldly concerns of religion. While he supported observance of the Mosaic Law, his harshest attacks were reserved for the sterile intellectualism of the Pharisees, whose meticulous outward observances oppressed the common people and stifled spiritual spontaneity. And though the Sadducees and the party of the Temple were most responsible for Jesus' arrest and trial, he dismissed them almost contemptuously. To him, religion was a matter of the heart and spirit, while theological pedantry was a barrier to both.

2. In his constant linking of himself as the Son of Man to the Almighty Father, Jesus finally broke with the doctrine of the total separateness of Yahweh from all creatures and clearly taught that *direct access* to God was possible through him and his example. This was, and still is, anathema to orthodox Jewish teaching. In the famous address to his disciples at the Last Supper recorded in John 17:21–23, Jesus makes it clear that he and the Godhead are

connected, as all those who understand him can likewise be con-nected. He prayed:

> Father, may they be one in Us, as You are in Me and I am in You, so that the world may believe that it was You Who sent me. I have given them the glory You gave to Me so that they may be one, as We are one, with Me in them and You in Me.

3. Despite every attempt, not only in his own public lifetime but in later centuries, to represent him as a King who would redeem Israel and restore glory on earth, Jesus steadfastly rejected any social and political mission. Rather, he taught that the disciples whom he had enlightened would act as a leaven and an inspiration to converts because of their holy lives and personal deeds. The Sermon on the Mount was certainly *not* a basis for 'Liberation Theology', but a series of assurances to the poor and downtrodden that they would be *spiritually* blessed and uplifted because of their sufferings. Again, in his words to his disciples in John 15:19–25, Jesus is quoted as saying:

> If you belonged to the world, the world would love you as its own: but because you do not belong to the world, because my choice withdrew you from the world, therefore the world hates you. . .If I had not performed such works among the people as no one else has ever done, they would be blameless. As it is, they have seen all this and still hate both Me and my Father. But all this was only to fulfil the words written in their Law.

The use of the possessive pronoun in 'their law' suggests that, by this time Jesus had completely broken with the old dispensation and was preparing his disciples for an entirely new vision of the King-dom of God. It was, as he remarked firmly to Pilate, a kingdom 'not of this world'. Yet such was the vein of social materialism that came to Christianity through its Jewish precursors that, for century after century, Christ has been hailed by social moralists as the kind of public reformer he neither was nor desired to be. The Master who prophesied the downfall of the old order after his death would hardly have any ambitions to lead it — Son of God or not.

4. While Jesus exhorted his disciples to 'teach all nations' it is unlikely that he ever anticipated the universal Church of Catholic ortho-doxy after the favours granted by the Emperor Constantine in AD 312. On the other hand, Christ's charge to Peter, as the Rock on which the church was to be founded — hotly debated by many

Protestants — does not seem to be a Scriptural interpolation. Jesus probably realised that his new teaching would need a coherent vehicle which was free from Jewish taboos, though unfortunately he made no known explicit provision for it. The cultural benefits of post-Constantinian Christianity which saved the West from complete barbarism in the Dark Ages were bought at the high cost of an exclusively intolerant persecuting religious system, of which it is certain that Christ would have disapproved.

5. It is also very likely that Christ had an inner, more profound teaching for his closest followers, which was privately transmitted and later garbled or lost. References in Gnostic texts, many of them older than the Gospels themselves, quite clearly suggest this. One secret teaching, echoing Hermetism and prefiguring Neo-Platonism, may have been that we are *all* sons and daughters of God, and the Lord Jesus is merely the Divine Exemplar. Such a notion is unlikely to have been tolerated by the hearers of Jesus in the synagogues any more than it sits well with mainstream Christianity today.

6. Jesus did not endorse the exclusively masculine emphasis of Jewish religious government, and it seems clear that he saw many women as close friends and disciples no less than his chosen Twelve. We know there was a high place for both his mother, Mary, and the reformed harlot, the Magdalene, in his inner company. The recorded preference of Jesus for the company of sinners seems to have been not merely to make a point about the virtues of repentance, but to show his hearers that conventional dignity and respectability counted for little in the eyes of God.

7. While Christianity was to be marked by its dynamic activism, emphasising works no less than faith, the famous rebuke of Jesus to Martha of Bethany — the archetypal 'busy bee' of practical religion who was critical of her contemplative, adoring sister Mary — shows that the Master valued spiritual awareness even more than deeds. He was not to foster a company of tense fussers and compulsives.

8. There is no evidence either in the canonical Gospels or in early tradition that Christ gave any direction concerning wealth or economic practices. (Indeed, the parable of the Ten Talents hardly suggests that he was an early socialist!) Contrary to constant guilt-evoking statements from contemporary Christian leaders the whole concept of 'social justice' is nothing more than a modern ideological fantasy. When Christ warned of the hazards faced by the rich in reaching salvation, he was not denouncing the means to, or possession of, wealth as such. Noting the greater temptations of the wealthy

and powerful toward wrongdoing, he argued that too much pre-occupation with goods or possessions was an obstacle on the path to God: 'What shall it profit a man. . .' and 'Seek first the Kingdom of God and all other things will be granted to you'.

Everything known about Jesus suggests that he wanted to raise the spiritual consciousness of his hearers. In that mission his cause was no different from that of Gautama the Buddha and the authors of the Bhagavad-Gita, and even saintly pagan teachers like Plotinus. For the rest, the claimed divinity of Jesus as Son of God, Redeemer of Man-kind and the Second Person of the Blessed Trinity is part of great myth and a matter for faith and devotion. What made Jesus unique among the great spiritual founders was his overwhelming emphasis upon divine and fraternal love and his insistence that even one's enemies should be cherished for that portion of God's presence within them. No other world teacher left such a difficult doctrine behind, and it represents an ideal to which millions have aspired but few have attained. Did Jesus, after all, expect too much of humanity? Perhaps, but the moving story of his Passion and death proved that he was prepared to suffer incal-culably to demonstrate his own precept. Any one who can still inspire people as a living force after twenty centuries is clearly a Great Being, and certainly the most vividly human and lovable of the great religious Masters. But he fostered no obsessions. No true spiritual master has ever done so.

THE CONCERNS OF THE EARLY CHURCH

The promise of eternal life was the pivot of Christ's appeal to the masses of the Roman Empire. It sustained Christians for over 150 years of cruel but intermittent persecution by the Roman State. The promise of eternity and the persecutions themselves, coupled with garbled re-corded prophecies of Jesus about the end of the world and the seem-ingly imminent 'last days', were etched so deeply into early Christian consciousness that such things must have encouraged a widespread earthly pessimism. This was intensified by the final destruction of the great Temple of Herod in Jerusalem, which fulfilled part of the proph-ecy of Jesus with dismaying accuracy. Gnostic dualism, which tended to regard the body as a mere prison for the spirit, was also influential. The impressive heroism of so many of the Christian faithful in the face of official persecution was accordingly tainted by episodes of sheer masochism. The promise of eternal life often produced a recklessness towards one's welfare in this life in order to win merit for the next. The teaching of Christ, that the Kingdom of Heaven is *Now* no less than *Then*, seems to have become quite obscured by apocalyptic fantasies that could not fail to encourage a kind of holy misery sufficient to daunt the most fervent hedonist.

All this is not to deny the lived ideals of the early Christians: their deep fraternal care for one another, their refusal of violence and their naked bravery in the face of atrocities, beginning with those launched by Nero in AD 68. These things were admirable in a way hitherto unknown in the Roman world. Such a 'witness' could not have failed to impress the intelligent pagan onlooker, even when it appeared to him or her excessive to the point of insanity.

It is against this background that the original misgivings about the flesh voiced by St Paul and the pathological austerities practised by the desert Fathers and applauded by such spokespeople as Irenaeus, Tertullian Justin Martyr and Jerome have to be seen. Marriage was considered a baser choice than celibacy. After all, the world's end might soon be nigh, and even scourging the flesh was thought a good way of forfeiting its perishable claims in favour of a virtuous death. This was an intelligible but very sick view of life in its human fullness, grounded in a quite wilful misinterpretation of Christ's holistic view of love. Furthermore, the world of great Rome — of the Julio-Claudian and Flavian emperors — was no longer the refined, well-served Athenian community of Pericles and Plato. The marital, sexual and civic virtues of Republican Rome had broken down, leading to the rise of coarse and brutal physical excesses, which repelled even pagan onlookers such as Pliny, Seneca and Tacitus. Many of the old Greek cities themselves, such as Ephesus and Corinth, had become decadent in supporting forms of worship which were little better than decorations for physical orgies. The spectacle of such lowered life could not have failed to offend the Jewish sensibilities of such a visitor as Paul of Tarsus, one-time servant of the Temple. The followers of Christ were expected to behave better and the Epistles of Paul tried to ensure that they did.

A whole chapter could be written about the complex contribution of St Paul. He is too often written off by cynics as the primary source of Christian prudery and sexual repression. In fact, no apostle ever spoke more glowingly of the supremacy of love, even if this were seen as Agape, or spiritual love, rather than Eros. Paul suffered from a mysterious physical disability he was too embarrassed to specify, so it may have been one affecting his generative and excretory organs. He preferred celibacy for the dedicated faithful such as himself, but he admitted that 'it was better to marry than to burn' (with lust). The oft-cited passage in the Epistle to the Romans where Paul condemns unbridled sensuality and deviations such as homosexual love shows the typical aversions of a devout Jew to practices condemned long ago in much more savage terms by Leviticus. There is no evidence that he singled out individual sinners for judgement, but merely attacked degenerate lifestyles. The other side of the coin shows that he had absorbed many Greek-Platonic influences during his early studies and later travels in Asia Minor. His magnificent proclamation of Christ Risen and Glorious has a note of almost mystical exaltation, far removed from the mundane imagery favoured by the rabbis of the synagogues.

By the end of the 2nd century AD Paul had been adopted posthumously by Gnostic Christians as their Apostle, even causing the orthodox Christians of Rome to refer to him as 'the apostle of the heretics'. Hence Paul, more than anyone, sought to create a free and separate life for Christians. In this he even opposed Peter who, early on, wanted all followers of Jesus to be circumcised within the Yahwist tradition. The compulsively austere, morbidly ascetic strain in Christianity was the creation of no one person, and certainly not St Paul. A lot of it was created by a later succession of gifted moral fanatics who practised and taught a view of life not only alien to that of the rich wholeness of being exemplified by Jesus, but even to the Old Testament sexual morality of the Jews, which was as much tribal and political as spiritual. Celibacy was in fact frowned upon by Yahwism, and sex within Jewish marriage was a lusty, full-blooded affair of which neither party had reason to feel ashamed.

Apocalyptic fantasies, the exaggeration of the redemptive virtues of martyrdom, the need for exceptional discipline of life in the midst of social danger, and certain Manichaean Gnostic-Persian influences all seemed to play their part in creating a lopsided Christian tradition favourable to compulsive ascetic behaviour. Assuredly, Christianity was neither the first nor last religion to harbour such behaviour from time to time — consider the excesses of the Hindu fakirs in Indian bazaars, for example. But early Christianity made such behaviour of mainstream importance.

There are some benefits in every moral extremity. Without the example of the most celebrated desert Fathers of the 2nd and 3rd centuries, who fled into the wilderness to commune with God in solitude, the West might never have reaped the intellectual benefits of monasticism or the teaching of the great enclosed Orders about the dignity of learning and labour in the eyes of God. Most modern people find it hard to accept that not all celibacy need be unhealthy, especially if it is chosen in maturity and with the sincere objective of finding social peace and spiritual concentration. Not only Christianity but Hinduism, Buddhism and many mystic Islamic groups have all suggested that the higher path to sanctity and spiritual enlightenment is best followed without the chase after worldly goods and constant sexual satisfaction. It was only the long period of ethical decay in the monastic orders at the end of the Middle Ages that helped to produce the violent Protestant reaction against celibacy in favour of compulsive — and often compulsory — marrying.

Nevertheless, some of the early Christian desert ascetics were virtually demented. Simeon Stylites practised revolting austerities on his worm-eaten flesh, while others carried out self-tortures which were as bizarre as they were disgusting. Yet they were at least done in solitude. The best of the desert Fathers showed a kindness towards wayfarers and natural creatures that even Francis of Assisi would have applauded. The most unnatural legacy of earliest Catholic Christianity was not so much its overvaluation of celibacy, but its warped attitude to marriage and toward the innocent emotional and sexual needs of the secular majority.

THE PARADOXES OF SANCTITY AND OBSESSION

Writing from Palestine in AD 408 to a wealthy provincial young man named Rusticus, St Jerome wrote revealingly:

> Your former wife, who is now your sister and fellow servant in Christ, has told me that, acting upon the Apostolic precept, you and she lived apart by consent that you might give yourselves to prayer, but after a time your feet sank beneath you as if you were resting on water, and indeed — to speak plainly — gave way altogether.[1]

This anecdote comes rather late in the history of the peculiar custom of 'spiritual marriage' between the sexes. One would have thought that if parties did not wish to consummate marriage sexually they would be better not going through the form of it at all. Early Christian zealots seemed to believe that couples could do better. Eventually the notion of spiritual marriage came to be discredited as the Church ultimately realised its folly, but the ideal persisted at least until the 6th century AD.

In earlier times it was not uncommon for eminent clergy to tour about in the company of chaste women who served their domestic needs. These prefigured the nuns and self-effacing secular housekeepers of later centuries. Some of these early Roman ladies were so attractive that the cantankerous Jerome was angrily sceptical about chastity being preserved.

Morton Hunt believes that due to such pressure as this, Christianity both strengthened marriage in one sense and poisoned it in another. In the best Christian marriages under the Empire, women and men imparted a dignified affection to each other which had been rare in early Imperial times. Yet the physical pleasures of married life were sadly blighted by the restrictions of eminent celibates who were apparently prepared to deny to others what they could not accept themselves: an archetypal prejudice that still lingers in Vatican pronouncements to this day.

As for the social status of marriage, it was held by some early Christian leaders that a second marriage was equal to adultery. There were numerous debates in early centuries as to what Christ himself had taught about divorce. The Gospel of St Mark reports his complete prohibition, but St Matthew clearly indicates that adultery could be a ground for dissolution. By the 4th century, the clergy completely dominated marriage which could not be solemnised except by priestly consent. In the 6th century the Code of Justinian made divorce almost impossible, and listed adultery as a capital offence. The great Theodora, former harlot and Empress to Justinian, was apparently not abashed by her own previous record, but active herself in eradicating conjugal sin.

There are obvious practical advantages to a strict pattern of monogamy. For one, it makes the rearing of children much more civilised and predictable. Indeed, one of the finest contributions of Christianity was a greatly improved view of children as being especially sacred to Christ, even though the merest lip-service was to be paid to the principle in later centuries. Yet in respect of women, the Christian Fathers reversed the considerable emancipation of wives which had developed under the pagan Empire. The idea of the wife was of an inferior and sinful person who should be left at home, dominated and even punished by her spouse. Clement of Alexandria told married people when they were allowed to lie with one another, and lovemaking was only considered sinless if there was not too much delight in it. Again, Jerome imparted a dour opinion on the subject.

It is disgraceful to love another man's wife at all, or one's own too much. A wise man ought to love his wife with judgement — not with passion. . .He who too ardently loves his wife is an adulterer.[2]

. Such injunctions help explain why sexuality and its enjoyment were associated with sinfulness and guilt from earliest Christian times, and why both Catholic Christianity and Protestant fundamentalism often treated sex as the primal sin. In finding justification for this, some early Christian moralists, alas, turned back to the questionable account of the fall of Adam and Eve in Genesis.

It was widely assumed that part of the sin by which Adam fell was the collapse of a continent coupling into sexual impurity; a notion that leads us to the effect upon the Christian mentality of the moral teaching of St Augustine, Bishop of Hippo.

THE AUGUSTINIAN LEGACY

St Augustine was easily the greatest doctrinal teacher of the early Church after St Paul. He exerted an enormous influence throughout all early Christendom by pouring out a flood of brilliant commentaries which are of prime influence upon Christian theology to this day. Yet in psychological and human terms this extraordinary sage had feet of clay. His *Confessions* have been termed the first modern book, indeed one of the first authentic psychological studies in Western history, since it seems certain that Augustine revealed more of himself than he realised.

Augustine was born in 354 in Numidia in North Africa, where his father was a local magistrate, staunchly loyal to the old pagan religion of Rome. His mother, Monica, was made of different stuff. She was a fanatically dedicated Christian, seemingly gentle and virtuous, but underneath a woman of iron determination with what seems all too evidently an unwholesome Oedipal fixation on her son. Many psychologists believe this fixation to have been reciprocated by Augustine, and it does much to explain his guilty lamentation about his wicked early life. Upon close examination, this life seems not to have been especially scandalous. When he was 17 he moved to Carthage to continue his studies and acquired a young mistress to whom he was quite faithful for fifteen years. She bore him a son, whom Augustine cherished, calling him Adeodatus, or gift of God. Hardly a life of dissipation!

The pious odyssey of Augustine and his journey towards the Christian faith is well known. After teaching in Rome for a year he won the post of Public Professor of Rhetoric in Milan. There he came under the influence of the great Ambrose, Bishop of the city. His mother then moved in peremptorily to take over control of his household. Monica managed to persuade her son to expel his unfortunate faithful mistress so that he could make a 'proper' marriage with a 12-year-old girl, which could not be legally consummated for another two years. This heartless connivance exposes the basic character of Monica — later strangely canonised by the Church — as that of an appallingly meddlesome and destructive woman. She was to become the prototype of many a pious, psychologically castrating Christian matriarch in the centuries to come.

In his writings and his pastoral life Augustine suffered many of the contradictions of the modern Christian. On one hand he was a fervent believer in the Neo-Platonic exhortation to allow the individual to experience God in his or her own way; on the other, he insisted on the sanctity and binding authority of the Church as an institution. In his greatest work, the *City of God*, he displayed the world-rejecting pessimism of one who had seen from afar the sack of Rome in 410. Only the heavenly city, prefigured by the Church on earth, would last forever, while the corruption of the world would soon pass. The gulf fixed by Augustine between spirit and flesh was repeated in his concept of a material world which was incorrigibly tainted and beyond redemption. Thus, the universe of Augustine remains obstinately divided and the holistic vision of the mystic seems never to have been granted him, though he taught that the Christ-spirit had existed throughout time and was greater than the historical Jesus of Scripture.

Augustine thus remains one of the most arrestingly influential examples of an obsessional neurotic reaction. It is from the prodigious Bishop of Hippo more than from any other single Christian figure that European culture derived its deadly ambivalence towards sexuality and the figure of Woman. On one hand stands the figure of the Madonna, sheltering all those Monicas whose admixture of maternal concern and psychosexual pathology parodies the figure of the Blessed Virgin. Opposed to her stands the glamorous, flamboyant figure of the Whore, obviously fascinating, but forbidden as a consort. No wonder that, despite her friendship with Christ, Mary Magdalene never seems to have made much impact on the Western consciousness. The notion that the worldly woman in her full voluptuousness can also be virtuous and holy (in the old sense of *whole*) is something the Augustinian mentality has never been able to accept. So in the later Christian centuries, woman began to appear in many strange guises — chaste Mother, the continent but powerful Mother-Prioress, the Whore and the witch Lilith, legendary evil first wife of Adam.

The Augustinian view of woman, in which the role of chaste mother and lusty wife could never be commingled, gradually produced a tragic but well-meaning male deformity as well. The good mother could only triumph through her children, rejecting the pleasurable sexual means by which they were brought to her breast. By devaluing the female, the early Christian theologians laid the foundations for her role not only as the alleged seductress of mankind, but also the frustrated emasculatrix who sends forth her sons as psychic eunuchs into the world, where they might be capable of Agape but usually renounce Eros in favour of a raw but hopeless sexiness.

From this came one of the primary fixations of many obsessionally guilty persons, in being born of the generative organs of woman, in being erotically drawn back again to those same organs — or in the case of the unfortunate frigid woman herself, guilt in possessing such organs of pleasure at all. Augustine himself summed up the Christian conflict: 'Through a woman, (Eve) we were sent to destruction; through another, (Mary) we were reclaimed'.

The prejudices of Christian zealots in Patristic times against the body extended even beyond erotic indulgence to the time-honoured pagan custom of bathing. When Jerome came to Rome as a young man he found 900 public baths which, characteristically, he thought would be better converted to baptisteries. One who had bathed in Christ apparently needed no further washing! This ready toleration of physical dirt continued in many Christian nations until our own century. The ascetic prejudice against both nudity and the pleasure of bathing gave rise to epidemics of disease in the Christian centuries which were unknown to antiquity, even though several great cities of the ancient world were more populous than their modern counterparts fifteen hundred years later. Far from being 'next to godliness', cleanliness had to wait until Lister and the late Victorians to enjoy the connection.

The eventual conversion of the dying pagan emperor Constantine in AD 337 brought about a change in the social outlook of Christian leaders which is still debated by historians. It has long been claimed by Christian apologists that, by the mid-3rd century AD, formal paganism in all its variants was a spent force, and that pagan Europe and the Mediterranean world were waiting for the medieval Great Church, with its superlative organisation already borrowed from the political structures of a waning Empire. A brilliant recent work by Robin Lane Fox, *Pagans and Christians*, has laid this fallacy to rest. Fox demonstrates that the triumph of Christianity was certainly no foregone conclusion. In the 3rd century the Empire was becoming splintered and weakened by successive barbarian invasions, but 'Immortal Rome' itself retained its cultural opulence and magnetism right up to the first sacking of the city by Alaric the Visigoth in 410. The distorted picture of a spiritually exhausted, ideologically bankrupt Roman Empire seems to be yet another dubious Augustinian legacy.

The reign of the Antonine Emperors in the 2nd century, culminating in the reign of Marcus Aurelius, one of the most wisely sober of pagan personalities, had purged the Imperium of much of the social grossness of earlier times. For the following century, Fox has unearthed countless records that show that the old gods in their myth and their attributed virtues were still revered. As Fox writes:

> People might adhere to one god as their particular protector, but they did not convert to one god only. Pagans never had a wider choice of god than at this period, and yet these various cults show no sign of competing for people's sole adherance. Competition for converts was the business of philosophies only. . .No pagan complained of bewilderment and multiplicity had its strength. . .It helped people to explain their misfortune in external terms, by error and not by sin.[3]

Thus we touch again on one of the themes of this book, that the worship of the Infinite by various polytheistic representations has always been easier for simple folk than a grand but remotely intolerant monotheism. Jesus had proposed a decisive remedy by pointing out that the Everlasting Father dwelt as a spark in every creature. Christianity, as a movement, however, was too ready to follow the path of Judaism, stressing the transcendence of God far beyond his immanence. As a result, the Church had to face the need for other connections between heaven and earth by encouraging the cults of saints and their relics, to say nothing of the later consoling doctrine of an individual guardian angel. Even up to the 20th century it was evident that, for many uneducated Catholics and Eastern Orthodox Christians, the reverence of the Blessed Virgin and the saints and their images was merely polytheism in another guise. Again, the need for divine or demi-divine figures one could contact for intercession to liberate one from guilt and the accompanying risk of obsessional torment was all too evident. Not the least of the various reasons for the later decay of Protestantism was its failure to cater for this deep psychological need.

However the faithful Christian today might rejoice in retrospect over the rise of the Great Church in what is *claimed* to have been the victory of Christ over the heathen, the behaviour of Christian leaders after their political triumph was hardly edifying. Within a few decades of imperial conversion, Christians were visiting the same cruel discrimination upon Gnostic and pagan dissenters as had been visited upon them in earlier times. There were many Christians then still living who could recount the last great persecution of the Christians under Diocletian, and one would have expected followers of the martyred Jesus to have been more tolerant. While it is true that the West owes much to monastic Christianity because of its partial preservation of ancient culture, Christian zealots in the early centuries destroyed as much as they preserved: much of Catholic Christendom seems to have applauded the decision of Pope Gregory the Great to burn the great Palatine Library in Rome with its irreplaceable pagan texts.

In addition to the tightening Christian restrictions over free thought after Constantine, a corresponding tightening of moral laws took place. There were elaborate proscriptions for married couples no less than for the banning of homosexual activity, making it punishable by death. These righteous sanctions were in force within thirty years of the death of Constantine. Of course the latter proscription did not put on end to homoerotic love, which continued, even in monasteries, for over 1000 years up to the Reformation and beyond. Arbitrary authority rarely learns from experience in such matters.

THE RISE AND FALL OF THE CHRISTIAN COMMONWEALTH

The Christian ascetic ideal had some benefits, as did even its intolerance of other faiths. The growth of the Great Church of Catholic Christianity produced a civilisation which was to develop public intellectual tensions and social and organisational vigour in proportion to its private frustrations. When love and sex are sundered from one another and the raw appetite of conjugal sex accepted as no more than a deplorable necessary exercise in sin, the human psyche is apt to turn its energies into the paths of aggression and powerseeking. Thus, by the high Middle Ages European civilisation was marked by contrast between the elegance and beauty of its ecclesiastical scholarship, architecture and art, and the quarrelsome brutalities of a civil order presided over by a relatively unlettered nobility. Like the priesthoods of ancient Egypt, the Christian clergy jealously guarded knowledge and education as their own prerogative. Before the invention of printing it was no wonder that some great nobles and even monarchs were *ignorami*, not far removed from barbarism. But the medieval world view was not without glory, for the great Gothic cathedrals such as Amiens,

Lincoln and Bourges are standing evidence of some sublime energies at work.

Unfortunately the dream of a universal Christian order was to be banished by the very arrogance and lack of humility shown by the Church's own leaders. It was not enough that the Church could proclaim her spiritual superiority over the conduct of secular affairs. Many popes of the high Middle Ages attempted to dominate the secular State as well. The power of popes to pronounce anathema upon the heretic, and even place whole kingdoms under interdict — whereby no Christian could receive the sacraments necessary to his salvation unless his rulers repented — placed an entire civilisation under the shadow of displaced guilt. The secular powers of Europe had uneasily supported the Papacy in the disgracefully bloody episode of the crusade against the Albigensians. Much of southern France was devastated and thousands of Cathars killed or burned. Secular rulers had even tolerated the interference of the Holy Inquisition in many instances of secular offence. But the final formal proclamation of the supremacy of the Papacy over all secular power was too much for the more fiery temporal rulers of Europe to endure — especially when it was known that greed, concubinage and political intrigue flourished as luxuriantly in the Church as did any of the wisdom and holiness inspired by such luminaries as St Thomas Aquinas, St Bonaventure and St Anthony of Padua. Even in the previous century, St Bernard of Clairvaux had complained: 'Whom can you show me among the prelates who does not seek to empty the pockets of his flock rather than to subdue their vices'.

The pretension of the Papacy to both spiritual and temporal power was too often a burden to the morale of clergy and laity in the national churches outside of Italy. This was never more evident than under Pope Innocent III, who received the tiara in 1198. At his death, Innocent left the Church at the summit of its earthly power, having presided like an eloquent despot over Christendom and a closed European commonwealth sealed off from other influences by Islam to the east and the uncharted Atlantic to the west. Any protest against the Papacy from the Eastern Orthodox church had been muted by the scandalous sacking of Christian Constantinople by the predatory Latin forces of the Third Crusade.

The century that Innocent's pontificate inaugurated, the 13th, was undoubtedly the greatest and most confident in Christian history. It saw the rise of the Franciscan and Dominican orders, the incomparable stained glass and transept portal sculptures of Chartres Cathedral, the art of Giotto, the commencement by Dante Alighieri of *The Divine*

Comedy, the subtlety and brilliance of the theological Schoolmen at the University of Paris, and the legendary power and piety of St Louis IX, King of France. It also saw the beginnings of Troubadour song and poetry and the Cult of Courtly love — which hardly owed anything to the Church. Out of this latter aristocratic cult of knightly worship of chastely unattainable ladies came some improvement to the status of women. Heloise and her brilliant theologian-monk and castrated lover, Peter Abelard (not so very long dead) still provided an ugly reminder of the cruelty imposed upon those who dared breach the lopsided sexual conventions of such an epoch. However, as later chroniclers including Chaucer noted, many a great abbess and prioress contributed a lively wit and learning to the medieval discourse, without trifling with her virtue or station.

Over all this activity soared the majestic enclosing arch of the Great Church inspired by the Gospel of St John, its prayers, hours, saintly cults and festivals, its sacraments and exquisite liturgy, all crowned by the mystery of the Mass, wherein Christ was believed to be truly present in the Eucharist. Despite much socio-economic squalor at foot of stage, it was a great spiritual drama which inspired fervent participation by countless good men and women of all classes. But, like the vertiginous vault of Beauvais Cathedral, it aspired too high and before very long came crashing down.

The decay that had already set in at the summit of power in Rome was soon to infect the wider Church with the illnesses of nepotism, moral corruption, arrogant abuses of power and the endlessly compelling petty tyrannies of canon lawyers. The Bull *Unum Sanctam* put out by Boniface VIII in 1302 displayed the ultimate folly of a Pope playing Caesar. 'We declare,' he wrote, 'that it is a necessity of salvation for every creature to be subject to the Roman Pontiff.' Still smarting from old memories of the ruin in Provence and Languedoc wrought by the papal crusade against the Albigensians, the French finally lost patience with Rome. Philip the Fair of France dispatched an armed band to the Vatican. Accusing Boniface of heresy, Philip placed him under arrest. It is recorded that the vain old Pope promptly died of shock. Thus began the French 'captivity' of the popes in Avignon, leading to the rival papacies of the Great Schism, which tore so completely asunder the great web of authority woven by the Church between the 11th and 13th centuries that it was beyond convincing repair. This was not the first time the hopeless bubble of a New Jerusalem *on earth* had been exploded, and this obsession, in other secular variants, is with us still.

THE FRANCISCAN VISION

St Francis of Assisi — Francesco Bernardone — was perhaps the closest figure to Christ in temperament and outlook of any Christian, yet he founded an order of friars which was to embody a great many of the tensions and paradoxes of medieval Christianity. In his youth Francis was familiar with the language, song and poetry of the Troubadours, and he knew of the ideals and practices of courtly love. In April 1206 he had a dream which changed his life. He was to revive the old ideal of Christian austerity in a form too beautiful to have been guessed at by earlier curmudgeons like Tertullian or Jerome. Francis reached out to the world with a love of all created things which some writers have considered closer to a variant of a sanctified Gnosticism than to tougher juridical Christianity. The temper and tone of Francis also contain echoes of Sufism, but his doctrine and devotion to Christ were orthodox enough.

With its humility, renunciation of all property and utter dependence upon random charity, the Order of Friars Minor under Francis was an outstanding rebuke to the magnificence and worldly opulence of the Great Church in its most triumphant phase. But in a nod to that same Church, let it be said that its leaders had the wit to recognise in Francis an idea so overwhelmingly spiritual and touching in its impact that permission for the Little Poor Man to found a new religious order could hardly be refused. Whatever can be said against formal Christianity in the high Middle Ages, it still tried to put spirituality and the affairs of God first, eschewing the tendency to 'baptise' various forms of materialistic social action which was to occur under Protestantism and the grossly secularised Christianity that is typical today. Despite the fleshly mortifications which Francis practised upon himself, he appears to have had no special obsession with sexuality as such. He practised, rather, an almost Gnostic renunciation of the body and most of its burdens and pleasures. Yet even this holiest of Christian geniuses in the West appears to have been unable to escape a vein of obsession: his special vow of poverty and his objection to the possession of worldly goods.

The first General Assembly of the Franciscans in 1219, with Francis as their Superior, brought together 5000 friars. This astonishing increase marks the degree to which a great new wave of spiritual enthusiasm had swept through the stereotyped and over-regulated life of Christendom. Yet the Order was soon to totter under the impact of the decision of Francis' successor, Brother Elias, to renounce Francis' undoubtedly impractical rule against the owning of any property. Elias argued that the Friars Minor could not possibly conduct the complex affairs of an ongoing congregation in taverns, open fields and wayside churches. The Kingdom of Heaven had not yet arrived, and men must still conduct their affairs upon a material base. The Order would have to have convents and estates if it was to pursue its work of teaching and conversion efficiently. The followers of Elias argued that it would be a dowdy, tumbledown sort of religious organisation which conducted its affairs while its members were dressed in lice and rags. Even the most ferocious of early Christian ascetics had practised their mortifications in desert places. Ever since, poor Elias has received a bad press and is often accused of corrupting the vision of the Franciscan order's saintly founder. His difficulty is testimony to a revived strain of economic puritanism in the Church which could not prevail in the face of a common desire for material security.

The pristine Franciscan ideal, however, was not to die so easily. It was the inspiration for a number of wilder visionaries who were often slightly demented and very ready to oppose the authority of Rome. Even before Francis the infectious notion of founding a Heavenly Jerusalem on earth had been in the air. In Joachim of Floris an Italian mystic and Cistercian Abbot who had died in 1202, the latent madness of extreme Christian historicism had once more erupted in an acute form. He had prophesied that a third age of the Church, that of the Holy Spirit, would usher in 'perfect liberty' in the year 1260. Joachim became an ancestor of several deluded movements of social redemption which were to culminate over centuries in such unlikely long-term political aberrations as Soviet Communism and German National Socialism.

After Francis, radical resistance to the canons and ethics of the Great Church increased in force. With the Papacy captive in Avignon for most of the 14th century, paranoid murmurings about the 'last days' again began to filter through all levels of society, punctuated by the disastrous natural carnage of the Black Death of 1348–51 which killed off half the population of Europe.

In the next century the rebel movements led by John Wycliffe and John Huss of Bohemia (whose burning left embers which were to ignite the Reformation itself) were to end, perhaps permanently, all prospect of a universal Christian commonwealth united under one leader and one doctrine. That dynamic restlessness which was becoming a fateful characteristic of European civilisation had become too strong to contain.

The late medieval crumbling of 'Christendom' both as a concept and a fact suggests that when any organisation, religious or civil, imposes compulsive aspirations and obsessive moral demands upon human society greater than human nature ought to bear, the deluge from pent-up frustrations will not be long in coming. Would there have been less greed and power-seeking in late medieval society if there had been less official cursing of the flesh and more honest recognition of the claims of Eros? Not for those privileged classes who so often indulged their sensuality while professing penance to their obliging priestly confessors. The tragedy of any culture which bases its compulsions upon guilt is that pain and pathology is generally induced not in those uncouth souls who can flout its pressures, but in those sensitive, faithful folk whose capacity for love is most easily crippled.

THE MEDIEVAL TWILIGHT AND THE RISE OF INDIVIDUALISM

Despite the failure of the late medieval Church to find a middle way in faith and morals, such as characterises Mahayana Buddhism, the two-and-a-half centuries after about 1250 produced an impressive series of liberal religious visionaries. Their healing influence might well have averted the Protestant revolt, if the Roman See had not been the plaything of Renaissance princes and popes without effecting any real change in the moral and social outlook of the faithful majority. None of these great figures was a half-crazy, millennial figure like Joachim of Floris. The revolution they sought was more in the hearts and minds of the faithful than in the decaying structural system. Three such figures will serve as examples:

1. *St Bonaventure*: Born in 1217 and elected Minister-General of the Franciscan Order in 1257 — one of the greatest mystical theologians of all time. Bonaventure studied theology at the University of Paris and quickly set aside the arid nitpickings of the prevailing Scholastics for a much grander vision. Had it not been for the equally majestic figure of his contemporary, St Thomas Aquinas, Bonaventure might have finally restored Neo-Platonic philosophy as the official basis of Catholic theology. In his marvellous essay, 'The Mind's Road to God', he taught that God was not remote from the human soul, as classical Judaism had believed.

   Reminding his hearers that the Kingdom of God was *not* some earthly paradise, ensuing after some wrathful social apocalypse, Bonaventure taught that it was possible to enter the depths of one's own soul to find God, whose everlasting image was always imprinted there. The Divine could be approached in three major stages: in the world of Nature, within the soul itself, and finally by a soaring ascent through ecstasy to the One God existing beyond time. The Seraphic Doctor urged a precise examination of Nature in all its facets in order to reveal the Divine plan in every creature and object of interest. This encouragement was to inspire Friar Roger Bacon of Oxford, perhaps the first true empirical scientist in the Christian world.

2. *Meister Eckhart*: The towering Dominican mystic who was, not surprisingly, accused of heresy in 1321. Confined by his superiors to influence in German-speaking lands until his rediscovery in our own century, Eckhart's mystical teaching is too exalted to summarise here. But he preached the doctrine of sane, contemplative detachment as rigorously as any Buddhist sage. He claimed that 'Christ' as a divine force could be coaxed into existence out of latency in any individual soul. Taking as his cue the mystic Gospel of St John, Eckhart believed that we can all become Christs ourselves if we follow the difficult and lofty way of Jesus. He spoke of humanity as being 'in' God and not merely subject to the remoter will of Heaven. Eckhart taught that beyond the personal God, and even the Trinity itself, was the cosmic, ineffable Godhead. The ravishing optimism of Eckhart's teaching about the divine destiny of good men and women was what his doom-haunted century badly needed: a counterbalance to the religious prophecies of disaster and divine chastisement which were widespread in Europe after the Black Death.

3. *Nicholas of Cusa*: Born in 1401, Nicholas was the last great thinker of medieval Christianity, and it was to be long indeed before Christians again heard a voice of such sanity, urbanity and loving forbearance. After his visit to Constantinople, Nicholas realised that the Eastern Orthodox Church was much closer to the spirit of early Christian piety and faith than the ceaselessly regulating and anathematising Church of Rome. He was deeply influenced by Eckhart and taught that there was good in all religions and that even polytheists 'adored the Divinity in all the gods' — 'for the names attributed to God are merely derived from his creatures, since He Himself is ineffable, above all that we might name or say'. Nicholas was also one of the first of the Christian Renaissance men. He had mastered mathematics, law, elementary science and philosophy as well as theology. His remarkably successful ecclesiastical career was a tribute to his social and intellectual agility; otherwise he could have

easily followed Eckhart into oblivion. Fortunately Nicholas lived at the time of the Renaissance popes, whose worldly and sometimes scandalous personal lives had at least the side effect of making them relatively tolerant of diverse opinion.

It may seem churlish to omit consideration of the great St Thomas Aquinas. Yet his superb synthesis of Christian faith in the *Summa Theologica* has that compulsive mark of a closed, rigid theological system which was ultimately to do Catholicism more spiritual harm than good. Thomas was quite compassionate towards the flesh and human frailty when compared to his tormented counterpart, St Augustine. Yet his remark: 'It is more shameful to be incontinent in lust than in anger, because the former partakes more of our animal nature', is a sentiment that our century could hardly endorse. Two horrifying world wars, the atomic attacks upon Hiroshima and Nagasaki, the continuing authoritarian madness of dictators, could hardly persuade a 20th century onlooker that anger could be in any way less 'animal' than lust! It was one of the great blunders of the resurgent modern Papacy under Pope Leo XIII in the late 19th century that Thomism was chosen as the basis of official Catholic theology. This was to again suffocate free speculation under a blanket of rationalistic structures which the rebels of the Second Vatican Council of 1963–65 were to tear down with almost gleeful alacrity. After all, Thomas himself was reported to have experienced a great spiritual illumination at the end of his career which led him to dismiss all his previous intellectual labours as 'straw'.

Catholic Christianity, notwithstanding its mania for defining and proscribing areas of private conduct better left alone, its regular outbreaks of Caesaro-Papism, its elevation of celibacy over marriage and its Augustinian distrust of the flesh, up to Luther's time never entirely lost sight of the Gospels and the example of Christ. A high medieval civilisation that could produce Aquinas, Dante, Abelard, Francis of Assisi and many others was a tribute to a culture that the Church had largely created, and around which it had put sturdy walls to protect human life against anarchy and barbarism. The mystical, healthily speculative Hellenic strain in Catholicism had never been wholly overwhelmed by the political moralism of the Old Testament. The sacraments of the Church, principally the Eucharist and Confession, permitted the worst sinners, and even the most defiant of intolerantly defined heretics, some chance of retraction and reprieve.

THE RENAISSANCE HUMANISTS

The Italian Renaissance was very much a late flower of medieval civilisation. It was hardly the revolution in learning, art and social consciousness that its own privileged elite figures imagined. Yet the fresh and bracing winds of individualism which once again blew through the aristocratic courts of Europe helped to cool for a while many of the old orthodox fanaticisms. Catholic faith was maintained while embracing that secular learning and pagan culture which the great medieval scholars had so often spurned. Thinkers like Marsilio Ficino and Giovanni Pico, the Count of Mirandola, proposed a grand synthesis of all wisdom, Christian and pagan, Gnostic and Jewish, without doubting their status as Christians. The retrieval of the original texts of Plato and other Greeks, when scholars fled to Florence after the fall of Constantinople to the Turks in 1453, caused a great stir in the scholarly circles of Italy. The Greco-Roman legacy had never entirely faded from the Mediterranean lands, and this social difference between 'North and South' was to be one of the great psychological departure points in Europe at the time of Luther's revolt.

To Ficino and Pico, there was something of God in all worthy cults and ways of life. Even from the earlier time of Petrarch, the great pagan and humanist writers — Virgil, Plato, Aristotle, the Hermetic philosophers and even some of the sages of Islam — were seen as worthy and lofty beings, revolving like planets around the central sun which was Christ. Again, their inspiration was the Hellenic Christ of St John's Gospel — not the prophetic turbulent Messiah of the Old Testament.

Pico's famous statement that 'man is the measure of all things' has often been misunderstood. He meant that humans were the middle term of existence between Nature and God, and that man was a complete microcosm of the universe that bore him. Thus, much could be learned about God and his universe by studying humanity. This attitude was a reversal of the typical theocentric preoccupations of the medieval theologians and the Old Testament prophets. As the Papacy itself competed with secular princes to purchase the art treasures and manuscripts of antiquity, a new tolerance — and almost inevitably a new laxity — settled over the Roman Church. With great art attesting a new appreciation of the Platonic beauties of life, a certain amount of honest appreciation of the loving sexuality could re-enter through the back door of Catholic life. This loss during the Renaissance of restrictive taboos imposed by moral obsession was not without some penalties, as the brutishness of earlier ages was often refined into new forms of blasphemy, conspiracy and murder. As merely one instance of this, it was the bell sounded at the elevation of the Host at High Mass in the Cathedral of Florence which was the signal for the callous assassination of Giuliano di Medici in 1478.

Meanwhile the peasant masses of Europe continued to toil, live and die in a largely agrarian economy, as they had done for centuries. For such unlettered folk the pieties of the Great Church still greatly mattered, despite the corruption of Rome and the exploitation of their credulity and generosity by wandering bands of monkish confidence men.

One outstanding figure on the threshold of the Reformation has great significance for any study of the role of obsession and compulsion in civilisation. He was Desiderius Erasmus of Rotterdam, one of the greatest foes of compulsion, who died in 1536. Erasmus was a new kind of man. By his own admission, he was neither physically nor politically courageous, but his was the greatest voice of sanity before the collapse of Christendom into warring factions. His satire on the entry of the late Pope Julius II into heaven left little doubt in the mind of the chuckling reader that he held the state of the Papacy in contempt. But as a Catholic with a strong sense of tradition, he regarded the rebellion of Luther with even greater horror. The Great Church had indeed become corrupt and disordered in its parts, he argued, but peaceful reform was possible. He had no intention of seeing Europe given up to a barbarous Nordic type of religious enthusiasm if he could help it.

Erasmus was born apparently the illegitimate son of a physician's daughter and a man who later became a monk. After spending six years at a monastic college of Augustinian monks, Erasmus was filled with anger at the decadent life he found there. He became an enemy of the frivolous and pedantic debates of the Scholastic theologians, and spent much of his life outlining the abuses in ecclesiastical life and calling for reform of the Church from top to bottom. In 1516 he published an annotated New Testament which was virtually the first Greek text available to the West and he tried to rationalise and humanise Christian doctrine. Not surprisingly, as one of history's great scholarly foes of obsession and compulsion in all its forms, Erasmus was to be abused by both sides in the coming religious conflict. Like his great admirer and friend, Sir Thomas More, he strove to become a voice of moderation and sanity in a world increasingly dominated by various forms of messianic madness.

In his brilliant criticisms of the prevailing order, Erasmus had done his work almost too well, and his writings were to be used to destroy rather than reform the Church he loved but found it impossible to admire. Many would consider him a compulsive vacillator and doubter, but he had none of the torment or urgency of nature which marks the compulsive personality. If Erasmus had been heeded, the Reformation and the terrible wars of religion that were to follow after it could well have been avoided.

THE PROTESTANT REFORMERS

The effect of the Reformation upon Western culture may be considered in two main ways — as either a reactionary rejection of the scholarly and individualistic interests of the Renaissance, or as a progressive outgrowth and enlargement of some aspects of these interests. In some ways, it was both. But the Reformation had the unfortunate long-term effect of throwing faithful Christians too much on to their private resources and cutting them off from the mythic benefits and consolations of a confessional church. They were to be without trust in the benign mediation between humans and God by the Virgin and the Saints. In choosing to wholly embrace marriage and the family and by rejecting the life of apartness and prayer, Protestant potentates both welcomed the wife and enslaved her in one measure. Moreover, Protestant leaders were often prepared to make common cause with secular rulers for their own advantage. This assisted the later rise of nationalism and the pugnacious obsession with 'self-determination' among various races and peoples which has become both the glamour and the bane of the last two centuries.

Perhaps most of all Protestantism revived the old dreams of a perfect City of God on Earth, partly refuting the ancient contention of Augustine that the two cities must forever lie apart. In so many ways Protestant doctrine represented a return to the ancient tribal view of life depicted in the Old Testament. It was not surprising that the reformers, particularly Calvin, were to refer constantly to the censorious teachings of the Old Testament prophets as their source of authority. Rejecting the rule of Rome and of the Papacy which claimed to derive its traditional teaching from the Apostles themselves, Protestantism rejected a powerful Roman Magisterium and opted for the literal teachings of an all-powerful book, the Bible, instead. It was no coincidence that the Protestant enthusiasm for Scripture coincided with the invention of printing and the possibility of widespread lay access to the sacred writings. Like the Judaic society it so unwisely copied in its first two centuries, Protestantism rested its claims upon a verbal and vocal culture. It knew even better than the Dominican preachers how to harangue and threaten from pulpits, to implant the kind of guilt in the hearts of the multitude which would make them docile for very fear of their salvation.

As Kenneth Clark has pointed out, Protestantism in the main, produced no great art. Like the Hebrews of old who had to build the great Temple of Solomon with the aid of Egyptian builders, Protestants were suspicious of visual imagery. Eros is never far from great art, even when lent for religious purposes. Protestant leaders were overwhelmingly interested in *logos* — the word which could not really encompass the Word made Flesh. Yet Protestant reformers, like it or not, still had to build the new structures of their churches and group life on the foundations of fifteen hundred years of Christian experience.

As their name suggests, Protestants partly formed their first doctrines on the basis of negation. They knew what they hated about the old Roman dispensation, and in developing a new, austere anticlerical religious style they destroyed far more of the better legacy of the Great Church than they kept. The greatest Protestant aim was to invigorate the person of individual force and enterprise, replacing the old Culture of Obedience with the new Culture of Will. Carl Jung, himself the son of a Swiss Protestant minister, saw all too clearly the dangers to which the rise of Protestantism had exposed the Western psyche. He wrote:

> The Protestant has lost the sacred images expressive of important unconscious factors, together with ritual which, since time immemorial, had been a safe way of dealing with the unaccountable forces of the human mind. A great amount of energy thus became liberated and went instantly into the old channels of curiosity and acquisitiveness by which Europe became the mother of dragons that devoured a greater part of the earth.[4]

Commenting elsewhere he also remarked:

> As soon as the dogmatic fence was broken down, and as soon as Catholic ritual had lost its authority, man was confronted with an inner experience without the protection and guidance of a dogma and ritual. Protestantism, in the main, lost all the finer shades of worship, the Mass, the Confession, the greater part of the liturgy and the sacrificial importance of the priesthood.[5]

Let us now turn to the personalities and impact of the two most famous Protestant reformers, Martin Luther and John Calvin. Luther has come down to us as a not unattractive figure, despite the explosive and neurotic inconsistencies of his nature. There was nothing cold or dry about him, and the contrast between his intellectual brilliance and industriousness and his later love of robust and earthly pleasures makes him in so many ways a stereotyped emblem of German genius. One can imagine his fury at the effeteness, luxury and squalid hypocrisy that he found in Rome during his fateful visit there in 1511. What he observed doubtless prompted his decision to use honest marital sexuality as one of his weapons in the war against Rome. Early on he sanctioned the marriage of priests and denounced celibacy, arguing that it had been invented by the Devil as a source of sin. Later in his career, he advanced to the even more radical view that marriage was not a holy sacrament at all but a civil affair, mainly a subject for secular contract and regulation rather than canon law. Emboldened by the success of his rebellion, he also seems to have thought that Christ probably committed adultery with Mary Magdalene, and possibly other women, so as to partake fully of the nature of man. Such was the extremity of a former Augustinian monk who had wrestled against the pressure of his vows long and honestly to the point of a virtual mental breakdown.

Luther was the son of a tough German peasant, who became a miner. He was beaten mercilessly for small errors and imbued with a vivid sense of his own wickedness. He was taught to believe in both the Devil and God with equal fervour, and he fully believed in demons and strange powers. The harsh factors which worked upon his nurture seem to have implanted in him qualities of hysteria, obsession and sanity in about equal measure. The hysteroid element in his personality enabled him to rid himself of many obsessions after his first great gesture of rebellion against the Church at Wittenburg in 1517. Always he retained the typical tendency of the obsessive personality to work, pray and preach with an eye to perfection. Afterward, his increasing indulgence towards fleshly joys enabled him to keep his balance in the course of a wild career. He remarked: 'If our Lord God may make an excellent large pike and a good Rhenish wine, I may very well venture to eat and drink. Thou mayest enjoy every pleasure in the world which is not sinful'.

Luther's words are those of an obsessive-compulsive personality who has in part overcome the fixations of his early life; but in his preaching he had an almost terrifying single-mindedness which is the mark of every religious zealot. At times he still spoke like the sin-tortured monk he once was. 'We are the children of wrath', he claimed, 'and all our works, intentions and thoughts are nothing at all in the balance against our sins'. The hysteroid quality in Luther's make up made it possible for him to espouse inconsistencies which the lay person wrongly labels as 'schizoid'. It is the hysteric, after all, who is usually capable of not letting his virtuous right hand know what his scurrilous left hand is up to. A man who could urge German princes to 'smite, stab and kill' the rebellious peasants of Germany for fear of the fate of his new religion was also one who could weep over a crushed cornflower he found in the winter snow.

Luther's genius lay in his personal charisma. Energetic, manly and affectionate, as well as coarse, bawdy, and abusive, he lit up the whole landscape of Europe like a lightning flash until his death in 1546. Yet his inconsistencies could be shameful. He espoused the cause of the common people when it suited him and betrayed them when he needed the power of the German princes to back his fight against Rome. Thus he set in train the fatal tendency in Protestantism to tack one's sails to the prevailing winds of secular power. However, he kept enough of the old Catholic traditions to preserve some continuity between Christian medieval civilisation and the ages to come, which is probably why Lutheranism has been more resilient than many Protestant denominations, in retaining some grip upon its adherents to our own time.

There can be no doubt that, with Luther, Europe had entered upon four centuries of a culture pattern marked by intense secular and religious striving, with guilt and sometimes despair as the driving social engines. The loss of Catholic confession and the Church's claims to absolve the sinner had incalculable consequences for the dilemmas of the Protestant conscience. In the rejection of contemplativeness and its higher corollary of promised spiritual bliss, Europeans were to plunge themselves into an endless round of compulsive doing. They believed more emphatically than at any time since St Augustine that they were remote from God, and were thus compelled to make as much of their secular state on earth as they possibly could. If Christians were undoubtedly history's first over-achievers, from the middle of the 16th century this was to be doubly true of most devout Protestants.

The effect of the second major Protestant reformer, John Calvin, on the religious and secular life of the Western world was an appalling one. Calvin will ultimately go down as one of history's greatest tyrants. His tyranny was the worse for having burrowed corrosively into the depths of human sensitivity and finer feeling. Far more than Luther, he caused millions to despair of their worthiness in the eyes of God. His infamous doctrine of predestination would be, for as long as it was held in totality, one of the cruellest doctrines ever taught among civilised people. Devoid of any of its original subtleties, the doctrine was soon understood by most Calvinists to mean that since God had known from all eternity who among men and women would be saved or damned, they would have little chance of obtaining any personal merit in earthly life to offset this predestined knowledge. Calvin's doctrine had originally been proposed by St Augustine, but it had never carried much weight among theologians until Calvin took it up and turned it into an instrument of psychological despotism. Moreover, whereas Augustine had tried to make a distinction between God's foreknowledge of human fate and the exercise of human free will, Calvin appeared to be saying that the exercise of free will made little difference to human fate or the Divine plan. Significantly, in the almost 720 000 words of Calvin's arid tome *The Institutes of the Christian Religion*, the word 'love' appears only twice.

Calvin was born at Noyon in Picardy in 1509. His upbringing by a harsh stepmother may help to explain the coldness of his later nature. He was plagued by headaches, indigestion and fits of anger; later on he acquired ulcers, kidney stones and tuberculosis. Nevertheless, like many obsessives of fanatical bent, he studied with deadly intentness to perfect his mind in law no less than sacred knowledge. Converted by Luther's teaching, he soon began to write his own blueprint for primitive Biblical Christian life. After becoming a preacher in the city of Geneva and already famous at 27, he eventually became the virtual dictator of the manners, mores and almost every facet of human life in the city. Geneva became a theocracy, ruled by a Consistory of religious elders with Calvin at its head.

Calvin's rule over Geneva was written into legend by its blasphemous trespass against the simple loves and pleasures which Christ shared with his friends and Apostles. It was punishable by fine or imprisonment to sing or dance (even at weddings), to use profane language, to serve too much food at dinner or wear ornaments or jewellery or anything other than the plainest of clothes and hairstyles. Sexual faults were not only transgressions against morals but they were treated as heresy. Fornication could cause the (lucky?) offender to be exiled, and adultery merited death by drowning or beheading. To be fair, many sinners were let off the extremity of these sentences, but only after being terrified out of their minds and given steep fines and gaol sentences. It was soul-terror that Calvin's grim band aimed at inducing, and he was too icy-natured even to rejoice at the sight of bloodshed. Calvin left no record of inner anguish or sufferings, but it is evident that he must have been a tormented creature indeed. As far as one can determine, he remained completely celibate until an unfortunate, good-hearted widow fulfilled his particular requirements as a wife and faithful companion-house-keeper. She died nine years later, and Calvin wrote about her some of the few kindly words he was ever known to have penned.

Like the early Fathers, Calvin reverted to the idea that marriage has two main functions — the production of offspring and the remedying of incontinence. He had the same woman-suspecting and body-fearing qualities as the early Christian ascetics. While commanding marriage of the majority he had nothing to say about companionship, affection, passion, or adoration between husband and wife. Oddly enough, a woman in Geneva could sue for divorce if her husband became impotent, but even Calvin's own stepdaughter and son-in-law were condemned for adultery. Furthermore Calvin comforted himself with the odious thought that Almighty God had sent syphilis to punish those who escaped the law in 'sly and naughty ways'.

With so many prohibitions placed upon interest in sexuality, enjoyment, the arts, food, natural joys and even the smallest of luxuries, there remained indeed only one activity whereby man could be justified: *work*. Commercial prosperity could issue from the compulsive pursuit of work throughout life. So arose the notorious puritan work ethic, which was to provide modern Europe with such a dynamic thrust toward material improvement and (as we now know) material destruction. Unable to earn salvation on their own merits, men and women could only strive by a grim combination of natural wealth and personal meanness of life to demonstrate to themselves no less than to their neighbours that they might indeed be among the predestined Chosen.

For the first time in Christian history, material success could be seen openly as a mark of God's favour. Every opportunity for gain was to be emphasised with complete confidence in God's 'calling' to hard work. Later this applied in ever larger extent to commerce and the business of making and exchanging money. In a sense Calvinism and its many Protestant offshoots laid the foundation of a world of specialised labour which taught men to work for work's sake. In the end, it produced the typical middle-class way of life to which we are accustomed in the 20th century. The original psychological principles involved were those born of religious compulsion and the baptism of Mammon which has today long outlived the religious impulse that once gave it sanction. All the words which we now associate with the world of business and commerce — 'growth', 'progress', 'development' — originally had their origin in the ascetic thrust of over-restricted libido into the channels of material acquisition. The view of St Thomas Aquinas that 'virtue consists in the good rather than the difficult' would have found little favour among 16th-and 17th-century Calvinists.

Calvinism not only promoted obsessive-compulsive traits in an un-paralleled manner; it was itself a complete system of obsessions and compulsions parading as godliness. His own words reveal the bleakness, and sadistic bent of his nature:

> Let it stand therefore as an indubitable truth. . .that the mind of man is so entirely alienated from the righteousness of God that he cannot conceive, desire or design anything but what is wicked, dis-torted, foul, impure and iniquitous; that his heart is so thoroughly envenomed by sin that he can breathe out nothing but corruption and rottenness; but if some men occasionally make a show of good-ness, their mind is ever interwoven with hypocrisy and deceit.[6]

Calvin's attitude toward human relationships was harsher even than anything the hardest of the early Church Fathers could have conceived It was little wonder that Puritanism in its later forms could not main-tain such restrictions, and that in England, at least, it had lost a lot of its power to compel and terrorise the imagination of the mainstream faithful by the mid-18th century. But the miserable parsimony of emotion and spontaneous feeling which the obsessive Calvinist con-science imposed infected almost every sect of Protestantism to a greater or lesser degree. Moreover, after the abolition of nunneries, women came to be regarded as mere bondservants of their sires. Richard Hooker, a founding theologian of the Church of England, remarked as much in the reign of the redoubtable Elizabeth I:

> For this cause brides were in marriage delivered unto their husbands by others. . .This putteth women in mind of a duty whereunto the very imbecility of their nature and sex doth bind them, to be always directed, guided and ordered by others.[7]

The tremendous diversion of energies which the espousal of evangel-ical Protestantism accomplished for Europe was also to have ironically valuable fruits in the furtherance of industrial techniques and science as well as commerce. For this, not only Western folk but humanity in general have some reason to be grateful. But as I shall argue in the next chapter, the Protestant climate in which so much of the science of Northern Europe grew up imparted to it a habit of *categorising* in-numerable facets of natural reality to the degree where, by the mid-19th century, the categories themselves had been turned into pillars of dogmatic secular truth. Science in the wake of Protestantism was not only to inherit the Greco-Christian curse of an exaggerated rationalism, but formed its brotherhoods and societies on quasi-religious, pontifical and exclusive lines.

Protestant theory cannot be said to have made capitalism possible, for history gives the lie to this. After all, early forms of capitalism were flourishing in Florence as early as the 14th century, while the rich merchants of the Netherlands were still reaping profits from the Spanish gold of the Indies before Luther's rebellion had fully begun. In fact, even by the mid-14th century the taboo imposed by the medieval Church on the lending of money for interest, or usury, had become an accepted dead letter. But what Protestantism in general and Calvinism in particular did accomplish was not only to make capitalism respectable but to have capitalists themselves regarded as the working arm of God busy transforming the world. This new commercial industrial, exploitative scientific world view was summed up in the early 17th century by Sir Francis Bacon, who exclaimed: 'We must interrogate nature with power'.

It was not until after Adam Smith wrote *The Wealth of Nations* that economic theory based upon work and profit as a sign of 'election' shifted mainly to an economic system based upon the secular energies of self-interest and hedonistic desire. The Calvinist note was to be softened yet again in the early 19th century by the doctrine of Jeremy Bentham, who outlined an economic regime which catered for 'the greatest good of the greatest number'. Yet even up to our own time, the Calvinist, Eros-avoiding obsession with work for work's sake has never really departed from the consciousness of the Western entrepreneurial classes. Moreover, it has too often been associated with emotional woodenness or sterility in one's role as spouse, friend, parent or lover.

Meanwhile, the mystical quest for spiritual liberation, which had always served as a pressure valve for the erotic confinements of medieval Catholicism, had eventually to show itself in Protestantism also, if only in exceptional cases. The gracious spiritual amplitude of Anglicanism in the time of the pious Charles I and Archbishop Laud produced the finest flowering of 'Anglo-Catholic' mysticism — among its special voices being the metaphysical poets Herbert, Vaughan, Crashaw and the extraordinary ecstatic, Thomas Traherne. The Lutheran Church likewise had not lost all of the old medieval inwardness, and it maintained a climate sufficient to nurture 17th-century mystics of the stature of Jakob Boehme.

A vital aspect of this argument has been that, far from adding to the narrowing and drying effects of obsession in human life, true practical mysticism often gives that life an elevation and fragrance which can bring both erotic love and spiritual striving into some sort of balance. The poverty of Calvinism and the sects of Baptists and later Methodism in their several forms was that they left so little inner psychic ground to which the over-sermonised and busy populations of evangelical Protestantism could retreat. So Nonconformism in all its radical variants became increasingly extrovert and associated with various worthy to cranky crusading social reform movements. These, at least, did some tangible good in Britain and America for the underprivileged classes in the harsh early period of industrial expansion. The sense of remoteness from a God who was exiled, not only by theologians but by scientists, to a realm beyond the stars left Protestant enthusiasts little choice but to proselytise fervently for Godly community life. In this pursuit they were to try to purify and ultimately to meddle in those secular affairs for which the clergy, due to their very calling, usually have so little talent.

THE CATHOLIC REACTION AND RECOVERY

The Counter-Reformation, in producing its own answer to Calvinist Protestantism, inevitably had to absorb a few of its influences. This was particularly noticeable in the rise of Jansenism in 17th-century France. Originating in Cornelius Jansen, a Calvinistically inclined Dutch bishop, this cult developed into a type of Catholic puritanism. Jansenism frowned upon pleasure, worldly ambition, secular learning and what it regarded as laxity of Jesuit confessors in particular towards immorality of all kinds. Although it ultimately died out as a real force in France after the destruction of the heretical Convent of Port Royal by Louis XIV, its influence upon exiled Irish clergy studying at French seminaries was to place a heavy Eros-denying incubus upon the Irish psyche. Indeed it is doubtful whether Irish Catholicism has ever recovered from the effects of the Jansenist heresy. After the English Protestant 'Ulster Plantation' under William of Orange, the only native Irish intelligentsia left to exert any influence on the population were a motley French-schooled puritanical clergy. Their work served to revive and intensify an intense Augustinian suspicion and repression of the flesh. This tainted outlook was later carried by otherwise devout Irish missionary clergy around the earth to North America, Australia and even parts of Africa. To this day Ireland has the most oppressive laws affecting sexual and conjugal affairs of any Western society.

As for the European mainstream of Catholicism, it was the aim of the reformed Papacy to cleanse its own house of former abuses, restate doctrine and combat Protestantism. To act as the spearhead of this task, Ignatius of Loyola founded the Society of Jesus. Because of Ignatius' own remarkable awareness of the dangers of excessive moral zeal, the Society won a degree of popular success which defied Protestant prophecies about the end of Popery.

However, the expunging of some of the moral squalor of the Renaissance Papacy was almost risibly typified by the acts of the former libertine Paul III, who ordered the expulsion of hundreds of prostitutes and clerical concubines from the city of Rome. An equivalent note of high clerical comedy was later provided by Pope Pius V, prowling about the Vatican art collection and ordering that suitably decorous coverings be provided for the formerly unabashed pelvic regions of many a sculptured or painted nude. Yet for all this revived prudery, throughout the Baroque movement in art the Catholic Church rarely failed to use the beautiful face or body to inspire religious emotion.

The Catholic answer to the various Protestant-inspired social movements up to our own century was to create a second renaissance in worldwide missionary activity, and to encourage the foundation of a large number of new religious teaching and nursing orders, which performed under the aegis of a spiritual rule a remarkable number of merciful services to the poor, the sick and the outcast. In Protestant lands such services had to wait until almost the middle of the 19th century to receive wide support from church leaders and secular governments.

Surely the greatest of Catholic figures in this sphere was the famous 'Apostle of Charity', Vincent de Paul, who died in 1660. Vincent may be considered virtually the founder of modern nursing care for the sick and poor. He left behind him not only several flourishing hospitals and his own Order of the Sisters of Charity, which he founded in Paris in 1634, but a radiant inspiration toward the service of the poor which spread not only throughout the whole Catholic Church but to non-Catholic nations as well. Vincent continued a tradition which had never disappeared from Catholicism — even in its most venal and corrupt decades — that of a true saint who accepted, without compulsion or neurosis, asceticism and poverty for himself while not expecting anybody to choose the same path except by their own desire.

Meanwhile, in the annals of mysticism the great Carmelite superior,

Teresa of Avila, managed to ignore the fanaticism of Spanish Catholic piety under Philip II by keeping a remarkable balance between disciplined commonsense and the most sublime outpourings of religious writing based upon her mystical visions. An authentic saint herself, Mother Teresa rarely forgot her sense of humour and she was not ashamed to use open erotic imagery in her celebration of Christ. In her renunciation of the body, she also achieved a magnificent sublimation of its demands. One of the shrewdest of Christians, Teresa understood the follies of bigotry and governed her sisters accordingly.

But despite rare souls like Vincent and Teresa, the evil fruits of the division of Christendom between Protestant and Catholic were expressed in relentless persecutions of one by the other, and by the devastating wars of religion, which were to last sporadically from Luther's time until the middle of the 17th century.

English-speaking Christianity and the spread of empire

It was in the British Isles that the drama of religious-cum-political obsession was most effectively played out within an entire social order. England had already been served a large taste of Calvinism after the death of Henry VIII with the accession of the Protestant Somerset as Regent. Over the border in Scotland, John Knox combined the dour legalism of Calvin with his own wrathful, choleric nature. Having broken the unfortunate spirit of Queen Mary Stuart and driven her from the throne, Knox continued to threaten sinners with damnation from his pulpit in Edinburgh even when he became blind, frail and prematurely old. The spell of devout but gloomy industriousness that he cast over the formerly turbulent Lowland Scots was to last well into the late 19th century, despite savage satire from free spirits such as Robert Burns.

Among the shrewder, more politically sophisticated English, however, Puritanism as a minority influence achieved its most adroit secular adaptations. These were to outlast the Civil War after which the Stuart monarchy was first abolished in 1649 then restored in 1660. Puritans exiled to the Atlantic colonies of America in the 17th century were to have a more profound effect upon English-speaking civilisation in the New World than they were ever to achieve in the urbanely compromising land of their birth. Oliver Cromwell and the Puritan movement are almost inseparable in the popular mind. But most of Cromwell's successors, with a shrewd eye to social advancement and the protection of their lands and purses, knew that they had to abandon his rigidity and his military brutalities if they were to secure a place in English society.

The Puritan and Nonconformist spirit was to provide a core for the successful British bourgeois class of the next two centuries. Yet by 1730 Montesquieu, upon visiting England, remarked: 'There is no religion in England. If anybody mentions religion, everybody begins to laugh'. It was a sweeping judgement, but aptly expressed the contemptuous weariness concerning most religious questions which had spread throughout the more educated folk of the British Isles. The English had seen the destructive effects of over a century of often bloody religious compulsion and were more than happy to become (in part) that 'nation of shopkeepers' of which Napoleon spoke.

Not so in the New England colonies, however. Many of the most odious features of Puritanism — its superstitious fear of the Devil, its taste for witch-hunting which had already begun to die out in Europe, its compulsive 'Bible-bashing', its distaste for the beautiful and impulsive — were to be preserved in America almost until the mid-19th century. As a French traveller visiting New England in about 1800 wrote:

> In this country as in others we find a mixture of vices and virtues but the virtues seem less attractive than elsewhere. They lack the charm which could make them lovable. The vices, on the other hand, seem more repulsive as there is a gloomy absence of any art which could hide them.[8]

In truth, the Puritan ethic with its regular urge for public denunciation and confession and its invincible self-righteousness has never really left American political and social life.

The socially redemptive and reformative thrust of religion nearly always tends to gain at the expense of the interior life of its adherents. Indeed, only saints seem to hold their faith, deeds and experiences in a well-balanced load. Calvinism, Wesleyan Methodism, and the 19th-century Baptist sects in the United States could only tap the spiritual and emotional aspects of religious confession by their ceaseless emphasis upon the theme of personal salvation as against damnation. Oddly, there was less thought of using Christ himself as a model for spiritual life. The Old Testament prophets were monotonously trotted out to present the faithful with the alternatives of strict conformity or doom. Overwhelming oratory and fervent popular hymnody were the hallmarks of Nonconformist worship, and never more than in the pulpits of the

Scottish Presbyterian 'low kirk', the Welsh Methodist chapel and in the later, barely literate, rantings of American Middle-West revivalism.

However it is easy enough for those who prefer the superior aesthetics and dignity of Catholic, Anglican and Orthodox worship to shudder over lugubriously vulgar styles of Protestant enthusiasm. Such sturdy evangelical communities of the 'saved' had at least the merit of stirring and sustaining millions of simple folk in the depressed urban working classes and among the hard-pressed pioneer rural communities of North America and Australia. Indeed, by the end of the 19th century in Wales, Anglican Church versus Nonconformist Chapel seemed to have divided the country entirely along class lines.

Even so, the missionary bulldozings of extreme Protestant enthusiasm were to be found far less bearable in the foreign communities they laboured to convert. For every reformer like William Wilberforce, who secured the abolition of slavery in the British dominions, every tolerant Quaker like Elizabeth Fry, who thought to offer comfort to the wretched in English prisons, there were dozens of high-stomached zealots who treated the religious practices of Asians, Pacific Islanders and native Americans as a challenge to their powers of coercion. It was never remotely conceded that the 'heathen' might have been innocently worshipping the One True God under other more accessible forms. Cultural practices that had sustained Asian and Pacific peoples for centuries were treated as devilish rituals to be expunged with fiery denunciation and bullying methods.

To be sure, the world was well rid of Aztec human sacrifice and such ugly customs as that of widows being burnt alive in Hindu *suttee*. Yet the muscular intolerance and lack of respect for other faiths which is typical of extreme monotheistic religion distorted the whole passage of Christian evangelism in foreign lands for at least a century and a half. For their part, the hapless 'natives' were to find that when men of the Christian cloth waxed too wrathful, the hostile guns of soldiers and traders would follow soon after. The cultural subversion of the native people of Hawaii in the 19th century by the members of the Boston Missionary Society is but one example.

Catholicism, too, had its own episodes of missionary folly in spreading Christianity beyond Europe, but it learned its lessons early. Within a decade of Cortez' conquest of Mexico the great Bishop Las Casas was pleading (with limited effect) with the Emperor Charles V that the conquered Indians be exempted from the usual charges of heresy, and that their customs be studied and preserved wherever they were found to be of benefit. Similarly, French Jesuits were anxious that military rule in Canada be not attended by the typical blood-letting, avarice and destruction which uneducated soldiers and freebooters brought in their wake. Out of this courage in the face of fierce resistance from the Indians arose episodes of alliance and friendship between races that were usually absent in the British colonies. There, the combination of pioneering courage, evangelical intolerance and greed for territory were to lead to a dozen broken treaties.

By the mid-18th century political, commercial and nationalistic concerns had largely obliterated the purchase of religion over the public affairs of Western nations. The relationships of parliaments and monarchs to popes, bishops, moderators and divines became more formal than real. What, then, had survived of the Christian rage for perfection, or Utopia on earth? Three legacies remained:

1. The Calvinistic notion that if one did not win merit and advancement on earth, one could hardly be sure of attaining it in heaven. After the decline of the claims of religion upon the restless Western intellect, it was an easy matter to let 'heaven' go and work feverishly against the dying of the light, obtaining a legacy of honour for oneself and one's offspring alone.
2. The loss of the indwelling mystic sense of God made it difficult for ordinary souls to hold on to the alternative notion of a remote and transcendent Deity. Scientific investigation had largely expanded the universe and this added to the individual's sense of loneliness and isolation from a post-Reformation God. Also, art, commerce, new medicine, science and the prolongation of human life, meant that earthly existence no longer needed to be so 'nasty, brutish and short'. As the ascetic privation of the senses ceased and geographical horizons expanded, the characteristic busyness and compulsiveness of Western intelligence had more chance to evade meditative inwardness and that deeper self-knowledge which can only come from some resort to it. Increasingly religion became, in the terms of Max Weber, a socially useful, validating membership which offered security rather than enlightenment. It was now not so much a means to salvation as a way of consolidating one's place in a tribe or caste. Little wonder then that the poor — especially in the English-speaking industrialised nations — found scant comfort in this sort of Christianity. It had won little enough for them on earth and now could not even hold out a convincing promise of life eternal. And this situation persists to the present day.
3. The lasting psychic deformity that Hebraic/Augustinian/Calvinistic

Christianity had inflicted upon conjugal and erotic relationships was to be a blight that even the most abandoned secular pursuit of vice could not shake off. The dichotomy between sexual restraint and 'sexiness', Agape and Eros, in the search for love in its natural expression, is a neurotic binary still to be bridged by Western societies. Pornography and prudery, rape and impotence, are the ugly contrasted stepchildren of sexual fear and oppression.

Hence, with the decline of spiritual inwardness, it was the moralistic, meddlesome guilt-evoking social concerns of Christianity that were to last most vigorously into our own time, making the Churches increasingly hostage to the doings of those ruthless secular powers they had once tamed and tried to uplift. Meanwhile, the still all-too-distant Christ stands beyond the crumbling margins of literal dogma, beckoning the faithful to that freedom of spirit he originally promised them. If the Kingdom of God is not 'within', it is unlikely to be found in any earthly Utopia humankind can hope to construct.

THREE

THE WORSHIP OF ABSTRACTION

A h, Liberty!
What Crimes are committed in your name.

Madame Roland (on her way to the guillotine, 1793)

Science has promised us truth...it has never promised us either peace or happiness.

Gustave Le Bon

There is a pertinent joke to the effect that Satan was walking through the world one day in the company of a senior demon. The demon nudged the Lord Lucifer and noted anxiously: 'Sire, look over there. Some person has picked up an important piece of truth. We had better look to our safety'. Satan smiled nonchalantly. 'Never mind, my dear fellow. We are in no danger. He will now try to systematise it.' Indeed, the world needs ordered systems — never more than today, with large populations burdening a crowded planet. But the obsessional mentality wants a *perfect* system which can lead in practice only to tyranny or its natural antithesis, which is revolution or anarchy. In all political and social systems, a craving for perfect government leads to a dangerous worship of ideological *abstractions*. Since the 18th century we have been brainwashed with many of these beguiling yet phantom abstractions. We know them now as well as the foods we eat: 'Liberty' — 'human rights' — 'self-determination' — 'social justice' — and, the most hypnotic ruling abstraction of all, 'Democracy'. Yet there is no true democracy on this earth and in view of the planet's increasing population, never likely to be.

The Church in its medieval heyday fostered few abstract concepts outside of theology. Before the rise of nationalism in the 16th century, even the concept of 'the State' was hazy by modern standards and only 'Christendom' seemed to have some ring of authority. Even so, the medieval Scholastic abstraction of 'Nature' and 'natural law' borrowed from Aristotle still lingers obstinately about our modern civic rationalisations of virtue and vice. The most notable sphere where 'natural law' was teased out into detailed canonical refinements was that of sexual conduct, especially adultery and homosexual love which remains categorised as 'unnatural' among pious Christians. The Catholic Church still extends a network of 'disordered acts' over everything from artificial contraception to masturbation and all kinds of mercy killing — frequently flouting currrent scientific understanding in the process. It seems that a simple designation of sin or virtue is not deemed sufficient in such matters.

By contrast, today's political and social abstractions tend to be interpreted and corrupted according to the ideology embraced by whoever uses them. One is praised or damned as much for convictions as acts. Sin now wears a particular political cockade, while virtue can be constructed by whoever wields civic power. Normally, who or what could realise such grand abstractions as 'science', 'truth' or 'freedom'? Yet such terms have long become the catchphrases of every cub journalist. Contemporary abstractions are what people commonly react to, rather than think about.

It is essential at this point to distinguish between *myth, symbol* and *abstraction*. So far, we have touched upon some of the great religio-political myths of the premodern world. A myth is not a mere synonym for a picturesque untruth. A myth often encapsulates a very important truth — sometimes an ineffable reality — in fictional or allegorical form. For example, the Resurrection of Christ is one of the most potent myths of Western civilisation. Assessed with a stone-kicking, literal-minded attitude, the Resurrection is a wild improbability. Yet as myth it embodies resonances of an event which still resounds across our psychic universe. In order to become more concrete, a myth must have its metaphoric 'shorthand' and this shorthand is a *symbol*. The Cross, the Crescent, Yin and Yang, the Union Jack, the Stars and Stripes, even the Swastika, are obvious enough symbols which embody both myth and historical circumstances in a way that every ordinary person can respond to in a non-intellectual fashion. Men and women have perished bearing standards emblazoned with such symbols — not as bits of cloth and plates of metal, but for the nobler or wilder myth they have evoked. *Abstraction*, on the other hand, is nothing more than an intellectual concept scribbled into social life by some political demagogue or weaver of scientific strategy. Thus the cry of Patrick Henry of Virginia shortly before the American Revolutionary War — 'Give me liberty or give me death' — might seem a piece of humbug when we examine what 'liberty' really meant to this colonial-Whig rebel in terms of his own self-interest.

The 18th century loved to style itself the Age of Reason. Yet no century had a more malignant undertow of explosive malice beneath its polite manners and seemingly ordered conventions. The air was full of sonorous political platitudes often removed from the behavioural realities of collective and individual life. These were invented as slogans for reform or revolution largely by middle-class intellectuals who wanted their own sort of oligarchy in preference to the traditional authority of kings or religious pontiffs. Alas, such slogans quickly passed on to become the property of ruthless fanatics and homicidal lunatics who were prepared to offer up thousands — indeed, millions — in bloody sacrifice. As Georges Sorel, himself a 19th-century political extremist, was finally forced to admit: 'Experience has always shown us that revolutionaries plead "reasons of state" but as soon as they get into power, they employ police methods, and look upon justice as a weapon which they may use unfairly against their enemies'.

Having experienced the first major political revolution in modern Europe after the Civil War of 1641–47, England later became the benign incubator for many sceptical political viruses which not so much encouraged the Revolution in France and elsewhere as gave radical intellectuals some basic weapons with which to undermine the legitimacy and credibility of the *ancien régime*. The contest between Anglican King and Puritan Parliamentary bourgeoisie in England after 1637 was less a contest of ideological abstractions than of wills and conceived rights and privileges. King Charles I was condemned to death by a Parliamentary tribunal uncertain of its real authority to kill a sovereign. Moreover, the death of this sovereign was received with no enthusiasm by the English masses, who felt a large measure of guilt by association. After the execution the fanaticism of extreme elements originally connected to the Puritan camp, such as the Levellers and the Scottish Presbyterians, never deeply influenced the Parliamentary seat of power, and still less the army of Cromwell's dictatorship which supplanted it. Wealthy London businessmen did as good a trade under the Lord Protector as they did under the monarchy, since affluent Calvinist merchants and squires could never rest easy with rule by a mob not of

God's elect. The desperate attempt by Cromwell's Major-Generals in 1655 to impose an extreme ascetic lifestyle upon the English people gave them a lasting hatred of militarism which was later to deprive many a despot of the instruments of oppression. Ultimately the code of 'business as usual' in England, as the first industrialised nation in the West, saved her from the worst excesses of revolution elsewhere.

The Constitution of Clarendon in 1660 which gave equal rights to restored king and Parliament was greeted with relief by the over-whelming majority of English people, and it provided the basis of a constitutional system that was to evolve quite sturdily up to the present time. Political licentiousness in England was henceforth to be confined mainly to political philosophers, poets and specialists in the lampoon. In this vein, John Dryden was able to remark that it was easier for the Puritans to put their lawful sovereign to death than to endure listening to a joke.

The Puritan hegemony in England failed mainly because of its frigid attitude to the basic and simple pleasures of life. Yet it was its aesthetic vandalism that more cultivated English people would remember with most resentment. Under the aegis of Parliament, more than half of the fabulous medieval and Tudor art legacy of England was sacrificed to iconoclasts and Bible-toting fanatics. They smashed every stained-glass window they could reach, ripped up paintings, defaced statuary, burned priceless Books of Hours and would have razed Hampton Court Palace to the ground had not a last-minute order prevented it. It is a mark of crusading obsessives that they find the emotional spontaneity in a work of art difficult to sustain in themselves. Consequently, such people find it easy to applaud measures designed to destroy any beautiful record of the spontaneity of others.

The Calvinist strain in its pure political form was almost dead as an instrument of moral discipline by about the mid-19th century, even in its heartlands — Protestant Switzerland and Presbyterian Scotland. But its *spirit*, prompted by the search on earth for a perfect society of solemn saints, had some interesting derivations and even inversions. Characteristically lowland Scotland, the second home of Calvin's doctrines, produced some of the most robust believers in *justified* material absorption — from Adam Smith, apostle of individualism and the free market, and David Hume, the unsettling sceptical philo-sopher, to several founders of the British Labour and Trades Union movement up to the day of Kier Hardie. The Protestant Celts in Scotland, Northern Ireland and Wales became the pillars of a society whose keynotes were to be sounded by the economic trinity of thrift, production and profit. The wrathful God of Calvinism has faded but its well-calculated economic imperatives are with us still.

ROUSSEAU AS POLITICAL SORCERER

Calvinism in Geneva even formed the early life of probably the most successful pamphleteer and inventor of political abstractions in the Western world — Jean Jacques Rousseau — born to shake the world in 1712 and dying a decade before the Revolution his ideas had done so much to inflame. No political or social theorist in modern history has exercised as much influence as Rousseau on such slender credentials and with as little moral credibility. In contrast to Voltaire, his amazing political success testified to the triumph of dazzlingly phrased abstract assertions over real social evidence. 'Jean Jacques' was the type of celebrity who would be adored by today's mass audiovisual media. As his scornful recent biographer, J. C. Huizinga, has shown, Rousseau cultivated much of his own 'press' and was busy and uncrupulous in his self-promotion. His *Confessions*, the first half of which were published in 1781, were even more sensational and revealing than those of their famous Augustinian namesake.

Far from posthumously demolishing his reputation as a sage and social saviour, the *Confessions* only enhanced Rousseau's social fascination. It did not seem to matter to his many followers that the latter years of his life were disfigured by crazy quarrels with loyal English friends and an ever-increasing persecution mania which convinced him that the British government and David Hume, his admiring philosopher ally, were seeking his life. Not unusually for a neurotic messiah of his type, Rousseau died insane in July 1778 — a condition worsened by an attack of cerebral thrombosis. Not even a saint has been hailed by so many philosophers, writers and politicians with so little convincing or objective reason for his cult.

Whilst acknowledging his splendid but unpractised advice about the rearing of children, one might feel that there must have been more to Rousseau. Not really. French was the intellectual *patois* of Europe in his day and the Genevan celebrity was expert in stroking and appealing to the discontented elements in the society of several nations. These were not the underprivileged outcasts of the Paris slums, or even an allegedly burdened peasantry. Rousseau was too much of a toady to powerful patrons in their chateaux to waste his time with nobodies. He flattered the influential political hostesses of the Paris salons, and his cultivation of the wealthy middle class and lesser aristocracy provided him with a rich medium for the dissemination of heady ideas concerning which his affluent patrons hardly understood the consequences. He was a man for whom the times were ready.

Rousseau's convoluted life of part enthusiasm and part expediency began when he ran away as a youth from Geneva in 1728. Pretending to be interested in Catholicism, he came under the patronage of a wealthy dame, Madame de Warenes. He became her general tutor and lover until she rejected him. Rousseau then began a lifelong liaison with Thérèse Levasseur, a maid at a local hostelry, whom he treated shamefully, and by whom he had five children. All of these infants he callously consigned to the care of a foundling hospital. So much for the sincerity of the author of *Emile*, a famous work on education which eulogised the charming traits of children and argued for a form of educational protection from society which would not warp their natural sensibilities!

It was Rousseau's masterwork, *The Social Contract*, that was to prove the most potent and enduring in effect. Full of plausible arguments and ringingly aphoristic statements, it became the primer of every social revolutionary and supporter of popular government for the masses over the next two centuries. Yet the famous opening assertion of *The Social Contract* — 'Man is born free and everywhere is in chains' — is logical and scientific claptrap which Rousseau himself had to qualify in his very next paragraph. We are, of course, *not* born free, but as heirs to a large number of genetic, social and economic limitations which no social system, however just or ingenious, could ever hope to equalise. The 'chains' of which Rousseau speaks were real enough, if one examines the fate of those intellectuals who spoke too fiercely against the enlightened despots of late-18th century Europe. But his proposals in *The Social Contract* have never banished such chains and have often supplied new demagogues and new tyrants with stronger manacles.

Rousseau's qualification of his original claim for our innate liberty is that a citizen somehow 'naturally' surrenders his rights and possessions to something abstract called 'the general will'. Individual rights, regardless of sectarian and private interests, must point toward the good of all. So, if a man acts against 'the general will', according to Rousseau's argument, he must be 'forced to be free'. This last telling phrase should have convinced any shrewd reader that beneath such lofty twaddle lurks the later despotism of the levelling bureaucrat and meddler in all manner of human intimacies and privacies. One is pushed to agree with Paul Johnson that Rousseau was the father of the modern totalitarian state. The seductive slogan 'Liberty, Equality and Fraternity', taken from *The Social Contract*, sounded the verbal trumpet and drum to which half the enthusiasts in Europe and a large part of the New World were to march.

THE FALLACIES OF REVOLUTION

When, each July, the Republic of France celebrates its inception on Bastille Day, even the fervent patriot ought to be caught up in a sense of irony. The Bourbon State that the revolutionaries overthrew in 1789 was not irreparably corrupt. Nor was it as savagely unjust and inhumane as claimed in the often venomous special pleadings of revolutionary pamphleteers, on which so much historical exaggeration is based. History generally favours the winners. There were indeed gross inequalities in the France of Louis XV (1710–1774). But his popular appellation — 'Louis the Well-Beloved' — was by no means sardonically applied. The royal government of France collapsed for three major reasons:

1. Following Louis XV's death, the vesting of power in a well-meaning but introverted and barely competent monarch such as Louis XVI, who was not helped by the impetuous miscalculations of his Queen, Marie Antoinette. Unlike his grandfather, the stolid hardworking King lacked the charisma to command loyalty at a time when this mattered as much as sincerity.
2. The vindictive jealousies of members of the lesser nobility and influential middle class who were determined to bring down the Versailles government by every means at their disposal. With the help of the treacherous Philippe, Duc d'Orleans, and a group of intriguers at court, the task did not take long to accomplish.
3. The blindness of the first two 'Estates', the nobility and the clergy, towards the need for radical social change and the immediate reduction of their ancient but outworn privileges. By the time they realised the folly of their delays and obstructions, it was too late to stem an insurrection.

The picture of the *ancien régime* popularised by such writers as Victor Hugo and Charles Dickens, stressing the sufferings of the populace of Paris and the destitution of the peasantry were at best half-truths when one looks at the last years of royal government. During the final phase of the reign of Louis XV, the once-hard lot of rural workers had considerably improved. Their control of land and their ability to profit from its products showed steady improvement right up to the fall of the monarchy. The conventional picture of the plight of the urban poor was true enough, but this applied more to Paris than to other provincial French cities. As for the aristocratic suppression of thought and the consignment of bourgeois freethinkers to the Bastille and other prisons, this was mild and infrequent when compared with the thorough practices of totalitarian regimes in our own century. When the Bastille was stormed and fell, it was found to contain only seven prisoners, all of whom were aged and reluctant to leave.

Concerning the alleged long-term provocation of the Revolution by Louis XV himself, no monarch, except perhaps Richard III of England, has been so consistently maligned and misrepresented. According to his latest biographer, Olivier Bernier, Louis XV was 'hard-working, conscientious, tolerant and kind'. He cared about the long-term welfare of the state and also about the comforts of the people; so most of his reign was an era of unprecedented prosperity. For fifty years he managed to preserve France from foreign invasion. This is hardly the portrait of the selfish, indolent voluptuary spread by the pamphleteers and scandalmongers who swarmed both before and after the crisis of 1789. Unfortunately, the king did not deign to answer the calumnies of his enemies. In fact, at the age of 60, Louis XV had been so angered by the growth of corruption in his government that he set in train thoroughgoing reforms to curb the power of a selfish elite so that the burden of taxation no longer rested so heavily upon the poor.

The truth was that the French Monarchy as an institution had become almost an *abstract* object of hatred to an ambitious bourgeoisie. To bring down the old nobility whom they resented and envied, it was necessary to topple the throne as well. Even at his stoical death from smallpox, Louis XV was not spared the merciless caricatures of his enemies. The major problem of France's last effective Bourbon monarch had been that he was set atop a pyramid of scheming nobles and officials, once shrewdly herded together for controlled observation at Versailles by his great-grandfather, Louis XIV. It was hardly surprising that after nearly a century their cooped-up frivolities and forced idleness had become faults blamed upon the monarchy itself.

Thus it was France, the turbulent Mother of Revolutions and one-time 'eldest daughter of the Church', who threw up as motley a collection of monsters and crazed perfectionists as any upheaval that succeeded it. Amid the chaos of warring factions which led to the Terror of 1793 and beyond, abstractions now bore the sword, gun and axe. 'We would rather make France into a burial ground than renounce ruling it in the way we think best.' These were the words of Carrier, Commissary of the Revolutionary Convention, which were to be endorsed by a succession of zealots intoxicated by the worship of the howling urban masses and willing to kill ceaselessly for a mere slogan or phrase. The French Revolution is too rarely examined in terms of the psychotic nether world which underlay the fine sentiments of its luminaries.

The three outstanding advocates of the Revolutionary Assembly were Danton, Marat and Robespierre. All three were bestial in their deeds if not their motives — Danton alone showing the saving grace of withdrawal when his blood-lust was dulled. Georges-Jacques Danton was born of peasant stock in 1759 and practised as an advocate in Paris at the time of the Revolution. Until then, he had seemed no more than a man in search of his career. He had even hoped, before the fall of the monarchy, to buy himself into the ranks of the lesser nobility. But the colossal energy of this 'Cyclops' was to thrust him in other directions.

Danton was a tall man, built like a bull, with a ferocious head set on mighty shoulders, a pockmarked face and beetling brows. His enormous voice urging the members of the Assembly to kill, he railed ceaselessly against aristocrats until there were hardly any aristocrats left to destroy. Afterward he wanted to sit down and enjoy his new comforts in company with a 'liberated' populace. He had been caught up by the obsession with abstract principles for all too long, but his innate practicality and sheer physical satiation persuaded him that there was no point in continuing to behave like a beast of prey, destroying human lives for mere phrases. He himself perished on the guillotine in April 1794.

Jean-Paul Marat was a different sort of demagogue. Eventually a murderous megalomaniac, his answer to every problem was to kill or maim. Ironically, Marat's early years were occupied in the study of medicine and natural philosophy, and he gained a doctor's degree while in Scotland. Already, however, he showed too much heat, too ready a tendency to abuse opponents for the coolness of scientific research. He decided that the science of a well-functioning 'social mechanism' was paramount if 'pure' science itself was to flourish, and from that he was drawn to Paris and the Constituent Assembly. Mounted on the tribune, Marat assured his hearers that the world would not be improved until '800 trees in the Tuileries gardens had been transformed into gallows'.

Propelled to the top of 'The Mountain', as the 'left-wing' seating of the notorious Jacobin party in the Assembly was called, Marat became the most loathsome figure of the Terror, forever calling for more and more blood, more wholesale executions, until even his supporters feared to sit with him. Like Hitler and Stalin more than a century later, Marat was busy with his own 'final solution' for the enemies of the

people. Not content, like Danton, with wiping out all of the aristocracy, he was propounding under the name of Reason, a program of
systematic butchery which would 'perfect' and 'purify' the French race
and the French state. Growing daily more frenzied, Marat neglected his
appearance and sat half naked without hose and in a greasy shirt,
forever scribbling at a large dirty table with a pile of papers. Here
he wrote one homicidal, denunciatory article after another: 'Cut off
two hundred thousand heads and you will have tranquillity, but not
otherwise'.

Eventually an intractable skin disease (probably psychosomatic) made
it necessary for Marat to spend all his waking time in hot water. Only
there was he free from painful itching. It was in a steaming tub, while
devising new infamies and dealing out new recommendations for murder,
that he was visited by Charlotte Corday, who gained access to him
allegedly with the names of new traitors. After stabbing Marat fatally
as he sat in his bath, she stated calmly and truthfully: 'I have killed a
wild beast, a monster, to save hundreds of thousands'.

The third eminence in this unholy trinity was perhaps the most
disturbing of all — Maximilien de Robespierre, a French lawyer from
Arras of Irish descent. Allied with his youthful but equally sinister
secretary, Louis de Saint-Just, Robespierre eventually made himself
dictator of France. He was a small, dandified figure with jerky gestures.
A man of intractable dryness, Robespierre's laugh was a grimace and
his small eyes gleaming behind spectacles inspired profound anxiety
in all those who knew him. For his part, Saint-Just seemed outwardly
to be a mere cherubic disciple, but his enunciation of Robespierre's
principles was devastating:

> For five years after their birth children will belong to their mothers,
> and thenceforth until the day of their death they will belong to the
> Republic. A taste for silence will be inculcated in them and a con-
> tempt for the flourishes of rhetoric; they will be the Spartans of the
> modern world.[1]

In Saint-Just's speech was encapsulated all the accents and ambitions
of an obsession with the idea of social control and yet more control.

At public ceremonies Robespierre spoke with a monotonous tone and
the pompously elaborate phraseology which denotes the emotionally
withered fanatic. Far from being an atheist like his colleagues, he spoke
against impiety and wanted to revive a deistic faith in God and immortality. But the God of Robespierre was a thing cut out of cardboard
— another empty abstraction out of his own mind. Robespierre's

decreed Festival of the Supreme Being, which was staged in Paris in July 1794, was surely one of the most hollow religious ceremonies ever conducted, especially when Notre Dame itself lay silent, damaged and desecrated in the wild orgies of the previous years.

Robespierre's extraordinary charisma saw to it that this almost bloodless figure inspired transports of admiration from those who saw in him rationality incarnate. Women sobbed at his boring addresses and exclaimed at his frigid face as if he had been another Apollo. Men too were 'inflamed by [his] republican virtues', as one citizen wrote to the leader. Rarely had the worship of windy abstractions shown how unreasonable a facade of reason unsupported by reality could become. At last, even the Convention rose in revolt against Robespierre, but the appalling Parisian mob was still on his side. While the dictator was still industriously signing new edicts for arrest and execution he was wounded in the face by a pistol shot from a soldier, under orders from the Convention, and guillotined a few hours later.

The most extraordinary aspect of the French Revolution was the lingering success of its propaganda. The young poet Wordsworth thought it was 'very heaven' to be alive at its outbreak. Indeed, Europe had been well prepared for the outbreak of the new order by the writings of such propagandists as Rousseau. Yet, as the entire ruling class of France disappeared in a welter of blood, the talented and conscientious along with the effete and corrupt, an appreciation of the true obscenity of the French Terror began to dawn upon many a fatuous mind. By Robespierre's time the old ruling groups had mostly died or fled, and the bourgeois children of liberty were now busy slaughtering one another. This was to be the case in every violent revolution up to our own generation. Yet the vein of populist romanticism that stirred the intellectuals of the West and agitated the more stagnant royal governments of Europe always covered up the fact that the mob, spurred on by alienated thinkers, can be a wilder beast than any dictator or royal autocrat.

Those patriotic French who would be horrified to compare the founding members of their Republic with eminent Nazis should recall some of the comparable deeds that were done. After the killing of the defenceless Royal Swiss guards at Versailles, their bodies were divided limb from limb and the flesh stripped from their bones until the skeletons were bared. A contemporary, Montgaillard, noted that there was a tannery set up for dealing with the skins of those victims of the guillotine whose bodies seemed worth flaying. He remarked that the leather made from men's skins would outlast chamois. The parents of one of Marie

Antoinette's maids roasted their daughter to death upon a log of wood sprinkled with sulphur because she was faithful to her royal mistress. For this they were given an ovation by the mob as signal examples of true patriotism and held up as models for other parents who still hesitated to sacrifice their children to the great ideal of equality. On such grisly credentials as these does the noble abstraction of 'liberty' which we embrace today partly rest.

By contrast, the Republic of the United States provided a rare alternative example of how a revolution might proceed without devouring its own children. But in truth it was a very strange upheaval, which is better explained as an only partly justified revolution of rebellious children against a slack-minded yet authoritarian mother. Behind the Declaration of Independence and the Revolutionary War in the United States lay a peculiar combination of puritan distrust of monarchical rule, economic resentment of merchants over taxes which were by no means crushingly severe, and the desire of more fiery frontier spirits to pursue their own self-interest without seeking permission from a careless and incompetent government across the Atlantic Ocean. It has been argued by many British scholars that there was actually less justification for the rebellion of the American colonists against England than there would have been for a similar rebellion of French-Canadians against their government in Paris, or for similar upheaval of Spanish-American colonists against the King in Madrid. Those who execrate colonialism and its evils — and evils there undoubtedly were — have forgotten that the British-American colonies of the Atlantic seaboard could never have maintained themselves satisfactorily before 1750 without the benefits of trade with the mother country or the assistance of a standing military force from England. In some decades the cost of British colonial rule exceeded the sum derived from it.

With financial assistance from the doomed government of Louis XVI of France, the armies of Washington narrowly won in the field and the American Founding Fathers were able to do their work. The Declaration of Independence from its first paragraph contains a series of abstractions in their finest form. It outlines a set of propositions as the spiritual foundations of a nation which are no more than noble half-truths at best. Yet 'We hold these truths to be self-evident', affirms the second paragraph of the declaration penned by Thomas Jefferson.[2] (Though what 'truths' in politics or purely human affairs are *ever* 'self-evident?') These 'truths' the Declaration avers are: '. . .that all men are created equal, that they are endowed by their Creator with certain unalienable rights; that among these are life, liberty, and the pursuit of happiness'. The rest of the Declaration cites a series of grievances against the mother country which, however exaggerated, had some basis in reality. There was talk of the perfidy of Great Britain visiting 'repeated injuries and usurpations. . .in direct object of the establishment of an absolute tyranny over these States'. Despite the 'proofs' put forward by Jefferson in the document, there was no indication that the then jovial and intact mind of George III of Great Britain ever entertained an absolute tyranny of this kind or that the lazy, disreputable Tory government of Lord North had any long-term object save that of forcing the colonists to abandon their rebellion and pay their taxes. At least half of the Declaration is simply wartime propaganda.

Meanwhile, there is something ghoulishly appealing about those despotisms which base their credentials upon the rebellion of a socially or politically deprived class. Such an origin is always held to excuse whatever later abominations may be committed by popular demagogues on its behalf. This was underlined by Auguste Comte who remarked that 'The chief malady of the West is a continual urge to revolt against antecedents'. Also, revolutions are infectious, and there was a whole series of such upheavals between 1789 and 1917, very few of them without bloodshed. What does it matter to a bereaved mother whether her son has been slaughtered in the antechambers of some right-wing dictator or cut down in the streets by random machine-gun fire from barricaded left-wing ideologues? Death is, after all, the only true democrat, and his judgement is final. No violent political revolution in the West since 1789 can be demonstrated to have changed *any* society notably for the better.

THE RISE OF THE MECHANICAL UNIVERSE

The process of harnessing reality to abstraction over the past three or four centuries has not been confined to politics, but also emerges in science and social endeavour. The world, as conceived by Plato and particularly Aristotle, is one in which inherent mind-like or 'spiritual' principles imbue matter through and through with some purposive development. Twenty centuries later some biologists and subatomic physicists are at last beginning to admit that this early conception may well turn out to have a core of truth. The mechanistic world of early modern science, which reached its peak after the discovery of gravity by Sir Isaac Newton, was considered to possess no inherent activity and no direction. As Newton saw it, the universe appeared to be the product of God's external action on mindless, unstructured matter. Without the gracious bestowal by God of active forces such as gravity, the world would have remained inert, purposeless and dead. He wrote:

> Were it not for these principles, the Bodies of the Earth, Planets, Comets, Sun and all the things in them would grow cold and freeze and become inactive Masses; and all putrefaction, generation, veg- etation and life would cease, the Planets and Comets would not remain in their orbs.[3]

To such early scientists, the world had no important function beyond that which God and people, as his agents, could impose upon it. And yet between 1687 and 1704, as Newton wrestled with the explanation of his theory of gravity, he remained a fervent Deist and a Christian of sorts. Nevertheless, on the side, he possessed what we now know to be an extraordinary interest in alchemy and the occult aspects of science. In the words of John Maynard Keynes, Newton was really 'the last of the magicians'.

From a spacious, holistic point of view, the picture of a great uni- verse populated by stars, planets and (ultimately) creatures as merely clockwork entities is a dismal one. Clocks had an abiding fascination for Europe, particularly after the completion of the great Cathedral Clock at Salisbury in 1380. At this time, an influential scientific amateur, Bishop Nicole D'Oresme, created the first metaphor for God as 'the perfect clock-maker'. Johannes Kepler was to take up the same idea two centuries later when he remarked in 1605: 'My aim is to show that the celestial machine is to be likened not to a divine organism, but rather to clockwork'. It is not a distant step from this to the notorious idea of René Descartes, philosopher and mathematician, that human beings were themselves merely ingenious mechanisms animated by a ghostly soul principle. This constituted a survival of the notion of a binary universe, which was first conceived of by the ancient Persians. Mankind was henceforth to become the operator, and the inert world of nature that which was operated *upon*. The implications of this useful but ultimately disastrous idea are clear. In our time, the whole ecology of the planet appears in danger from those who have followed the idea to its ultimate conclusion.

One of the most extraordinary drives among intelligent Occidental people has been the ceaseless urge to explore, and somehow contain or enchain the natural order. For example, whilst the compass certainly came from the Chinese, it took Western curiosity to use it extensively on the great oceans. From this thrust came the virtual denial, in practical terms, of the seamless nature of the globe and the intrinsic interrelationship of its parts. It had to be divided into encompassable and measurable bits, so that its separate fruits could be mined or enjoyed. Gerardus Mercator published his first large map of the world in 1538, and in so doing added another hemisphere, thus 'doubling the world' as a later contemporary significantly put it. The whole idea of meridians of longitude and degrees of latitude was an abstraction which hurt nobody and served many — as long as those who used it realised that it was merely a *convention* and did not make any deep statement about the nature of the world *in itself.*

It is a vulgar superstition deriving from late-19th century and early-20th century science that it has made adequate statements about the fundamental nature of almost any general phenomenon. Science had already gone public by the late 18th century. Each new savant and scientific innovator had his lobby and his fashionable following. Those today who think of science as being a calm and unflurried dialogue of fine minds should realise that it has seen almost as much acrid controversy as there was among clerics and theologians. There was a great argument as to who had demonstrated that water was not an element but a compound of oxygen and hydrogen. Cheerleaders lined up to claim that it was Cavendish, Watt or the Frenchman, Lavoisier. Sir Humphry Davy, who died in 1829, opposed the election of Michael Faraday to the Royal Society simply because it was *claimed* that William Woollaston had beaten Faraday to the discovery of the principle of electromagnetic rotation.

Scientists themselves had arisen from many a notorious party of sinners. Medieval soldiers of fortune had founded Balliol College at Oxford, assuring their entry into heaven in return for all the plundering they had done, and it was to be the same in the 19th century and beyond. In 1896 Alfred Nobel tried to make amends for deriving his fortune from manufacturing dynamite for armaments manufacturers. After 1901, Nobel's legacy was devoted to a prize for peacemakers and other servants of humanity. Although earned for much less frivolous work, the Nobel Prize gradually became like the Hollywood Academy Awards. In conferring a *cachet* of honour upon its winners, it granted such persons a *general* social distinction which was never originally intended apart from recognising an excellence they had shown in their specialty.

By the end of the 17th century the convention of detailed scientific classification and subdivision of phenomena had reinforced the obsessive style of Western science and ideally suited its desire to *control* nature usefully in all her facets. One of the prototypal workers in scientific classification was Carolus Linnaeus, born in 1707 in Sweden to become the founder of systematic modern botany. After his appointment as Professor of Botany at Uppsala in 1742, Linnaeus expounded a system of classification of plants based upon their sexual characteristics. In this way, he made possible the categorisation of literally hundreds of thousands of species. His work paved the way for such later botanists as Sir Joseph Banks to establish great gardens, conservatories and societies of horticulture. To produce such a prodigious body of detailed knowledge required a meticulous mind of virtually compulsive bent. Such industriousness betokens one of the valuable, practical uses of obsessive traits in the service of knowledge, though this still indicates nothing about the breadth, perspective, character or world view of scientists themselves. Happily, unlike politics or religion, scientific endeavour only rarely throws up a Frankenstein. The greatest area of vulnerability in science, as atomic physicist J. Robert Oppenheimer ruefully admitted, is that pure scientists too often live a socially naive and sheltered life, remote from the epoch-making consequences and applications of their work — like monastic clergy in earlier epochs. Since 1900 it is the journalist-popularisers of science who have often proven more arrogantly subversive, making a 'press' for the omnipotence of science and scientists which practitioners themselves usually have more modesty than to endorse.

This interest in organic life forms led to the fading of the idea of the clockwork universe toward the end of the 18th century. So much in the life of plants, persons and living tissues appeared to argue for a subtler force than mere mechanics. Thus arose the idea that there must be a mysterious animating energy or vital forces which somehow modified and made more malleable the rigid machinery of creation. The dying abstract world of the mechanists was thus brought again to indirect life, but now appeared to contain no place for God. As Laplace replied to a query by Napoleon: 'God? I no longer need that hypothesis'. Indeed, it seems strange to the modern informed mind that so much energy was consumed in the 18th and 19th centuries in trying to accommodate new scientific discoveries to the literal Creation account in the Book of Genesis, when it had long been obvious to true religious mystics that this account was a myth or allegory at best.

The new science of geology emerged in the early 19th century and culminated in the great work of the British geologist Charles Lyall, who was determined, in his own words, 'to free the science of the earth from Moses'. It is amusing to recall that not very long before, the fatuous Anglican Archbishop Ussher had announced that, by his calculations, the world was created precisely 4004 years ago at a certain hour in the morning.

The stiff-necked presumption and naiveté of religion concerning Nature, particularly in its extreme Protestant fundamentalist forms, was to receive a drubbing from 19th-century natural science, from which it has never really recovered. But alas, crude Biblical obsessions were being defeated by an equally rigid form of bigoted scientific debunking. Zealots can be as readily found in the lecture room as in the pulpit, and the final flower of all this mockery of religious belief was the principle of *reductionism*. Among bodies of scientists after 1800 there was a growing tendency to believe that the best and most elegant hypotheses are those which *reduce* all natural occurrences to the simplest possible explanation. Even if all higher-order activities in nature — ranging from the behaviour of large populations or the activities of the human brain, to the larger operations of the universe — seemed complex, these should always be reduced or fragmented to a simpler lower-order explanation. Thus it became widely accepted that 'good' science was the natural foe of complexity and ambiguity. Myth, allusion and 'the hunch' all became officially disreputable. In the applied sciences to this day it is still rarely appreciated that the *whole* of any phenomenon is not merely the sum of its parts.

By the early 19th century there were two contending ideas in natural science. Those like German anatomist Caspar Friedrich Wolff who upheld natural autonomy or 'vitalism' claimed there was an inherent force in nature which was indivisible and governed all its operations. On the other hand, reductionists saw in Wolff's same biological and anatomical discoveries not an interrelated field of vital energy but a mere mechanism.

The most outspoken exponent of biological mechanism was Jean Baptiste Lamarck, the first biologist to propose a theory of natural evolution. Lamarck is better remembered today for his argument (contradicting the later view of Charles Darwin) that creatures could inherit recently acquired biological characteristics. Yet Lamarck's determination to *reduce* complex biological phenomena to the actions of so-called invisible 'fluids' had a far more important effect upon the science of his day. He believed it was unnecessary to refer to a spiritual or divine principle of man to explain the faculties of mind, and he also thought these existed without much difference in all higher animals. As so often happens with propagandists, Lamarck was as dogmatic as any medieval canon lawyer. Though a careful enough observer of animals, he never made a practical experiment. His description of the working of 'fluids' in animal tissues was sheer fancy and his mechanistic biology had no future. Yet like many another suave abstraction in Western thought, Lamarckianism provided a reductionist model which was to dominate scientific outlooks in biology up to World War I. It also helped to buttress the stubborn obsession with mono-causal explanations — the this *or* that version of how organisms functioned.

The consequences of the publication of Charles Darwin's *On the Origin of Species* in 1859 could provide a chapter unto itself. Apart from Marx and Freud, no other thinker has had more impact upon people's view of themselves over the past century and a half than this modestly spoken British naturalist who journeyed thousands of miles to remote areas of the Southern Hemisphere to collect the data for his conclusions. All but the most myopic of Christian fundamentalist sects eventually had to accommodate themselves to some notion of human evolution. While Darwinism in its pure form faces extreme sceptical pressures from research workers today, the quality and ardour of Darwin's labour did more to place the study of biology and palaeontology on a sound footing than that of any other scientist.

Despite his own misgivings as a Christian humanist, the effect of Darwin's work was to strike at Pico's Renaissance notion that 'man is the measure of all things' to its very roots. God had seemingly been displaced from the heart of the universe and now evolutionary theory had come to do the same thing for the central role of humankind — or so it was thought. Of course, Darwin did not argue that man was descended from the apes: merely that *homo sapiens* and the higher anthropoid apes had been derived by natural selection from a common biological stem hundreds of thousands of years before. This did not seem to avert a perennial fixation by palaeontologists with finding or exploding the so-called 'missing link' between fossil ape and human, as if this somehow could demonstrate the presence or absence of a higher spiritual principle in people. Thus Darwin touched off one of the most obsessive of modern controversies without wishing it. The mere physical evolution of organisms has nothing proper to say about the existence or non-existence of 'spirit' and suggests very little about the nobler aspirations of humankind over the past forty centuries.

THE TRIUMPH OF THE MACHINE AND ITS CONSEQUENCES

As previously noted, there is much that seems machine-like in obsessive and compulsive thought processes: the same tendency to endless repetition, to seek balanced predictability in behaviour, to thesis followed by antithesis, as expected from the fixed motions of a mechanism. The relative lack of preoccupation in Eastern and primitive civilisations with mechanisms other than those machines developed out of practical necessity prompts the conclusion that the love affair between Western mankind and the machine has been really a circular, self-perpetuating phenomenon. Yet obsessional human traits *preceded* the machine as their partial expression. In one way, the most ingenious forms of moving apparatus produced in Western nations are no more than the projections of the restless, order-seeking, security-promoting intelligences which created them. Even during our own time the brilliance of technologists in creating all manner of machines from the automobile to the computer has brought about new forms of idolatry which will be discussed in Chapter 6. The modern machine age was an outcome of the Western mind's desire to put a chain about the earth. The machine in its turn was to exercise a hypnotic fascination over its creators. In the worst cases, a kind of pathological symbiosis started to grow up whereby human and machine were regarded as extensions of one another, machine imitating human — human taking on some of the characteristics of the robot.

When describing the household of Penelope, Homer remarked that, in the Greek Heroic age, twelve slaves were occupied in preparing bread for some thirty persons. By the mid-20th century, the labour of seventeen workers using the most modern milling machines could supply the entire United States with flour. In 15th-century France there was so little linen that Mary of Anjou, wife of King Charles VII, was the only person in the realm who had more than two linen shifts. By the mid-20th century, one spinning wheel could do 1300 times as much as the work of the human hand, and hundreds of kilometres of linen could be produced in a single day. Yet it was the power of the machine first to free and then to enslave people and take from them the meaning and end product of their labours that was to become the poisoned fruit in the new industrial garden of Eden.

Many pioneers of modern technology, first arising in England, are now household names. In 1738 one Lewis Paul took out a patent for the mechanical spinning of wool. His specifications described the machine as 'a device able to spin without fingers'. In 1766 James Hargreaves, a weaver and carpenter, invented the 'spinning Jenny' which could spin several threads at a time. Richard Arkwright, a barber by trade, showed himself to be a better businessman than Hargreaves. He bought Hargreaves' discovery and later invented the spinning frame which provided the warp threads that could not be spun by Hargreaves' invention.

Edmund Cartwright was a clergyman and writer who, until the age of 40, knew nothing about the textile industry; but he learned in conversation that the new spinning machine produced more yarn than the weavers could utilise on their hand looms. He at once set to work upon the invention of a mechanical loom on which weaving activities could be multiplied as spinning had been. The British textile industry became the mightiest in the world as a result. Only shortly before the British had had to import huge quantities of textiles from India; by the early 19th century, she was exporting cotton goods to India instead.

The first machines were undoubtedly to create enormous wealth for the few. The world's first railway line from Stockton to Darlington in Northern England was directed to transport not people but coal from the pithead to the waiting colliers at the waterfront. James Watt's discovery of the motive power of steam provided the most powerful of all known energy sources until the refinement of petroleum and the harnessing of electricity at the end of the 19th century.

The same new genius of technology was applied to rural life, and was to transform it in a way nobody could possibly have foreseen. In the 18th century, France was the most powerful nation in the West because she possessed agricultural wealth more than double that of any of her neighbours. The rise of British industry and the use of new agricultural techniques in the British dominions and the New World was to end French economic hegemony forever. The small farm was to persist throughout much of the Western world until World War I, since the attachment of people to the land and soil could not be loosened so swiftly. Yet whereas nearly 30 per cent of the population of the United States was engaged in some form of agrarian labour in 1900, only 5 per cent was still engaged in farmwork by 1980. The ancient attachment of the human creature to earth, sun, rain and the elements has now been weakened to the point where millions never have any direct contact with the cosmos or the earth as their mother, beyond watching images of it shown on a television screen.

It took the compulsions and the meticulousness of the Western mind to perfect industrial machinery, but it was that same compulsiveness unbridled by any sensible overview of the relationships between person, task and environment that was to produce a technological civilisation which seemed to be progressing under its own momentum. Jobs that had previously required the skills of a master craftsman with long experience, practised muscles and nimble fingers could now be done by unskilled labourers. For the first time the capacities of great masses of competent people were rendered superfluous, and unemployment came about not through scarcity but through a strangely lopsided prosperity.

Early industrial reformers remarked of the new poverty that while England's machines were spinning and weaving for the whole world, England's own children were going naked and hungry. 'I have seen them; famine has thinned them to skeletons, and they are dumb with despair', reported Lord Byron in the only speech ever given by the poet in the House of Lords. Thomas Carlyle, a generation later, claimed that in no previous historical epoch had the lot of dumb millions been so intolerable. It was not even death from hunger, he remarked, that was the worst of it. What was intolerable was to live in misery without knowing why. Having to work hard to earn a mere pittance, to be sick at heart and exhausted while lonely and uncared for was the lot of the great new herd-aggregate of England's industrial towns.

Britain, of course, only originated the disease which quickly spread to the rest of Europe and to the United States. Poverty appeared to take on a life of its own, but it was structural poverty caused by the machine and not by a lack of natural resources. When the first machines went to work in India, the British Viceroy reported to his government: 'The bleached bones of the old cotton weavers are now whitening the plains of Hindustan'. By 1900 it was believed that the Boxer Rebellion in China was largely exacerbated by the introduction of European machinery. As René Fulop-Miller noted, the central press organ of the British Chartists had remarked in the 1830s:

> The very topic of the machine seems to inspire alarm. Even while bringing about the greatest of all revolutions, it completely transforms the mutual relationships of human beings, yet no-one dares to say a word about the matter.

Thousands fled the industrial mills of England only to find much the same labour conditions in the congested cities of the Atlantic seaboard of the United States. Shrewder migrants preferred South America, Australia or Africa, where the new monsters of steel had not made as much headway. Even those artisans who were sent across the Atlantic to install the new machines often ran away into the woods of New England and would not be lured back into the factories by offers of high wages.

The machine had created a huge gulf between employer and employed and was far more impersonal than anything in the days when nobles had exploited peasants. Industrial workers had turned into a class, an urban 'proletariat', and henceforth were an instrument upon which many a dangerous ideologue masquerading as saviour was to play.

THE ADVENT OF THE SOCIAL SAVIOUR

In one and a half centuries since the Reformation, philosophy as the study of the relationship between God, man and the universe had suffered something of a decline. The intellectual promiscuity and preference for brilliant polemic of writers like Voltaire and Rousseau had pushed philosophical speculation more and more in the direction of social reform and political interpretation. In the 19th century, philosophy was to take a turn back towards fundamental metaphysical questions, but its new centre was to be Germany rather than France or England. After the well-argued doubts cast by Immanuel Kant on the sufficiency of pure reason to solve the great questions of life between 1781 and 1786, speculative philosophy began to revive.

Kant himself was the epitome of the mainly well-adjusted, civilised, obsessive personality — orderly, meticulous, punctual and awesomely diligent. It was said that the people of Konigsberg could set their clocks by the daily walks of the Prussian sage through the town. In many ways Kant was to be the father of liberal thought, and he was to have as much effect upon the freethinking wing of modern philosophy as English empiricists and sceptics like John Locke and David Hume. Like them, Kant steadfastly avoided fervid messianic hopes and millennial expectations. Perhaps Kant's most famous legacy was his Categorical Imperative. His ethical theory could be summed up as: 'Act only upon that maxim which you would wish at the same time could become a universal law for all'. This provided the basis of a humanist ethic which appealed to the common good without any reference to any kind of divine requirement from God. Kant also rightly argued that intellectual knowledge of objects *as such* (noumena) was impossible, since we can know only our sense impressions of them (phenomena). This was to be a valuable distinction, which science and its popularisers had forgotten by the end of the 19th century. Nevertheless, the Industrial Revolution had forced philosophers and social thinkers to tackle the problems of the new industrial state, and it was in France once again that some of the most bizarre and adventurous thinkers were to be found. Here arose the cult of the obsessive social saviour, who frequently never budged from his library or desk to find out the realities of the social situation for which he was prescribing.

The two most notorious examples of this salvationist convention were Claude Henri de Saint-Simon and his secretary Auguste Comte. Saint-Simon was an aristocratic adventurer. He had joined Washington's army as a volunteer and made purposeless journeys through Mexico, France, Holland and Spain, always on the lookout for some scene of inspiration. One of the silliest of his early schemes was a plan to connect Madrid by canal with the sea, totally disregarding the fact that the terrain on which the city stood was a vast plateau of solid granite. It was Comte's duty to try to systematise the erratic and increasingly indigent count's latest brainwaves and order them into some kind of coherent presentation — a task which he detested.

The two men evolved the notion of three stages of knowledge through which humanity had to pass: the religious, the metaphysical and the positive — the last of which was the only practical reformative stage. From this grew the theory of Logical Positivism, which created a school of thought that was to persist into our own century. Its disciples denied all reality that could not be verified by the senses, and all theories that could not be tested by physical measurement. Ironically, even the boasted 'reality' of Posivitism was just one more abstraction, since sense-verification is no sure test of what is real — nor are those devices designed to extend the range of our senses.

After seven years of service, Comte broke away from Saint-Simon to follow his own path of knowledge and develop their theory to its conclusions. The break between master and servant, however, proved too great, and Comte's mind began to crumble. He developed delusions of persecution after quarrelling with Saint-Simon's habit of plagiarising his ideas. And so the paranoid founder of modern philosophical 'objectivity' found himself confined to a locked room in his own house and eventually, like many another messianic luminary, died insane.

The next French messiah was Charles Fourier, who had a sound basis of work in commercial life to support his grand theories. He journeyed throughout western Europe, carefully studying industrial life, the layout of towns, the practice of finance, architecture, and even the behaviour of the local inhabitants. Fourier began to build his own model of historical progress. In his view, there were eight epochs between the primal beginning of humankind and its perfection. It had passed from a state of nature, through savagery, by means of patriarchal rule and barbarism to civilisation. Fourier considered the last three stages that remained to be traversed were those of 'guarantism', 'community', and finally 'harmony'. In order that people might plan this perfectly evolved society, he envisaged vast archetypal complexes for state planners, which were called 'phalansteries'. These were to be public services hives, much like bureaucratic complexes of the future such as the Kremlin and the vast Pentagon in Washington. In these enormous cloistered edifices would be housed thinkers and clerks who would redesign the world. They were to be the archetypal sanitised ancestors of modern civil servants employed in a perfect (and, needless to say, obsessive) scheme. Such phalansteries were to accommodate between 1600 and 1800 persons who would actually live in the buildings where they worked.

Of course, European authorities were not disposed to listen seriously to a person who also argued that the North Pole would change its climate and become subtropical, and that the monsters of the deep could be replaced by new species such as the 'anti-shark' and the 'anti-whale'. The wonder is that Fourier found anybody to listen to him at all.

THE BRITISH AND GERMAN REDEEMERS

In Great Britain, the harsh reality of the Industrial Revolution and the terrible plight of the industrial poor inspired a less demented, more attainable approach. Robert Owen was a young man full of cheerful benevolence who had become part-owner of a textile mill at New Lanark, and he was fortunate enough to have substantial capital, even in his late teens. Starting with one hundred pounds, he established a prosperous textile factory and became wealthy enough to put plans for improved industrial conditions into effect. Enthusiastic rather than obsessed, he questioned why there should be poverty, distress and suffering in the world. Owen considered that the cause of every problem in the world was not to be found in the genetic inadequacy of the human being. Rather, environment was at fault since people were mostly a product of their environment, and hence environmental change would bring about human change. Here we have a foretaste of the much more radical later theory of Marx and Engels. Owen set about using his own factory as a proving ground. Upon arrival in Scotland he had the inhabitants of New Lanark tear down the old workers' hovels and cottages and commence work on new, clean and tidy houses and streets.

So successful was Owen's experiment that even the future Tsar of Russia stayed with the saviour and urged him to provide two million men to establish his new paradise in the great territory of all the Russias. Ambassadors, parliamentarians, all flocked to New Lanark to admire what Owen had done. Proving that he could do as well at another site, Owen gathered together half a million pounds to create another model manufacturing town in the village of Motherwell, after which the industrial wizard journeyed to the United States to address the Congress in Washington in 1825. He later established a new foundation in Indiana, where the Rappists, a fundamentalist sect from Bavaria, had already made a similar experiment.

Robert Owen was undoubtedly a cheerful sort of redeemer with a sanguine temperament, sufficient practicality, money and energy to make his system work — but only up to a point. He had overlooked the basic cupidity and cantankerousness in human nature, particularly among poor folk, who did not always know what to do with the fruits of their prosperity and their new leisure once they had attained it. When he returned in 1828 to the colony of New Harmony, as Owen called his Indiana settlement, he found that the system had broken down, that alcoholism, friction and *dis*harmony had taken the place of his demi-paradise. Even this did not discourage his belief in the essential goodness of mankind. But when he tried to install his system in Texas — then still under the control of Mexico — this too collapsed, and little by little Owen's great dream faded.

Robert Owen's experiment had shown that small-scale reform was possible, and that some lasting degree of success in redeeming the industrial and social order could be brought by concentrating on a local microcosm rather than upon obsessively grandiose plans for the redemption of the entire planet. Owen had seen from the beginning that for any economic program to succeed it would do well to avoid partisan political fanaticisms of all kinds. The failure of his plans for his human subjects came from Owen's inability to recognise that the good in humankind is amply commingled with evil and folly. In that sense he was yet another seeker after perfection in an imperfectible world.

Britain was to produce another equally cheerful and much more influential social redeemer in Jeremy Bentham. Styled the 'Napoleon of liberal thought', Bentham was probably the most influential political and economic theorist in the English-speaking world, and his ideas were to be woven into the forms of many representative governments during the 19th century. Far from being deeply obsessive in the definition of this study, he appeared to be nothing more than a brilliant and perennially optimistic adolescent. Like many a reformer before him, Bentham scarcely budged from his well-furnished house, out of which he poured a stream of theoretical advice, and which became a mecca for intellectuals, colonists and politicians from all over the world. Simon Bolivar, the great liberator of the South American colonies, turned to the British sage for help when devising constitutions for five independent states he had created. King Pedro I of Brazil did not think it incongruous to seek the same advice in organising his new monarchy. Even as late as 1831, at the age of 82, Bentham greatly influenced educational and social planning in the development of the Australian colonies.

Nevertheless, like so many Utopian planners, even the sane and urbane Jeremy Bentham had caught his dose of the Rousseauvian flu. It was evident that he too had not wholly abandoned what Robert Ardrey has called Rousseau's Illusion of Original Goodness. Bentham was an immoralist in the doctrinal sense, though he would have been indignant at being accused of advocating any sort of anarchy. As the founder of Utilitarianism, his chief doctrine was expediency, and hence his natural ancestor was as much Machiavelli as any philosopher of the Enlightenment. Bentham's doctrine of 'seeking the greatest happiness of the greatest number' implied a subtler, more ennervating tyranny than the old upper-class oligarchies it opposed, but it was still a tyranny in terms of the spirit. In Bentham we again encounter the pernicious idea of Rousseau that men *must* be organised and educated and even 'forced' to be free!

Rejecting Christianity as a harsh father-religion, and believing St Paul to be the Antichrist, Bentham's attitudes displayed the marks of the pampered but well-adjusted mother's son in revolt against any form of paternalism. John Stuart Mill recognised this, and commented as follows:

> Bentham had neither internal experience nor external. . .he never knew prosperity in adversity, passion nor satiety. . .he lived from childhood to the age of 85 in boyish health. He knew no dejection, no heaviness of heart; he never felt life a sore or weary burden. He was a boy to the last.[4]

Abstraction, if well applied by other practical and ingenious people often *does* work. The modern liberal State and the representative government that the free West enjoys today owe a lot to Bentham's inspiration. In choosing the middle way of expediency in government and social organisation, he set the scene for many a dull and lazy bureaucrat. But at least the British dominions were to be saved from the excesses which shook France from 1789 to 1871, and which were to inspire such deadly ideas in some thinkers abroad in late 19th-century Germany.

Utopian intellectuals weaving comprehensive schemes for social improvement rarely conduct any solid social research which might disturb their complacency. The French economist Jean-Baptiste Say made a devout pilgrimage to Scotland in 1815 to visit the tomb of Adam Smith, the spiritual founder of modern capitalism. In order to reach the tomb he had to pass through some of the industrial towns of northern England, where he found factory hands half starving, clad in rags, wasted away to living skeletons and huddled in foul, dark and damp slums. He listened to their tales of woe and learned that in Yorkshire, Birmingham, Manchester and Glasgow there were similar horrors and similar famished and destitute human beings. This told the other side of the plenty and wealth poured out by the new factories of Britain. Sadly disillusioned, Say turned back before reaching the grave and never again read a single paragraph penned by Adam Smith. An economist from Geneva, Jean-Charles Sismondi, was also filled with enthusiasm for the writings of Adam Smith, and had dedicated treatises of his own to the author of *The Wealth of Nations*. He crossed the English Channel and saw the same terrible poverty that existed in the wake of the machine and the enrichment of the great factory owners. Disillusioned, Sismondi set to work and composed a savage indictment of economic liberalism.

Yet tattered and decrepit as it has become, liberalism has been the only politico-social middle way thought to be available to the West in one and a half centuries. Developed 'free' societies, now bereft of the old tribal loyalties, sovereign rulers, religious myths and symbols, have had to totter along pretty much on the basis of Bentham's doctrine of 'the greatest happiness for the greatest number'. The alternatives — either harsh autocratic despotism or rule by an ill-informed and frequently lazy rabble — have been too disquieting to contemplate.

Flanking liberalism, of course, there has always been an enlightened *conservatism* which has had the unpopular responsibility of rejecting abstractions and being suspicious of all dogma. Its attitude to public affairs is best summed up by one of its finest spokesmen, the Anglo-Irish parliamentarian Edmund Burke, who remarked: 'Society cannot exist unless controlling power upon will and appetite be placed somewhere; and the less of it there is within, the more of it there must be without'. Burke was to be supported over eighty years later by that most persistently misinterpreted of philosophers, Friedrich Nietzsche, who remarked in 1866:

'Equality of rights' could all too easily be converted into an equality in violating rights. By that I mean, into a common war on all that is rare, strange or privileged, on the higher man, the higher soul, the higher duty, the higher responsibility, and on any wealth of creative power and mastery.[5]

Liberalism was the advancing politico-social face of the 19th century. Indeed, its hearty wish-dreams have been hardly dispelled, even by the terrible wars and pogroms of the 20th century. Liberalism's allure lies in a persistent appeal to individual self-interest and its constitutionally hedged appeals to the vanity and envy in us all. Not even the discoveries of biologists since Darwin, and the terrible rebuke to human *hubris* dealt by depth psychology since Freud (to say nothing of the impotence of liberal policies in the face of the armed might of totalitarian states such as Hitler's Germany and Stalin's Russia) have been able to topple liberalism from the affections of intellectuals and entrepreneurs. Liberal doctrine of the type typified by Benthamite Utilitarianism lingers on because of our belief that nothing, however small, can be put into effect without devising a workable social dogma. This is another archaic legacy derived from both Judaism and Christianity. Progressive liberalism also lingers because of the Enlightenment heresy that no social order should be left to evolve naturally without some wrenching kind of innovation. To the average Westerner, glory and excitement have for too long been based on social externalities rather than a quickening of the inner spirit — a matter for strong muscles, heady change or heated debate, not solitary reflection or quiet devotion.

Late 18th-century philosophers, principally Rousseau, placed the blame for the human condition on environment and the pressure of faulty social institutions. Rousseau insisted that savages were natural and pure (although it is doubtful whether he had ever met any) and therefore man was perfectly good from birth. Post-Revolutionary 19th-century Europe was far less sanguine. Some English philosophers, beginning with Thomas Hobbes, in particular, had taught before then that humans were naturally corrupt, selfish and prone to follow the dictates of their self-interest. Hence, Western people with their assertiveness and selfish impulses themselves provided the best regulators of human contractual relationships. From this arose one more miasmic abstraction called the 'free interplay of forces', much favoured by Adam Smith. One individual's untrammelled search for prosperity and satisfaction could meet and be balanced and checked against that of another. Egoism became enthroned as a useful engine of social policy, and liberals persuaded themselves that as long as this 'interplay of forces' prevailed, individual pursuit of wealth and power need not be a menace to one's neighbours. Ironically, the burgeoning factory age and the proliferation of machines was believed to have supported and proved this doctrine. Yet all the machine had done up to 1900 was to drive an even deeper chasm between employer and employee, master and servant.

Against this apparent failure of bourgeois liberalism to alleviate industrial misery arose a new messianic figure whose shadow still lies uncomfortably across the Western world — Karl Marx, and his supporter, Frederick Engels. Since he has inspired such an avalanche of commentaries, it is difficult to say anything new about Marx, except to stress that he was one of the greatest of all builders of abstract systems. He personified so many of the familiar weaknesses of the personally flawed obsessive neurotic who cannot govern his own life, but who nonetheless feels compelled to rearrange the lives of others.

Like so many visionaries who have been mad, unpleasant or merely self-deluded, Marx was not an attractive person. He often penned prose of such stupefying density that it is a miracle that an arid work like *Das Kapital* survived to become an instrument of revolution. Even as a student of 18 wandering the streets in thought and poring over books and manuscripts, Marx was seized with a redemptive urge. He hated the Jewish tradition in which he had been reared and detested Christianity even more. At the University of Berlin he encountered the teachings of Hegel, in which it was argued that all human progress came out of a fruitful conflict between ideals. 'Contradiction is at the root of all movement and all life', Hegel had stated, 'and only insofar as a thing incorporates a contradiction, does it possess impulse and activity'. Turning this idea on its head, Marx conceived the idea of a violent conflict between contradictory interests, classes and people to bring about the fulfilment of his dream of a 'classless society'.

Marx took the new Socialist movement which was then abroad in Europe to its relentless conclusion. The complete levelling and equality of humankind would only be made possible by force. In this, he was thoroughly in accord with such figures as Danton and Robespierre. Driven by his fixations, Marx suffered the not unusual ills of a persecuted prophet — headaches, constipation, sour ill-temper and continuing disregard of the needs of his friends, wife and children. In Cologne, Frau Marx was forced to sell or pawn their available possessions, even beds and bedding, in order to settle accounts. Marx complained to Engels that he could not send for a doctor, having no money, and had to feed his family on bread and potatoes. Yet even when rubbing shoulders with the poor, and impoverished himself, Marx never once scrutinised any detail of the conditions of industrial life about which he wrote. For that he relied heavily upon his factory-owner ally Engels, who at least had some practical experience of what was being talked about.

Marx's true metier was scribbling reams of prose, attending endless meetings and making dire prophecies. He posed almost as an Old Testament prophet who had received some new revelation from upon high. But like his disciple Lenin, he had the sense to see that his Utopian dream could not succeed without roots in bourgeois capitalism. The old obsession could provide the basis of a better obsession:

> Fanatically bent on making value expand itself, he [the capitalist] forces the human race to produce for production's sake: he thus. . . creates those very material conditions which alone can form the basis of a higher form of society. . .[6]

Marx continued to hail with delight the increasing misery he saw around him. He did not want harmony, compromise or reconciliation. He believed that the fanning of the flames of social misery and discontent was 'the most effective means for the unfolding of life, for the elaboration of the abundance of social forces'. Marxist doctrine was that the worse things become, the better the new millennium will be. But even recently the followers of Marx have refused to consider the fact that Marxism in application has been brutally tyrannical wherever it has been temporarily successful, and unsuccessful whenever it has shrunk from imprisoning or murdering an enemy. Marx's revolution came not out of the sophisticated and polarised groups in modern Western nations, but out of semifeudal Russia. Meanwhile, the bourgeoisie, which Marx so hated, have become the dominant class in developed society to the degree that it is hard to determine any more what the 'working class' really is. In an age when trades unionism defines its own hours, proposes restrictive work practices and wrings maximum wages out of employers — and can bring industries to ruin — the harassed junior executive class now forms the newest oppressed group.

Out of Marxism and its ugly, reactive, right-wing stepchildren Italian Fascism and German National Socialism, have come the vast wars and hecatombs of dead in our century. Yet Marx railed at those who had 'no knowledge whatever of the laws of history'. Once again, secular thought had returned to the obstinate religiose idea of movement towards a New Jerusalem of shining millennial advancement and progress. For the Jews, this was the fulfilment of a Covenant promised at the end of time. For the Christian, it was the Second Coming for which mankind must be prepared by the mortification of the senses and by unquestioning obedience to the Church. For the disciples of the Enlightenment, it meant a new age of fraternity which, ironically, had to be established by force and murder. For Marxian socialism, it was to be something called 'the dictatorship of the proletariat'.

From the progressive disillusionment of Western peoples with this endless succession of bankrupt historical panaceas, there could be only one outcome — an attack upon all abstractions, all myths and symbols, both useful and useless. For the nub of this attack we must turn to modern psychology in its coldest central variant — Behaviourism. In order to rid human beings of the phantasms of the mind, it was now thought best, after all, to deny the reality of mind itself.

THE RISE OF BEHAVIOURIST PSYCHOLOGY

Just before the outbreak of World War I, a professor at Johns Hopkins University in Baltimore named John Broadus Watson published a paper in which he proclaimed: 'The time will come when psychology must discard all reference to consciousness. . .its sole task is the prediction and control of behaviour; and introspection can form no part of its method'. According to Watson and his followers, the words 'consciousness, mind and imagination and purpose', together with several others, were declared to be unscientific and to be excluded from the vocabulary and attention of the 'behavioural scientist'. All subjective enquiry into oneself and one's impressions was useless, since the result was an elusive merry-go-round of untrustworthy imagery which could not be objectively pinned down or *measured*.

A recurrent theme in modern experimental psychology was the dictum that there was essentially no difference between the mental life of human creatures and lower organisms, except in terms of an increasingly sophisticated apparatus of perception served by networks of stimulus and response. At one hit, Behaviourism in its several forms provisionally abolished all *fundamental* problems — religious, political, humanitarian and perhaps even economic. If people could be conditioned into desirable sets of reinforced social responses, they could be taught to abandon disquieting abstractions such as 'self-determination', 'human rights' and 'dignity'. Peace would come upon the world and a final ordered animal contentment would arrive. Behaviourists believed that most wars, for example, were fought about abstractions, which was not too far from the truth.

In its more elaborate working out by Watson's successors, Clark L. Hull of Yale and B. F. Skinner of Harvard, behaviourism has become the central orthodoxy of academic psychology up to our own time. It has endorsed the words of Skinner: 'Since mental or psychic events are asserted to lack the dimensions of physical science, we have an additional reason for rejecting them'. Thus experimental behaviourism became a kind of solemn parody of mid-19th century mechanistic physical science. To this day it has not caught up with developments in molecular biology, neurology and physics, which have long since moved away from the crude life models of stimulus-response theory. Small wonder that behaviourism has gained little established acceptance outside English-speaking countries.

Despite all hostile commentary, the seductive as well as repellent nature of the teaching of such behaviourists as B. F. Skinner, particularly in his controversial work *Beyond Freedom and Dignity*, lingers on in several observable realities. Skinner is right to claim that our genuflection to political and social abstractions over the past 200 years, has caused Westerners to travel in an ever-contracting developmental circle. This has left a huge burden of subjective human misery, violent carnage, planetary exploitation and pollution as its legacy. Not only would it be far more convenient to have most of humanity reduced to a mass of conditioned, contentedly labouring, pleasure-seeking organisms; it would put an end to the endless, rape of resources and personal lives which has so often followed in the wake of the Western dogma of 'progress'.

More cogently still, Skinner and his followers grasped an unpalatable fact that redemptive pied pipers from Rousseau to Marx and Gramsci have never been able to accept. Most of humankind, during most of its waking hours, *does* behave in an unreflecting, automatic fashion based upon generations of habitual conditioning. Once having granted genetic transmission, we are indeed mainly products of parental moulding, academic teaching and peer-group pressure, and of numerous appetites imposed upon us from without. Most people are not dissimilar to programmed sleepwalkers; yet the majority of the great spiritual teachers of mankind came to call humanity out of this social somnambulism to the potential of a higher, more fully aware sort of life. This is a life that behaviourists cannot quantify and so prefer to dismiss or doubt. Yet an impressive minority of divines, adventurers, statesmen, artists and gifted social mavericks have exemplified the reality of the non-conditioned life in every season of their endeavours.

It is doubtful whether the races of the West have ever been lastingly uplifted by even *one* universal and comprehensive social plan or theory — certainly not since Plato wrote *The Republic* 2300 years ago. Almost all real advancements in human decency, compassion and refinement have been brought about by satisfactorily balanced and sometimes unspectacular people with no illusions about themselves and doing at least *one* important thing. Sustained successful endeavour is less a symphony of Utopian aims than a series of halting steps towards the practical realisation of a single beautiful or serviceable idea.

Consider only five notable examples:

Abraham Lincoln (assassinated 1865), had two primary aims — the abolition of slavery in America and the healing of differences between North and South after the Civil War he dreaded but pushed forward with anguished determination;

Anthony, 7th Earl of Shaftesbury (died 1885), spent most of his political life improving the wretched conditions in English factories. His tireless work led to the abolition of child labour throughout the British dominions;

Ludwig van Beethoven (died 1827), by every definition was an obsessive of the most sublimely inspired type. A man of slight general education but profoundly perceptive of people and their worth, this musical genius surmounted deafness in a manner almost preternatural, leaving to the world the prototype of the artist as a hero;

Jean Henri Dunant (died 1910), after seeing the sufferings of the wounded in 1866 at the battle of Solferino, inspired the foundation of the International Red Cross. He was responsible for the creation of the Geneva Convention for the proper treatment of war prisoners.

Marie Sklodowska-Curie (died 1934), twice received the Nobel Prize — in 1901 and 1911 — for her research into radium and radioactive elements.

None of the philanthropists, reformers and creators typified here believed in abstractions. They saw what humanity really needed and bent their noblest energies towards the provision of one or two shining creations. For this they needed no plan, no bombastic assertions about what they regarded as the destiny of humanity — merely a desire to be creative and useful. Any political sympathies were immaterial to their great work. Though not all were devout or godly, each had that divine spark which leaves humanity in a slightly better condition than it was before their coming. Beside such special geniuses even the best of the world's reformers of political and social systems seem flawed and a little blind to the facts of the human condition; even those as admired as Simon Bolivar, Mahatma Gandhi, Mustapha Kemel, Sun Yat Sen, Charles de Gaulle and T. E. Lawrence of Arabia. In the final appraisal those who help humanity most are those who *love* most. As we have learned so far, the tragedy of the obsessive or compulsive personality is that he or she only knows how to either serve or dominate.

To sum up, then: obsessional traits have been observed occasionally in all of the earth's peoples, but only in the West and those countries influenced by Western egoistic humanism and Utopian politics have they so frequently assumed the status of a disease.

The evolution of compulsive personalities and obsessive structures is closely linked with the Western bondage to historical time and the progressive desacralisation of the world since the Roman Empire. Exclusive monotheism and the idea of a God separate from creation — as in Yahweh of Sinai and Allah of orthodox Islam — has left no room for a tolerant mythic-animistic view of nature or any spiritually dynamic forces which humanity could mould into supportive local 'gods' and local cults. Throughout the forty centuries of first Jewish and then Christian and Islamic experience, there has been a steady pressure toward an exclusion of all divinity from the natural world. Far from being the indwelling Spirit which moved through matter from rocks to persons, an over-personified Deity was first removed to the height of a mountain top or the secrecy of some sanctuary and then thrust out of human consciousness altogether.

Thus Western men and women over the past two centuries have been left alone to make what they could of a world progressively purged of the Godhead by numerous disturbed, egoistic intellectuals. According to Nietzsche's famous assertion: 'God is dead, and it is we who have killed him'. And for an influential portion of European society he was correct in saying so.

With the excitements of geographical discovery and the rise of physical science, it had *seemed* as if humanity itself might be ultimately equal in innovative power to the Creator. The hubris of humankind, which has lurked in the European intellect since the Greeks, became inflamed to the point where intellectuals had begun to leave consideration of their own frailty and presumption out of the contest between themselves and nature. Having forgotten the indwelling of Spirit in themselves, people were prone to such an obsessive enlargement of their personal ego that (bolstered by such charismatic neurotics as Rousseau, Comte and Marx) they believed that they could redesign a human society and even primal nature itself on the lines of the perfect machine. It was to be an elaborately secularised version of the Great Church over again, with the scientist as priest and sociologists as mad mullahs.

In 1914 the whole human cauldron of psychic denial and repression and the compulsions which were built upon such vanity exploded with terrifying military force. So the West, in the chilling words of Nietzsche, began to enter upon 'night and more night'. Lulled by the distractions, fluorescences and sheer noise of our mega-technology, we are still oblivious to the steady deepening of the psychic twilight about us — with midnight itself not so far off.

• FOUR •

THE RISE AND DECLINE OF INTIMACY

T he credulity of love is the fundamental source of authority.

Sigmund Freud

The micro-medium of all social and psychological trends is the family. Within the confines of its laxities or restrictions, its natural responses or acquired obsessions, the child has developed almost half of its personality and at least two-thirds of its early social repertoire. Over two centuries of modern Western industrial life, the family became a laboratory for creating new forms of social continuity and social mischief in varying measure. Deeply affected by social change in vital instances, it contributed more of itself to social revolution than is popularly supposed.

Change within families fundamentally alters all other human institutions sooner or later. The triad of father, mother and child existed long before the modern state and the contemporary economy. Yet it is only in our century that some understanding of the history and significance of childhood in human affairs has been effectively studied. Merely a few great writers ranging from Shakespeare to Tolstoy have always guessed with Wordsworth that 'the child is father to the man'. Victor Hugo exclaimed, in about 1842, 'Christopher Columbus only discovered America. I have discovered the child'. Appearing in its French edition in 1960, Philippe Ariés' *Centuries of Childhood* was one of the first important works of psychohistory. It attempted to look at the psychological causes of historical trends instead of forever relying upon politics and commerce as a means of explaining social and institutional change. Indeed, Ariés argued that the very concept of the child as we know it today is a relatively modern invention.

Prior to the 19th century the child was regarded very much as a small adult, either to be treated with indifference or regarded as a miniature reflection of the life of surrounding adults. The relative shortness of human life before advances in modern medicine and nutrition made it necessary for those children who survived to grow· up rapidly and to assume their social responsibilities early. This was particularly true of the upper reaches of society. Edward, the Black Prince, won his spurs in battle at the age of 16; Joan of Arc saved France when she was only 18; William Pitt the Younger became Prime Minister of England at the age of 24; John Keats was already a great lyric poet by the time of his death at the age of 26. Adolescence, as we now know it and separately define it, scarcely existed before about 1820.

Speaking of the relative lack of psychological distinction between the sentiments of youth and age in the Middle Ages, Ariés remarks of children over the age of 7:

> They immediately went straight into the great community of men, sharing in the work and play of their companions, old and young alike. The movement of collective life carried them along in a single torrent of all ages and classes, leaving nobody any time for solitude or privacy.

This slowly changed:

> Between the end of the Middle Ages and the 17th century the child had won a place beside his parents to which he could not lay claim at a time when it was customary to entrust him to strangers. The return of the children to the home was a great event; it gave the 17th-century family (and after) its principal characteristic. . . the child became an indispensible element of everyday life. Parents worried about his education, his career and his future. He was not yet the pivot of the whole system, but he had become a much more important character.[1]

Ariés' main argument is that Western society lost as well as gained by the increasing enclosure and protection of the child within a nuclear family home. Before the early 19th century, children were exposed to the rough brutalities and profanities of their elders no less than they were carried along by the more useful currents of extended social life. Ariés believes that there had to be a trade-off between the claims of a new family intimacy as against the old sociability. Whereas children had once been the absorbers of diverse social influences ranging from the precociously maturing to the retarding, children became increasingly the focus of mental pressures from parents, as well as physical nurture. No longer at constant physical, social and sexual risk, they became the increasing target of adult desires for emotional self-extension beyond the grave. Thus after a slow transition between 1600 and 1800 from relative parental indifference to increasing parental enfoldment, there occurred within children a growth of an internalised domestic guilt-imperative, instead of the old realistic social imperatives of duty and shame towards a wider community. If Ariés is right, the domestic soil which nurtures personal obsessive and compulsive characteristics has become *more* rather than less fertile over the last two centuries.

An authority who disagrees with Ariés is American psychohistorian Lloyd de Mause. Writing with a group of colleagues in his work *The History of Childhood*, De Mause takes an uncompromisingly futuristic view of the progress of childhood experience from ancient times.[2] He remarks: 'The history of childhood is a nightmare from which we have only recently begun to awaken'. While he admits that there have been fond and devoted parents in every age, De Mause argues that the greater opportunity for socialising offered to children of all classes before the late 18th century was often little more than an exposure to mismanagement by wet-nurses, abandonment to callous strangers and to the uglier sorts of physical and sexual abuse. Even five centuries into the Christian era, he claims, the lot of children was little better than if they had lived in the worst of the pagan cultures. He points to the 2000-year-old custom of tightly swaddling children and notes that this retarded not only their physical and neurological development, but produced an enforced passivity which must have rendered millions socially dull, timid and unadventurous. Thrashing a child until he or she was almost insensible was a common custom only gradually being abandoned by the end of the Napoleonic era.

Six modes or stages of child-parent relationship from antiquity to modern times have been identified by De Mause. Stage 1 he terms the *Infanticidal Mode*, in which children were frequently killed or neglected and allowed to die by their parents. This state of affairs was common up to the 4th century AD, he contends.

Stage 2 was the *Abandonment Mode*, which the author locates in the period from the 4th to the 13th century, which had greater respect for the child as a vehicle of a soul. When people were forbidden indiscriminate infanticide, the habit was promoted of abandoning children to the care of religious orders and monastics, nuns, servants and wet-nurses. Sexual abuse of children is alleged to have diminished in the Middle Ages because of the warnings of the clergy on this subject, but the habit of regarding the child as a future vehicle of evil, tainted with the sin of Adam and Eve, prevented the development of any widespread compassion.

Stage 3, the *Ambivalent Mode*, which dates from the 14th to the 17th century, suggests a realisation that the child was not just a little adult, a potential sinner and scapegoat, but a being whom parents bore some responsibility to shape and mould.

By the 18th century, the *Intrusive Mode*, according to De Mause, was one of a closer warmer parental approach to the child. Mothers began to suckle their own children more frequently, and they were toilet-trained more rationally, played with more often and whipped less — but (oddly enough) punished more often for masturbation than ever before. There were signs of parent-child empathy at last.

Stage 5 is the *Socialisation Mode*, which brings us to the 19th and early 20th centuries when the raising of children made them vehicles of the parents' own wishes and responsibilities. The child's will had to be conquered; he or she must be trained to a social conformity which had to be taught for the child's own good as much as for that of society or parents. For the first time the father appears to take more than an occasional detailed interest in child training — sometimes even relieving the mother of the chores of child-care.

The final stage, obviously admired by De Mause (and indeed rather prematurely) is the *Helping Mode*, beginning in the middle of our own century. The Helping Mode embraces the proposition that the child knows better than the parent what it needs at each stage of its development and this involves both parents in the child's life. As the author admits, the Helping Mode involves a great amount of time, energy and discussion on the part of both parents, especially in the first six years. This means that the parent is the servant of the child rather than the other way round. It also means an abandonment of physical restraints and controls to a large extent in favour of interpreting the emotional conflicts of the child and attempting to resolve them. De Mause makes much of this mode, concerning which he claims from studies and books that: 'It is evident [sic] that it results in a child who is gentle, sincere, never depressed, never imitative or group-oriented, strong-willed or intimidated by authority'.

The portrait thus painted of De Mause's ideal child is somewhat worrying — is he in fact describing the potentially narcissistic, social 'yuppie' of our own time, who is certainly often unintimidated by authority but also frequently selfish, emotionally predatory, unstable in attachment and constantly greedy for material solace and stimulation? What is so backward or naive about the traditional notion that children *cannot* always know what is best for themselves? Among the duties of parents to their society is that of erecting useful containing boundaries around child behaviour, so that not only do children avoid undue risks to themselves, but they also do not offer too much insult or violence to their peers and elders. To devote *too much* care to the child is as much a robbery of his or her integrity as giving too little — and, of itself, a type of obsession.

Assuredly, the New York School of psychohistorians has thrown down a long-overdue challenge to those sociologists and historians who tend to interpret human welfare in purely political and economic terms. Yet the weakness of the New York School is that it relies far too heavily upon a Freudian psychoanalytic-erotic model of human intimacy. This valuable but quite limited perspective promotes the idea that the present American libertarian-permissive style of family relationships provides the best of all possible worlds. The high rate of youthful crime in the United States and the anarchy which reigns amid group life in so many American cities and troubled educational institutions hardly promotes much confidence in De Mause's *Helping Mode* beyond the confines of an educated Anglo-Celtic-Jewish middle class with the time, economic resources and teacher sophistication to make it work.

We are still not rid of the fallacious Enlightenment conviction of Rousseau that formal re-education is the panacea for all private human ills. Both teachers and parents are heirs to the triumphs and disappointments of their own nurture pattern, all too frequently coming up with either imitative or reactive educational solutions derived from their own childhood and family backgrounds.

The enclosed type of modern nuclear family, largely isolated by urban industrial circumstances from community ties and extended kinship networks, is scarcely older than the Industrial Revolution. Economic determinists have a modestly compelling case when they argue that the construction of the small family home as a nest, with a child requiring to be protected from strangers flocking into the new factory towns of Europe and Britain, was more a matter of industrial necessity than fond design. Fathers having become mainly absent bread-winners, the mother was frequently left alone to manage domestic tasks. Only in the poorest parts of industrial or rural society was she forced to work alongside her husband. Thus the mother was increasingly confined to her house, which had now become a seclusive home. Her chief task was to be the care of the children. In this she could be more fussily invasive yet comforting than was either fashionable or indeed possible for her distant female forebears. There was even a period in early 19th-century Britain where it was more common for under-age children from poor households to perform miserably paid outside work than their mothers.

This strong domestic containment of female working energies during the Victorian era, particularly among the urban middle classes, tended to produce the mother-centred 'hothouse' pattern of child nurture. This was the 'Oedipal' milieu familiar to Sigmund Freud at the end of the 19th century and on which he was to base so many of his cases and theoretical conclusions. And it was to prevail until the early 1960s. Despite the steep rise in the number of working or career mothers in English-speaking societies over the past thirty years, this pattern remains strong in millions of households. It has lingered longer as an influence in societies like those of North America, Britain and Australia than has ever been the case in Europe. But even on the Continent it has retained a tenacious subterranean hold on the thinking of even loosely attached *de facto* couples.

SOCIABILITY VERSUS INTIMACY

It is worth repeating that the embattled and crumbling closed nuclear family, *circa* 1990, is only two centuries old. Before this time, in common with other world communities based upon a largely agricultural economy, Western nations saw the family more as a channel for biological and social transmission than as an independent entity. Household ties were linked closely to an elaborate network of clan and community obligation. In pre-Revolutionary France, which has one of the best preserved parish records of any Western nation, community participation fully equalled family loyalties. Births, deaths, baptisms and marriages were not so much close family affairs as communal rites involving large numbers of relatives and acquaintances. By contrast, today's carefully orchestrated wedding rite, for example, is a pallid secularised mutation of the communal customs of celebration in old Europe.

Prior to about 1800, young people had their own separate religious sodalities, secular societies and meeting places in houses, taverns and even village squares. Yet they were allowed to participate in and even organise obsequies, rites of passage and even festive celebrations of their elders. Baptisms, marriages, betrothals, funerals and public wakes were occasions for eating, drinking and tale-recounting in which any courteous passer-by might join. Births were only barely conducted in private. Guns were fired and church bells were rung to ensure that every family special event was a special event for all who might be interested. The cold contraction of all this into a classified notice in the columns of our daily newspapers denotes only the privatism of our own century.

The superficial similarity of this ancient communal cultural life to today's peer-group rituals in America and Western Europe should not deceive us for a moment. Today's youth culture is commercially insulated from the life of its elders — moving to the contemporary currents of media-inspired opinions, music and fashion. This pattern has emerged from the decline of the old privatised nuclear family, leading the less serious and privileged young of Western cities to a rootless, nomadic and often dangerous street life. Only in the power of the purse and the choice of education have most families retained much external control over the behaviour of adolescents.

The significance of today's seeming apartheid of youth and age should not mislead us. *Inner*, though warped, controls have replaced outer taboos, allowing youth unparalleled freedom of choice and movement. This apparent freedom conveys the *illusion* of full physical independence, but without real social strength or spiritual substance. Communal control by bourgeois society over its young since about 1950 has been replaced by subtle domestic devices of emotional manipulation. The physical chastisement of children has been replaced progressively by strategies of reproach, withdrawal or deprivation: though also with much genuine affection. Only in the homes of the poor, disturbed and industrially coarsened have the ancient habits of direct verbal command, neglect and physical brutality still persisted. The wife-beater and child-abuser in East London, the New York Bronx or Sydney is not really very different from his 18th-century counterpart.

In earlier ages than ours, harshly unequal, aloof human relationships — between master and servant, husband and wife, landlord and tenant, teacher and pupil — were common. Yet our scarcely half-century-old division between the experiences of youth and age would have simply astonished peoples of even the last century. Since World War II, consumer objects have been astutely presented as a media focus of quasi-erotic desire. Such objects now help to determine or distort the very shape of human relationships, the avid worship of the automobile being the most outstanding example. In middle-class circles, *having* is now seemingly more important than *being*. Indeed, even intimate relationships themselves are now commercially modelled and marketed.

THE CHANGING FACE OF CONJUGAL LOVE

In his careful study, *The Making of the Modern Family*, Edward Shorter suggests plenty of evidence from Western Europe that, before the late 19th century, there was not much affection between couples within marriage.[3] Since each of the partners had defined roles to perform, some division of breadwinning husband and home-making wife existed even before the Industrial Revolution. Shorter feels that this division only became significant when the father had to be *absent* for long periods in the 'dark satanic mills' of the industrial cities.

In rural France and in England in the days before the great Enclosure movement which deprived so many small farmers of common land, few sentiments of tenderness appear to have been exchanged between husband and wife, or parents and children. Hence, there does appear to be, in the terms of Philippe Ariés, a kind of balance between sociability and intimacy. Before 1800, this balance was firmly tipped in the direction of sociability, at the expense of intimacy. The problem with this evidence is that it leaves unanswered the question of where men and women derived their love, or whether they found much love at all. Poor folk, labouring from dawn until dusk for a living in subsistence economies, rarely have time for the nuances of affection. There must have been countless exceptions to this rule, but these cases were rarely recorded. Shorter remarks:

> What was important, was doing the essential work of society — grinding the grain, transmitting the property from generation to generation in an orderly way, clothing and feeding the members of the family sufficiently so that they would not become a burden to the rest of the community.

This was what marriage was all about for the typical couple; it was not a means of finding mutual erotic satisfaction.

Here we have the nub of it. For many centuries, Western marriage was only rarely undertaken between young folk on the basis of any kind of chosen courtship or passionate love. By contrast, today we tend to interpret or praise the essential worthiness of marriage mainly in terms of its charged emotional content. Law, custom and Christian tradition had little to say about conjugal love, and both Protestants and Catholics saw marriage as a duty rather than as a passionate erotic commitment. If the young husband was handsome and the bride was pretty and responsive, sexual rapture was possible, but this was a bonus to the contract. Otherwise, the best that traditional marriage could offer was an ordered and disciplined companionship that might well mellow into good-humoured maturity. There are worse marital sequels than this.

Perhaps one of the most unlikely revelations is that frequent reference to tender love as an active force in the life of a married couple apparently begins with the Puritans of New England. A paradox of the moral harshness of communal life in the sprawling and restless communities of the New World was that the public regimentation provided by evangelical religion did not necessarily prevent private tenderness between husband and wife. From the beginning, American Puritanism showed a curiously ambivalent interplay between some measure of domestic individualism and rigid public conformity. The sea change from Britain and Europe to the United States had a definite loosening effect upon the tight Calvinist ethic, imparting a domestic softening which would never have been tolerated in Edinburgh or Geneva. The early settlement in Massachusetts Bay provides historical records and letters which suggest that the word 'love' was frequently used in describing the desired course of marriages. The Anglican settlers of Virginia often mentioned domestic tenderness as one of the fruits of a good marriage. Indeed, the inclusion of romantic tenderness in the hopes of newlyweds as a matter of custom may well have been originally derived from early American Atlantic settlers of most religious persuasions. This was to have far-reaching consequences for married life throughout the modern English-speaking world. By contrast, the injection of any romantic element into conjugal life in Britain, Europe and Australia had to wait until after the Napoleonic Wars.

The Growth of Eros in Family Attachments

If the injection of romantic and erotic expectation into marriage increased so dramatically in post-Revolutionary Europe, was an increase of sexual permissiveness in some way responsible? Shorter believes (not without recent academic dissent) that there have been *two* sexual revolutions in modern Western history — the first occurring (and perhaps influenced by) the rise of French Enlightenment teachers and the ensuing Revolution; the second in the 1960s. His evidence is one of the primary indices of sexual promiscuity before the free use of chemical contraception, the incidence of illegitimate children. Given the timeless sexual impetuosity of young people a better measure of promiscuity in our own time is the incidence of medical abortion.

During the 18th and early 19th centuries, the chief opportunities for matchmaking as distinct from lovemaking occurred upon the few holidays and festival days which were available in communities which had long hours of tiring work. There was an unusual degree of autonomy in the behaviour of young people in these decades — more than one would expect. However, full youthful acquaintanceship was slow in progress. Elders constantly made sure through gossip, scorn and advice that young people behaved themselves as far as could be expected when it came to sexual intercourse. Limited opportunity and lack of privacy thus continued to be vital factors in the incidence of premarital sex experiments. How far the social rules for courtship were obeyed is unknown before the more carefully kept records of the 19th century. After that, the vogue of greater sexual freedom arose mainly in large cities. Here, size of population and anonymity made sexual experiments of all kinds uncommonly convenient. Numerous seductions of young girls occurred across social classes. In the early 19th century intercourse with servants working in the same household or neighbourhood was commonplace. Even a century earlier, employers were still heavily represented among the ranks of seducers. This is not surprising, since the sexual freedom and the liberation of women (outside the noble class) had to wait until our own century.

We may never know with what frequency young people have ever truly been sexually continent before marriage, but it is hardly cynical to suggest that complete sexual continence in most age groups is observed only by a small, pious minority. Even so, the powerful taboos of Judaism and Christianity have been perennially present to cause guilt about erotic experiments, though frequently dishonoured in the observance. As well, alternative forms of sexual satisfaction, such as masturbation and casual homosexual contact, appear to have been common enough in former centuries. In Western literature, the very lack of reference to masturbation before the late 18th century suggests there was a good deal *less* shame or special concern about the matter than in later times. By the early 19th century, a wave of grim warnings about 'solitary practices' in clerical, medical and educational circles steadily rose until it peaked in its last two decades.

These concerns of medics and moralists coincided with an increased frequency of individualistic sexual preoccupation and a type of romanticising of sexual pleasures and outlets which hardly existed before about 1750. Some evidence indicates that there was a good deal of early adolescent sexual titillation of the heterosexual as well as the relatively innocent homoerotic type, which allowed many young people to get through the long fallow years before marriage.

Perhaps one of the most important aspects of the *two* sexual revolutions — in the early 19th century and in our own time — has been that of youthful sexual experimentation with several sexual partners. This appears to have been surprisingly rare in earlier centuries, except in the houses of the gentry where there was plenty of opportunity for the young sons of the household, at least, to play about with servants and young distant relatives. In Scandinavia the sexual life of many a couple began before marriage since time immemorial, as that country had none of the Catholic taboos against prenuptial intercourse that applied in others such as France, Italy and Ireland. As for England, the lingering influence of Puritanism had a similar dampening effect. Prostitution, on the other hand, was always hotly condemned, even when winked at. In societies where Lutheranism prevailed, there was little toleration of it at all.

The century from 1750 to 1850 'witnessed a crescendo of complaints about amoral sexual activity among the young'. Shorter believes that, despite some exaggeration, authorities were in fact picking up, as he puts it, 'a shift in the fabric of intimate life about them'. Yet by the end of the century, due to the pressure of the Victorian moral code and its puritan equivalents in Europe and the United States, society was again able to impose tighter social controls, as a significant drop in the incidence of bastardy in the late 19th century indicates.

The easygoing morals of Regency England were gradually eroded in mid-Victorian times by any number of 'wholesome' books, pamphlets and educational exhortations towards manly/womanly chastity and virile continence. For countless people, these reapplied taboos were uncommonly successful. It seems that more young unmarried men and women were likely to be celibate in the years between 1860 and 1900 than at any time in Western history since the Reformation. How, then, was this earlier temporary explosion in sexual promiscuity effectively contained by the end of the 19th century? 1 believe that it was accomplished by a powerful increase in detailed obsessional controls implanted in young minds. Four summary factors assist this:

1. The increasing delegation of moral authority to the enclosed nuclear family in ever-enlarging industrial cities. The tight little nuclear nest could guard its offspring more zealously than in the sprawling communities of the past, and it was expected to do so;

2. A great revival in formal Christian piety, and with it the never-banished Augustinian anxiety about the flesh. Guilt rather than shame became again a powerfully effective sentinel over libido;

3. The increasing replacement of the old *public* suppression of erotic
   or aggressive misbehaviour with private exhortation and detailed
   'examination of conscience' urged by parents, teachers and clergy;
4. An increasing displacement of sexual libido among the middle and
   upper classes into the pursuit of 'filthy lucre' (an interesting Freudian anal association). The rising classes of Britain under the Empire
   at its zenith and in America during the Gilded Age were rather less
   scrupulous in their business dealings than in their sexual ethics.

We are still heirs to the late Victorians in our morals, even while mock-
ing them or revolting against them. Moreover, people showing obsessive
and/or compulsive characteristics are every bit as unspontaneous in
sexual behaviour as they are in joining emotions to numerous other
thoughts and deeds. Spontaneous romanticism is only coupled to obsession in the case of artistic talent or genius; the two elements are
rarely found in combination within the personalities of ordinary folk.
Shorter argues, with good evidence. 'With pre-marital sex, it is the
lower orders who kick things off and the middle classes who tiptoe
behind. But', he adds, 'with childcare and a fondness for the hearth's
warm glow. . .the situation is reversed.' Interpreting this in psychological terms, the writer appears to be implying that tenderness toward
children exists in inverse proportion to the amount of sexual licence.
Speaking very broadly, this would also be true of romantic sexual
behaviour in our own time. Erotic passion in marriage has little to do
with conjugal duty and the adequate care of children.

Must, then, parents embody some obsessive or compulsive controls
in order to be responsible, stable, and adequate as spouses and child
role models? The answer appears to be 'Yes', but in very prudent measure.
Middle-class parents of the Victorian Age believed that they had attained their ideal of moderation, but in practice this was achieved at
the cost of considerable tension and an apartheid in sexual roles. These
attitudes gradually formed the Oedipal mother of Freudian lore, who
frequently nurtured her children, especially her sons, in a contradictory
web of comfort-bearing solicitude and intense brainwashing. This
occurred in the process of accepting the removal of the father to the
perimeter of moral and domestic influence. The obsessive pattern of
conjugal and parental duty obtained from the perennial Christian
tradition often lost its moderate, usefully sheltering aspects in one
generation to become a cluster of guilt-edged, disabling emotional
fixations in the next. This is particularly true of parents from extreme
Protestant evangelical families such as those in Britain and the United

States; and in families of Irish-Catholic descent, who have produced many an emotionally gelded son and anorgasmic daughter.

The nuclear family — vehicle or cause?

Shorter's book on the rise of the 'modern' family finally settles for the fashionable economic explanation of the change from *community*-based family to the eroticised *private* marriage bond we have known in recent times. Yet, he concedes that: 'The nuclear family is a state of mind rather than a prevailing kind of structure or set of household arrangements'. This state of mind has brought about claims for the privacy and sanctity of marriage and family life over all other relationships, and also for its newly privileged and secretive emotional climate. Meanwhile Shorter is *partly* right in pointing to 'capitalism' as an engine of greatly changed community relationships after 1800. The steady shift from a largely agricultural and trading economy to a heavy manufacturing and capital-intensive one over the past two centuries has taxed the ability and flexibility of a travelling labour force whose mobility partly uprooted Western humanity from its roots. This made the elaborate kinship and friendship networks of immemorial small-town life increasingly difficult to preserve. The *loneliness* of the new isolated urban nuclear triad of father, mother and child inevitably forced it to look inward upon itself, with both enriching and warping consequences for each new child generation. This tight, isolated small family began, almost of necessity to feed upon its own emotional resources, rather than turning to a variety of people for the satisfaction of its intimate needs.

The late 19th century in Europe, America and the old white British Commonwealth marked the triumph of the Splendid-Awful Family. Its every domestic sentiment and pious nuance was celebrated in popular novels, its mother elevated to the status of a demi-goddess whose erotic desires it was pretended were utterly separate from her tenderly asexual functions as a parent. The father was frequently a business patriarch, who presided *above* the nest, with only a minor social impact upon the core of its experience. Middle-class children were more sheltered from the carelessness and cruelties of adult life than at any time since Ancient Rome. Yet the cost of being so potently identified with the emotional desires and mores of their parents meant that security for children had to be paid for in the currency of less inner freedom to pursue their own dreams in their own way. The Victorian family circle indeed carried on the patriarchal traditions of the ancient extended kinship network, but by means of an unrecognised clandestine gynarchy in which the mother, grandmother and governess were the real bearers of emotional and moral power. In the case of boys, this was only partially corrected in the upper class by the masculine harshness of the great British public school system where despite the vigilance of schoolmasters, the family's ministrations could frequently backfire into later homoerotic relationships.

A prototype of the Splendid-Awful Family could be found in the brood of the remarkable woman who gave her name to the whole epoch — Victoria Regina et Imperatrix. The royal family which ruled the British Empire typified the new mores in microcosm, together with their paradoxes. Her reign combined with matriarchal tenderness towards children a ruthless moral and psychic control. It placed Victoria the widowed Mother-Queen on a pedestal of unassailable virtue in the midst of her once lusty fecundity. It was essentially a bourgeois model that Victoria and Albert helped to present as a universal norm. The old aristocracy of Britain, like its Continental counterparts, was glittering and often fecklessly arrogant, but it was neither moralistic nor especially controlling of the hearts and minds of its offspring. Rather, its special mark was unconcern about the needs of children, and the delegation of nurturing duties to servants.

The family of Victoria and Albert was to set a quite different pattern. Their son, Albert Edward, Prince of Wales, was reared in an atmosphere of suffocatingly humourless Germanic rectitude. Throughout his life his mother kept him, as Heir Apparent, from any practical involvement in the affairs of state. His moral flight from the royal nest into a dissolute private life, while outwardly supporting the iron code of the Victorian ethic, has often been cited as an example of Victorian hypocrisy at the summit. In truth it was not. The future King Edward VII was a bored fugitive from matriarchal controls, while never really doubting their value or ceasing to love his formidable mother and Queen.

Victorian family life was rarely hypocritical in the clichéd sense, but more a victim of painful compulsive dissociations in conduct — the moral right hand of its male members rarely caring to admit what the lascivious left hand was up to. The enormous libidinal and aggressive tension caused by the ritualistic controls of Victorian social mores must have contributed greatly to the displaced executive energies of a small nation which came to control the greatest empire in human annals.

A century later, in the early 1990s most Anglo-Celtic families are still only mutations from the Victorian norm: the abolition of the stigma of illegitimate birth, the vogue of de facto marriage and condoned single-parenthood being the only major departures. This is because the 19th-century nuclear family model has been and still is one of the most potent agencies for the transfer of emotional, social and ideological attitudes to the yet-to-be-born since Ancient Egypt. It is not surprising, therefore, that parents with longings to extend their own emotional aspirations beyond the grave should still seize upon the child as an ideal vehicle.

Yet this very parental futurism inevitably carries the virus of a time-haunted compulsion. The evocation of simple shame and sometimes cruel physical punishment for misdeeds in olden times has been replaced by the unspoken proposition of nuclear parents to their children: 'I will love you if you cause me to feel pride in you as an extension of my personality and my posthumous ambitions'. In order to win the ever-receding bait of parental love and approval, children are bent increasingly to obsessional doubts about their social worthiness. Parents foster elaborate sets of compulsions to assure the child that this worthiness can somehow be won.

Once this basis of family conditioning was established, the apparatus of business, government and public life could expect future conscientious servants who felt worthy through constantly *achieving*, rather than by being merely pleasant, diligent persons. Given the time-ridden historical perspectives prompted by the Christian religion and a connected scientific world view, few upwardly-mobile families with children could escape into a simple working enjoyment of existence. In this way a social superego, which was once only loosely imposed on Western populations by priests, kings and barons, became part of the close emotional fabric of domesticity itself.

The triumph of the separate family in the late Victorian era ensured that the futuristic striving-achieving mode in middle-class life would become the norm for most children up to our own time. The outcome in terms of practical ingenuity, organisational energy and general physical betterment has been amazing, if we consider the great leap which now separates us from the Victorians in such spheres as medicine, applied science, engineering, communications and transport. Yet the coarsening (and often debasing) effect of this on those products connected with evoking emotions and intuitions — mass entertainment, religious piety, the arts, literature and music — shows how much we have lost as well as gained since at least World War I. Not without good reason has George Steiner dubbed our present over-packaged, mechanistic civilisation as a 'post-culture'.

PARENTAL IMAGE AND SOCIAL BEHAVIOUR

However one might prefer to regard the family as being a pawn of so-called 'socio-economic forces', we still fashion our behaviour throughout life through a series of imitations or identifications with potent or admired *persons*. Amid the contemporary feminist emphasis upon the long social subjugation of women, the continuing emotional and moral *power* of the mother in the modern nuclear family, particularly since World War I, has been persistently overlooked. Suburban Australia is an outstanding example. As a largely Anglo-Celtic frontier society, dominated early in its history by a preponderance of city-based males, Australians grasped eagerly at the nuclear family and the civilising influence of women as a remedy for the loneliness of life in a vast, sparsely populated island-continent. In these Antipodes, the traditional extended kinship ties of Europe had no like conditions in which to develop. Until 1860 the family, for most Australians was not only the nub of society; in isolated rural areas there was no other society.

'The hand that rocks the cradle rules the world' is only a recent adage which has grown up alongside the enclosed family. Countless distinguished special cases illustrate this. So many eminent men and women have came from homes where mothers were the dominant influence, throughout the Western world and more recently in many Afro-Asian societies touched by Western values.

By contrast, studies have shown that the dominating father is as likely to create a reaction by his children *against* his demands as a desire to follow in his footsteps. He rarely has grandiose plans for his offspring, in particular since the achieving father does not care particularly for youthful competition: indeed, he may retard or block the ambitions of his sons, while being indulgent towards his daughters provided they do not challenge the convention of male supremacy.

The mother of architect Frank Lloyd Wright believed in planning for her son even before he was born: she decided then that he would be an architect. Annette Bromfield, the mother of the novelist Louis Bromfield, decided that her firstborn son was to be a writer and placed enormous pressures on him to excel in literary studies. Many musicians had dominating mothers, a famous example being the cellist Pablo Casals, whose dominating mother was so fearsome that he reported later in his life that he had had only two options — to become a prodigy or simply to go mad. In the large family of Giacomo Puccini, the men provided all the physical bullying but the mother applied all the emotional pressure. His uncle was forced to assume the unwelcome task of teaching the young Puccini to play the organ after repeated pleas from the boy's mother. If ever young Giacomo made an error, he was kicked in the shins by his uncle, causing him to develop a muscular tic, which made him jerk his leg whenever he heard a wrong note.

One normally thinks of famous soldiers as being reared in a strong masculine tradition. Yet the mother of General Douglas MacArthur was the principal force in his life. His mother was his only school-tutor until he was 13, and she was determined her son would carry on the family military tradition. Young Douglas reported that he was so spoiled by his mother that his fellow students at West Point mocked him unmercifully because of his aloofness. Although he much later made a happy marriage, the future Allied Commander did not escort any girlfriend along West Point's famous Flirtation Walk. This was a ritual reserved for mother and son only.

Jewish mothers have had a formidable reputation as being forceful motivators in the lives of their sons. This is particularly true of many brilliant musical virtuosi, and others such as Theodor Herzl, the founder of Zionism. Herzl's father was constantly involved in financial triumphs and mishaps and it was Theodor's mother who had to support her son emotionally. Sometimes dominating fathers drive their sons and daughters into the arms of a more potent but understanding mother. Late in the 19th century, Lieutenant Colonel H. H. Kitchener was a British administrator of a very poor Irish county. He was an arrogant chauvinist who taught his son to regard the Irish as an inferior race, and his rules for his children were so stringent that his wife, a delicate, sickly woman nearly twenty years his junior, felt obliged to protect them — particularly her delicate, withdrawn son. Loving his mother and reacting from his father, the young Herbert spent a lifetime compensating for the excesses of his mother's love and for his father's cruelty. He became Lord Kitchener, Commander-in-Chief of the British forces at the outbreak of World War I. The Field-Marshal never married, surrounded himself with men and was displeased if a member of his close staff married.

Many mothers retain a powerful influence upon their sons and, indeed their grandchildren, until the very time of their own death. This was true not only of General Douglas MacArthur, but of the family of

Luther Burbank, the great horticulturist whose mother dominated his life to the end of her own. Research workers who conduct longitudinal studies have noted that sons tend to survive or rebel against father-domination, but seem to become lifelong victims of mother-domination, because of their mothers' greater persistence, subtlety and talent for instilling in them the detailed observances of life. Traditional domestic women have had a great many devices of child control at their disposal. On the other hand, their daughters, not unexpectedly, may clash violently with mothers who excessively dominate the household. Such daughters are capable of using the same controlling devices against their mothers in maturity as were employed on them in their childhood.

Often the failures of the father rather than the dominance of the mother render a woman central in the life of her children. The father of novelist F. Scott Fitzgerald was a wholesale grocery salesman. Fitzgerald senior was such a disaster as a provider that his son was sent by an aunt to a school for wealthy Catholic boys. Unfortunately, the future novelist's gentle demeanour and most feminine good looks made him a social failure. He always felt a poor relation among rich and patronising folk. This is a theme which crops up more than once in Fitzgerald's fiction.

Alfred Nobel, who left his fortune to promote world peace was a mother-smothered boy who hated his father intensely — possibly because his mother's pervasive influence prevented him appraising that parent justly. Young Alfred once wrote a long poem justifying parricide. He was so overwhelmed by his mother that he did not even dare introduce his mistress to the formidable lady, and when the mistress bore a child he paid another man to marry her.

William Avery Rockefeller was a travelling vendor of quack patent medicines. He was forever in and out of money, and his son John D., one of three brothers, used to sit by the road waiting month after month for his father to come home from another money-raising tour. 'Big Bill' Rockefeller cheated his sons and swindled them regularly, allegedly to make them clever in handling money. Not surprisingly, John D. Rockefeller, who was for a time America's richest man, was originally parsimonious with his fortune, resolving that he would never again be subjected to the ups and downs of fortune like his feckless father. His mother was probably the only person the oil magnate ever loved, but unlike many other influential women she seemed to have no desire to impose her will upon her sons. Her son was thus an exception among many famous figures.

As one further sidelight on the darker underside of the nuclear family, clinical worker David M. Levy undertook a famous study of maternal over-protection and found that the husbands of overwhelming nuclear-family mothers were often passive or unable to deal with the relationships which grew up between possessive mothers and their children. In the family of Rainer Maria Rilke, the great Austrian poet, the father was unable to communicate or show affection to his son at all. Sophia Rilke was, by contrast, a foolish, impulsively emotional woman full of flights of fancy who encouraged her son's creativity while warping his life. She pretended that Rainer was a girl; she let his hair grow long and kept him in girls' frocks and taught him to dust and clean, even calling him 'Sophie'. The uncommunicative Joseph Rilke, Rainer's father, was a soldier who was disappointed by never being advanced in life. Ultimately the unhealthy Oedipal preference of the wife for her son over her husband led to their separation. Joseph Rilke could never accept his effeminate son as a poet. It is a story which would have exercised the imagination of any orthodox Freudian.

The sheer inability of many fathers to accept the confined domesticity of the nuclear home because of the traditional freedom beckoning husbands out of doors, has caused many young men to accept the pious values of their mothers rather than copy the incorrigible restlessness, drinking and philandering of their fathers. One such case was novelist Count Leo Tolstoy, whose father Count Nicholas had only two passions — cards and an infinite number of mistresses. In his memoirs, Tolstoy remarked of his father: 'God knows if he had any moral convictions. He certainly gave us no hint of any'. The complications of Count Nicholas's life were even more bizarre than those to be found in the novels written by his son. Thus Leo was left to the consideration of his vain and rather stupid grandmother and his mother, who tended to agree with everything the older woman decreed.

Many gifted but tormented sons and daughters have come from homes divided by conflict between a spirited wife and a restless husband. Such a person was Charles Lindberg, the famous aviator. His father wanted to be a poet but turned to law, and some of the restlessness of a conflict-prone household was imparted to Charles. The families described here often encouraged creativity at the expense of serenity. The constant drive to follow the dream of an ambitious parent, or to compensate for parental disharmony and disappointment, is a frequent cause of painfully obsessional, if often highly productive, artistic or social striving in a child.

In a notable study by Victor and Mildred Goertzel, who conducted enquiries into the backgrounds of over four hundred early 20th-century men and women, it was noticed that actors and actresses are the professionals most likely to come from very disturbed homes.[4] Authoritarian politicians (such as Hitler and Mussolini) came next, accounting for 95 per cent of their grouping. Military leaders who came from unbalanced homes represented 86 per cent of that group. It is quite evident from studies such as this that the basically obsessional character of Western civilisation can be traced back to and reinforced by primary psychological and moral experiences, rather than by the abstract dictates of some social or economic order.

Among the world-shakers of the West there has been an extraordinarily high proportion of obsessive and compulsive personalities. Their gifts have enabled them to harness obsessions to the point where a creative contribution transcending neurosis could be conveyed to the world at large. Alas, it is quite otherwise with the ordinary or ungifted person, whom such a pressured environment is likely to warp or crush rather than inspire.

THE POTENCY OF THE FEMININE

If we accept the dominance, or at least firm centrality, of the mother-figure in the nuclear family home, it can be asked *how* this can be considered to have increased or extended obsessive drives in Western communities. It is already noted that the futurism of the obsessional mentality and its active compulsive component occurs more frequently in the traits of the male, if only by the fact of his traditionally self-imposed social burdens. Most of the so-called 'forward planning' in the developed world is still done by men. But a closer look at the domestic politics behind such public behaviour will reveal the 'matriduxial' core of our now-decaying patriarchal system. The stubborn Judeo-Christian preoccupation with millennial dreams and its hidden links with the industrial scientific order continues to be presided over by male clergy, professors, managers and, of course, fathers. But it is the woman and the mother, who from the earliest years of her children, accepts the detailed implications of this world view and makes sure that her sons in particular are well imbued with it. This is why the rise of feminism and the emergence of powerful career women have only mildly altered the ideological climate of English-speaking societies since the Vietnam War. Women have generally been more concerned with gaining *entry* into the corridors of political and economic power than with attempting to change the ideological agenda. Hence the observation made of Margaret Thatcher — a wife and mother as well as Prime Minister — 'she is the strongest man in her Cabinet'.

How have women been so useful in helping men maintain their striving, compulsive life-mode? If we accept that the Christian religion and the secular-humanist dogmas of the Enlightenment, (which either distorted or diluted its message) make up the basis of today's ethical outlook, it is women rather than men who have been the more steadfast and convincingly humane indoctrinators. Amid the decline of institutional Christianity as a social force, it is women in the churches who are still providing much of their dynamism. Even in the Church of Rome, which is the last bastion of male ecclesiastical power, it is mainly the influence of the female that keeps the sap moving through the arteries of parish and diocesan activities. Following the perennial 'Monica-Augustine' pattern, the power of the Catholic mother could never be underestimated. Even the more heavily patriarchal Protestant-evangelical churches and small sects show that it is the womenfolk who ensure that the detailed practical precepts of religion are kept and that children are well-versed in its requirements.

Over the past century or more of compulsory primary and early secondary education in English-speaking societies, it is again women who have been among the most potent and influential classroom mentors. The American primary education system has been dominated by female teachers for decades and even the coeducational high schools of the US have contained an increasing quota of women teachers. The same pattern has developed in the United Kingdom, Scandinavia and large parts of Western Europe, to say nothing of the old British dominions such as Canada, Australia and New Zealand. After the extension of free, compulsory education to all females in Western countries in the mid-19th century, women proceeded to share the desires and dreams as well as the dogmas of their menfolk. Greater access to formal knowledge and the social power conferred by it enabled them to do this. Aristocratic women had always had access to the sources of literary and scientific knowledge if they wished. For 250 years the shrewd hostesses of the intellectual salons and courts of London and Paris were often clandestine feminists, in outlook if not behaviour, whilst the bourgeois wife was, by contrast, even more enmeshed in the details of socio-economic observance than her husband.

THE RISE OF THE PSEUDO-FAMILY

The key words that denote the mammalian family are Procreation, Protection, Attachment and Adaptation. What used to be fixed and determined in all higher mammals — even in primitive humans — the endless cycle of fertilisation, parturition, growth, decay and death, has become ever more negotiable in Western civilisation. Only our physical death is unavoidable, and even this can be postponed by the sorceries of modern medicine and surgery. Once one accepts the power of genetic transmission, it becomes clear that the enormous power of the human family to shape social destiny originally lay in its role as nature's own laboratory for our species. But in our time, its age-old secrets and exclusive prerogatives have been compromised and weakened by other forces. Science and education have become the allies of parenthood, but also their subtle subverters. The mass media and the oppressively large urban peer group also undermine the old paternal prerogative of conveying skills and values to the young. Parents too share a new bewilderment in proportion to an expanding range of often trivial social options and consumer goods. The old blood loyalties and tribal coercions are now confronted by a new class of affinities. The loyalties of the nuclear family are challenged at every point by new individualistic or peer-dominated living arrangements. Only the strongest and most gifted offspring can adopt these loose arrangements without extreme risk to their later social maturity.

Using the antitheses of Philippe Ariés, we may note that, once more, 'sociability' — often of the most debilitating and abysmally empty kind — now challenges family intimacies. The nuclear family was given a dose of slow-working poison at the very pinnacle of its potency after 1950 by a stream of outsiders bearing it gifts — psychologists, educators, social workers, media moguls and commercial salesmen. Most of all, the nuclear family has been undermined by new variants of Romantic Love. Born centuries before in Southern France, romantic love has been celebrated anew in a world influenced by America. After World War I, the United States became the second home of erotic optimism. Such optimism had all the magical power of Hollywood and the most strident ditties of Tin Pan Alley to assist its propaganda. Alas, like all traditions which have outstayed their usefulness, the renovated notion of Romantic Love merely offered new obsessions for old.

Romanticism in literature and culture has enjoyed a bad intellectual press since World War II. Yet it used to be a worthy opponent of unbridled rationalism and greedy economic compulsion, only becoming their unwitting ally since the advent of the audiovisual media. Without the protective fence mounted by former romantics in favour of sentiment against scientism, we children of the industrial age might have become even more entranced consumer-automatons than we are. Even so, the romantic construction of the world — its worship of nature, its celebration of art, the five senses, the joyous, the passionate and the macabre — was never intended to be incorporated into daily family relationships, especially when fortified and yet debased by the media for mass consumption. The new romantic expectation of endless physical love and fulfilment is something which family life can rarely satisfy. Moreover it retards that necessary emotional growth of both husband and wife which is essential for the rearing of well-adjusted children.

We must never forget that it is Eros, and not the Philia of lasting conjugal friendship, which is at the root of most longings in modern marriage. In erotic terms, Lloyd de Mause's vaunted *Helping Mode* in child-rearing tends to turn back on itself. Over-liberal patterns of marriage and child-rearing inevitably lead to greater sexual promiscuity and, carried too far, this erotic freedom always threatens the security of the next family generation. And, as modern statistics show, divorce and marital fracture are likely to lead to a similar chain reaction of fracture in the marriages of offspring. Unstable families tend to beget unstable families. Yet much of this serial calamity comes from the contemporary romanticising of marriage itself — a folly in which both church and secular society have conspired since late Victorian times. The very words of the modern marriage bond itself represent an uneasy amalgam between the old hard-headed Christian commitment to contractual fidelity and the near-impossible romantic expectations of lifelong erotic devotion. 'Forsaking all others' and 'Till death do us part' are vows easier to fulfil when there is remarkable compatibility between husband and wife and when the social opportunities for extramarital philandering are limited. Today, aside from the fear of sexually transmitted disease, opportunities for random fornication and the casual *affaire* are virtually limitless. The preromantic marriage was strong enough to withstand some infrequent infidelity, whereas contemporary couples commonly head for the divorce court at the first sexual flirtation.

The true mark of romantic love has never been, after all, a search for a continuing intensity of *sexual* pleasure. The troubadours of 12th-century Provence founded a convention in which the subtle denial or postponement of sexual satisfaction was a means of heightening emotional intensity. Hunger for the unattainable or the barely obtainable is one of the greatest incitements for heightened desire that humankind knows. Cosy availability and the lambent flame of passionate love are rarely found in combination. In many primitive societies, such as the Barrow Island Eskimos (or Inuit), extramarital sexual outlets are frequently condoned as a *game*, and it is decided by consensus that this need not threaten a marriage or family. This is simply because emotional intensity plays little part in the adventure. There is not the desire for endless pursuit and possession of the loved one which is so much a feature of romantic passion. Yet as many contemporary couples have come to realise, the tendency of romantic love to consume itself to ashes can never provide a realisation of limitless passion.

Denis de Rougement, in his famous work *Passion and Society*, argues that the darker unconscious objective of all romantic passion is consummation in death — something that the great medieval legend of Tristan and Isolde actually celebrates.[5] This legend echoes what is felt in the deepest recesses of our consciousness. Spiritual love *may* transcend death but passion, with its cargo of physical lust, cannot survive the sepulchre.

On a less grim note, we can observe the paradox of an age of easy divorce where there is endless marrying and remarrying throughout Western societies. All of it constitutes a denial and even abuse of the traditional marriage and family contract where the romantic *affaire* was always thought of as an *alternative* to marriage rather than one of the elements contained within it. A simple state of adultery, or merely an agreement to live together, would surely be a more honest appraisal of what a questing potentially unfaithful partner really needs. So many partners in Western society want it both ways — they seek within the respectable confines of marriage a Don Juan and a breadwinner, or a madonna and a whore — in the one impossible package. Little wonder that almost one in two American marriages now break up, with a corresponding two of every five in Britain, and nearly one in every three in Australia and on the continent of Europe.

All this rapid legal coupling and uncoupling has produced a new phenomenon in Western society, one which has not happened since the Dark Ages: that of the *pseudo-family*. This is betokened by a couple who live together sporadically and unpredictably, expect the State to worry about their neglected offspring and enter into new, confused family relationships complete with stepdaughters and stepsons, or who may decide not to bother about children at all. This untidy situation has ushered in a revolution in the changing role of the woman in human intimacy, particularly her attitude to herself, and her recognition that men may be less essential to her well-being than she imagined. Men, on the other hand, lately seem more inclined towards compulsively dependent womanising instead of forming comradely bonds.

Conditions for the rise of the late 20th-century pseudo-family can be listed as follows:

1. An increasing lack of commitment to lifelong monogamy, coupled with inconsistent hope that marriage may endure without much effort on the part of either party.
2. The decline of the religious concept of marriage as a sacrament, with God as witness. This has played almost as large a part in change as the heavy freight of romantic/erotic love contemporary marriage is now expected to carry.
3. Failure by the majority of spouses to arrive at individual psychological and social maturity before taking their vows. In the old small-town. and village communities there were fewer developmental tasks for young men and women to accomplish. Marriage used to be the *culmination* of a young man's rite of passage to full community initiation. Today it is often merely the conclusion of a prolonged sexual pre-adventure with no assumed consequences. The marriage contract is falsely assumed to denote technical arrival at an emotional maturity which has actually been retarded (especially among men) by a whole variety of other social involvements and erotic indulgences. The result is often a kind of Peter-Pan-and-Wendy syndrome where the parties marry without having really grown up and where at least one partner fails to mature thereafter.
4. The lack of natural human kinship systems for the newly married couple to rely upon. The extended family has gradually turned sour in most Western urban societies. Relatives have been reduced to mere 'in-laws', sometimes helpful but as often interfering, rejected or malignant. Such elders too often lack the communal charisma, knowledge and social authority to help newlyweds establish some concern for children and immediate posterity.
5. The trivialisation of the marriage bond by a now near-automatic divorce process. The abolition of all fault in divorce proceedings in many countries plainly suggests that there is no longer a *responsible* partner in any relationship. The less culpable partner in a physically or mentally abusive marriage suffers equally with the more culpable. The marriage ceremony remains, but increasingly as an object of trivial display, with the bride as glamorous focus and the bridegroom largely a reluctant hostage to the performance. As Goethe wrote nearly 200 years ago: 'Among all festivals, the wedding feast is the least appropriate. No other festival is so much in need of being celebrated in seclusion, humility and hope. Rather should we celebrate happy endings than uncertain beginnings'.

6. The relegation of the child-bearing process to an afterthought. Future offspring now must contend with the house mortgage, automobile and labour-saving household devices, to say nothing of the frequent persistence of both spouses in maintaining a full-time career. With such pressures operating upon its future parents, the child starts at risk of being either a pet to be randomly cosseted or a mere parcel to be handed around to the care of others. In most English-speaking societies external child-care facilities have increased six to seven-fold since World War II, while populations have only shown a two to three-fold increase. The importance of the child in the middle-class home, which reached its zenith *circa* 1950, is now in steep decline, even in the US.

7. The ill-omened rise of hundreds of thousands of single-parent families which, in truth, do not make up a family at all in terms of normal anthropology. Whereas before World War I patriarchal laws in such nations as Britain gave the father almost complete power, custody and authority over children, it is now mostly the separated mother who is given a monopoly of her younger children. The father must fight for lengthy access to his children in those cases where he is actually interested in gaining it.

Out of this mélange of influences, as often abetted by smart sociologists as deplored by them, comes the Pseudo-Family where the parties assent to stay together as a unit until it becomes traumatic or merely uncomfortable or boring to do so. Adultery is rapidly becoming a pejorative ecclesiastical term, as the 'meaningful relationship' (meaning the erotic abandonment of one partner for another) has taken over. The children of such fragile and often disposable marriages lack the one thing children need most of all — a *consistent, predictable*, rearing pattern — which, though it may sometimes entail little expressed parental or parent-surrogate love or competence, at least spares the child the frightening prospect of being passed around among outsiders. Indeed, for the thousands of homeless children who now drift about the industrial cities of the West, with their susceptibility to social, sexual and criminal exploitation, the situation is now not so very different from that of the 17th century.

Yet to talk about the 'breakdown of the family' is one of the glib staples of weekend journalism. Such talk ignores the fact there has *always* been a disturbingly large minority of families in Western civilisation that were hardly families at all, and that served the needs of the rising generation indifferently at best or brutalised it at worst. It is *the loss of the sense of communal ties and of true social friendship networks* that makes the situation of the isolated 20th-century family so forlorn. But why was the nuclear family unit such a successful (and sometimes oppressive) socialising agent half a century ago, in such contrast to its increasing enfeeblement today? English social critic Jonathan Gathorne-Hardy believes that this has something to do with the widespread narcissism and ego-satisfaction which marks what he calls 'the Privilege Bulge' — that large generation of contemporary parents who reached their majority in the mid-sixties and who were members of the large post-World-War-II 'baby-boom'.[6]

In common with several other writers, Gathorne-Hardy points out that the generation born in the mid-forties and in the immediate postwar years, particularly in the United States, were the most indulged, cared for and 'liberated' children in history. They epitomised the result of Lloyd de Mause's *Helping Mode* of rearing. Today we are beginning to realise that this mode did not, after all, bring us the best of all possible cultural worlds.

Gathorne-Hardy argues that the selfish pursuit of wealth, power and social significance of the baby-boom generation represented only a climax of a steady movement over fifty years away from the customs of lifelong marital fidelity and the deferral of some personal comforts for the sake of child needs. He claims that the narcissistic trend began in the 1920s when the 'flappers' were discovering the multiple orgasm along with the Charleston and the One-Step. The terrifying carnage and social dislocation wrought by World War I seemed to create a fever, particularly on the part of men, to live a fuller, more intense life. Their prevailing obsession seemed to be with pleasure, which, of course, could not bring full satiation because obsessive people never know how to enjoy themselves for very long. These between-wars folk were the parents of the post-World-War-II generation, and their influence still lingers in English-speaking society, despite the chastening effects of the Great Depression.

The offspring of the between-wars generation who were parents in the early 1950s, denoted the first generation which no longer relied upon its own practical capacities or the sturdy folklore of its forebears, but sought advice increasingly from doctors, social workers, broadcasters, magazine columnists and batallions of (often contradictory) child-rearing experts from Truby King to Spock. By the 1960s the outcome was a quite different youthful generation which had been more written about, observed, protected and overindulged than any in human experience. It is hardly surprising that these privileged youngsters who formed the 'hippie generation' were mostly the rebellious sons and daughters of a bemused and increasingly shocked middle class. Sixties youth had the material security if hardly the common sense to ride out the social storm they had created. The Vietnam War was merely one focus of their discontent, not the cause of it. Alas an unseemly nostalgia for the era makes this reality difficult to acknowledge today.

The hippie generation brought a new sort of emphasis to the 'dating' and coupling pattern between the sexes. This was the notion fostered by such therapeutic gurus as Dr Fritz Perls in California, that the parties existed to complete one another's hedonistic wants. 'Make love not war' could have been better translated as: 'no cooperation without copulation'. Compared to such delights, making a home, preparing for a new generation, and even the long-admired compulsive goals of securing money and social esteem began to take second place. This was a generation which began to talk incessantly about 'human growth' and 'self-fulfilment'. For a minority of the over-observed young people of the 1960s and early 1970s, the cultural opportunity for a more adventurous spiritual growth was well used. But for the majority, 'growth' could mean the tasting of dozens of grotesque and ephemeral experiences from hard drugs to campus conflicts, most of which led to spiritual dead ends. It is this rather disillusioned, but still relentlessly ego-absorbed generation which has entered the forties age-range and which, in the terms of Oscar Wilde, knows the price of everything and the value of nothing. It is hardly surprising that their offspring, the bewildered but 'nice' late teenagers of today, have no idea what a contented and yet dedicated family life might be like.

THE CONSERVATIVE REACTION

The challenge to the nuclear family nest has not gone uncontested by conservatives. Nor has the power of its transferred traditions and compulsions been any less potent in large numbers of middle-class families which astutely seized upon the labour-saving trappings of contemporary post-industrial civilisation but resisted its throwaway values. Doctrinal religious piety and logical-positivist optimism combined with a self-validating pursuit of affluence are the rocks to which the old-style nuclear family is still strongly tethered. Perhaps the most striking element has been the degree to which the Christian churches have remained the most trenchant defenders of the 'traditional' nuclear family against all alternative lifestyles.

The Catholic church, despite its one-time elevation of the values of religious celibacy and the maintenance of Augustinian clerical doubts about the flesh, became rampantly sentimental about the sanctity of the family after World War I. In the 1950s the mother had become the lesser prototype of the Madonna in every Catholic family. The official Catholic refusal of any contraceptive check to maternal fecundity seemed peculiar, in view of the image of the admirably restrained virginity of Mary. As we have seen, the intense combination of chastity with marital fecundity was to maintain one of the most powerful yet limited of the feminine stereotypes — that of the perpetually child-bearing and caring asexual mother. Alas, it was on her that the increasing complexities and wayward example of pagan urban life were to place intolerable strains. For his part, the Christian husband has been, ultimately, required to place little check on his conjugal appetite. Nor, in so many cases, is he yet an observant or even overtly caring father to the children he has sired. The great imbalance between maternal and paternal emotional contributions to children still holds powerful sway, particularly in middle America among Catholic and Protestant Evangelical communities. Some of the pressure upon Catholic women has been alleviated by the indifference shown by 80 per cent of Catholics to the Papal prohibition of artificial contraception. But 'Momism' is by no means a spent force in any English-speaking society.

Analyses of the early family backgrounds of technologists, scientists and more conservative business entrepreneurs have shown that they have been powerfully formed by the old logical-postivist, materialistic world view. It is they who embrace the old obsessive-compulsive style of child-rearing which, not unexpectedly, still results in the largest number of intact families in the Western world. Furthermore, a rigidly traditional rationalistic type of Christianity is not, as is often supposed, in conflict with the modern scientific industrial world view, but in fact coextensive with it. It is *radical* Christians of various persuasions — those interested in ecology, spiritual issues and so on — who are most likely to reject the detailed compulsions of the old nuclear family in favour of alternative lifestyles.

As for the Protestant achievement-ethic, this is still alive and well. With the collapse of more authoritarian socialist alternatives in the former USSR and its satellites, the Protestant capitalist tradition is very far from showing signs of decline. While one should never underestimate the residual power of the Left-libertarian alternative establishment in English-speaking societies, particularly in the mass media, the persistence of great private wealth is still one of the main reasons why the old family structure continues to validate itself. This is if only for the shallow reason that is remains as an incomparable vehicle for privileges and transmission of property.

However, one should not be too cynical about the side-benefits of the WASP family style in terms of the political, economic and ideological cohesion conferred by the family upon Western communities, nor about the persistence of its ambitions and compulsions. The *positive* contribution of the obsessive-compulsive style to all those institutions that have redeemed social and economic life from chaos has already been noted. Further, the danger posed by most of the Utopian alternatives since the time of Rousseau has become all too plain. The real problem of family obsessions and the ambitions that elders still nurture in the hearts of their children is in what these fixations *exclude*. Those fighting a rearguard action for what they imagine to be God, country and family too often are sadly one-dimensional people in whom all human excellence tends to be seen in terms of quantity, of over-specialisation, of contempt for visionary speculation in favour of logical-linear thinking, of purely physical answers to health and well-being and of deep suspicion or hostility toward any lifestyle not leading to tangible or 'useful' outcomes.

Little wonder that the Christian family commonweal, or what is left of it, is torn asunder today by the contending claims of the old Jewish/ Calvinist/Catholic fideist views on one hand and radically destructured or 'gnostic' views of religious priorities on the other. One stands for what is left of the old compulsive Establishment order while the other demands an end to it all and a return to a lifestyle more in harmony with the notion of a world and its inhabitants as a spiritual unity. Alas, without some collaboration between the Children of Obsession on the one hand and the Children of Liberation on the other, the planet is just as likely to be destroyed by the dreamy incompetence of the latter as it is by the rigidly organised myopia of the former.

Despite all doubts about the future of the family as a unit, most couples in English-speaking societies still tend to share the unquench-able optimism of Americans when it comes to permanent mating, even though the rate of legal marriage has fallen off steeply since 1970. The gap has been amply filled by 'trial marriages' and *de facto* living arrangements. The sheer rapidity and variety of the involvements undertaken by young people, the blurred lines between numerous erotic encounters and a final marital commitment have complicated things even further. In spite of all our improved psychological knowledge, the absence of mature articulate counsel from older adults and the abrupt disinclination of youth to listen to it has made marriage or serious coupling at a young age more hazardous than at any previous time.

Not the least of the changed variables which now affect marriage and family life is the increasing longevity of one or both partners. In the early centuries, rife with wars, epidemics and dangerous working conditions, death resolved many a strained and hurtful family situation. The relative tranquility of English rural life in the Caroline Age before the Civil War of 1641–47 made for as contented a family life as the Western world could offer. Yet figures from a series of studies of English villages after the war in 1688 suggest that one-third of all marriages in Stuart times were second marriages. Today, many vexatious partners outlive their long-suffering spouses. The greater longevity of elderly women in particular has made them a heavy burden upon the welfare systems of many a modern society. This has not only changed marital expectations of permanency but has had subtle social effects and put strains upon most human intimacies.

The compulsive lifelong bourgeois marriage of this century up to 1918 often resulted in a dutifully correct household frozen into cold avoidances and bitter unspoken hostilities. Many of these chilly bourgeois families produced the 'grey people' D. H. Lawrence portrayed with such merciless perception in such works as *Women in Love* and *The Virgin and the Gypsy* and whose latter-day counterparts were scrutinised so powerfully and painfully by the later Dr R. D. Laing.

There are good reasons to believe that only genuine, lasting conjugal love can justify maintaining lifelong marriage when the arrangement has simply outrun the romantic affinities which brought the couple together. Indeed, there is an ancient Hindu custom whereby ageing males, having provided for their womenfolk and grown offspring, may surrender their married life to seek spiritual improvement as hermits or disciples in a religious community.

Another consequence of the decline of the nuclear nest is the exploding prevalence of step-parents when one parent forsakes a marriage only to take his or her children almost immediately into another union. The evidence for the effect of these newer arrangements is so far rather equivocal. Sometimes the new marriage gives youngsters greater freedom from tension and a better chance for socialisation with new step-siblings; at other times all the mythology of the wicked 'step-mother' or 'stepfather' comes into unpleasant reality.

Gathorne-Hardy has suggested that there is some Jungian merit to monogamous marriage. He points out that it can be a pathway to salvation which a weak or inadequate person could not tread by him or herself. That marriage can lead to growth of a spiritual and social kind, if it is resourcefully used, is not a new idea. Such an evolving marriage is not expected to be as happy or hedonistically fulfilling as a romantically contracted marriage is supposed to be. It is a process of *self*-discovery as well as discovery of the partner. Many of the sacrifices of unwed ego-fulfilment which such marriage requires are amply rewarded by the spiritual elevation which can often come at the end of a rewarding companionable life. Alas, the operative word in this scenario is 'can', rather than 'will'. This noble ideal is in fact rarely fulfilled. Moreover, the notion that marriage can be a maturing vehicle for immature single people is a fallacy exposed daily in every divorce court.

Since the mother is the child-bearer, she is the most potent transmitter of both biological and psychological influences. What she is willing to accept and settle for now more than ever influences the success of family life since not unreasonably, women are demanding much more in the way of enlarged consciousness and cultural opportunity than their grandmothers had. Unfortunately, the extremes of militant feminism accentuate one of the most dangerous of the several negative stereotypes of family life — that of the aggressive, destructive female who is competitive, suspicious of or dominant over her male partner.

The 'castrating' female has been amply discussed in Freudian literature, much as this may infuriate feminists who like to portray the male as *invariably* the aggressor in marital situations. Not until the era of Susan Brownmiller, Kate Millett and Shere Hite have women appeared *publicly* in a destructively anti-male guise. After 5000 years of decidedly variable modes of patriarchy it is doubtful if the matriarchal family of prehistory could ever re-emerge without turning Western culture upside down. The only realistic alternatives are a greatly modified patriarchy (which already exists) or broadly egalitarian shared responsibilities. As noted British psychiatrist Anthony Storr has pointed out, families where one spouse is heavily dominant over the other are almost invariably unhappy or tense affairs. Regardless of the sad history of the *physical* abuse of women by men, this is particularly the case where the female is the psychological aggressor. Her mental hostility to the husband contrasted with her active concern for the children produces signals of such confusing ambivalence that offspring cannot be other than harmed.

On the other hand, the late Margaret Mead was probably right when she believed that the chief motive at the bottom of all feminist activity, even at its most militant, is the simple desire of women 'to be what they want to be'. As long as this does not include a neurotic denial of woman's uterine possibilities, such a desire can only accord with natural justice. It can hardly be refuted that nearly twenty centuries of Christianity have cast the woman in such an auxiliary role that she has rarely had the same freedom as the man to accept or reject parenthood as her destiny. After all, it was the teaching of Christ himself that the *individual* is supremely important, and that it is not right that one person should be so subordinate to another — master and servant, husband and wife — that spiritual integrity is violated. It is a teaching that many conservative Christian dogmatists have ignored even up to our own day. Their failure to learn it has led to many a Christian family being governed by a male bully and living in a state of sanctimonious misery. Yet 'family-bashing' by politically militant women only compounds this problem. Even when stripped of all repressive pieties, motherhood remains the most potent of all civilising roles and we downgrade it at our peril.

Much of what has been said so far about family conventions concerns the imposition of customs and structures which are failing to supply the emotional or spiritual fulfilment of people who obey them. This too is the stuff from which compensating obsessions and compulsions can be fashioned — the constant reiteration to oneself or by others that this is what one *ought* to do or *should* do, to the exclusion of what one might *want* to do if left in a state of emotional and conjugal openness. All social structures still benefit from a small ingredient of inner compulsion. Intimate *personal* attachments certainly do not. Obsessive catchphrases such as 'working at your marriage' and 'love is a decision' are part of the stock claptrap of 'inspirational' books on marriage, and they merely reinforce the old fixations to the joy of neither spouses nor children.

Forces at work on the family today impose upon it altogether new social obsessions and compulsions that have not been directly derived from the fixations of our forebears at all, but come from quite impersonal or even alien sources. These are the most powerful of such forces:

1. *The return of the working mother and the increase in latchkey children.* In addition to creating costly early child-care burdens for the taxpayers of several Western nations, this development leaves the child once more at the disposal of outsiders. This promotes the sort of premature socialisation which, before the Industrial Revolution, was handled by a conscientiously disposed local community. With community consciousness rapidly vanishing from urban life, children are left without adequate adult models for long daytime periods.

2. *The influence of the mass media.* As the presence of the solicitous mother fades, the mass media become substitute childminders — making TV and the cinema in particular the most powerful influences outside the nuclear family itself.

3. *Increasing sexual precocity.* Both biologically and socially, children are arriving at post-pubescent awareness much earlier than in previous times. The child therefore becomes sexually aware in mid-childhood. The old 'latency' period talked about in Freudian literature narrows to the point of vanishing. The child is exposed to erotic titillation long before it receives adequate education.

4. *More permissive school environment.* Due to the influence of figures such as Rousseau and Dewey, and educators like A. S. Neill, the child is subject to fewer and fewer controls and sanctions over his or her behaviour at school. Into the vacuum left by the teacher as a once-authoritative person, the peer group has moved as the main guide to conduct. . .with often undesirable to even criminal results.

5. *The greater mobility of the parental culture.* The combination of the automobile and job which forces the father to go wherever his employer wishes means that families constantly change domiciles and neighbourhoods. The child rarely strikes down deep roots and important early friendships are constantly being ruptured.

Until quite recently, then, it was possible to trace the transmission of obsessions and compulsions related to one's personal worthiness in intellectual and social matters to the pressures exerted by the family and closer peers. If undamaged by these pressures, young people could escape into the various adult arenas of social and political life and use some of the more positive energies gained from the old kinship compulsions as a means of serving ego and society at the one time. By contrast, youth in today's age of the audiovisual media have to cope more with increasing dispersion of trivial compulsions and addictions throughout the *public* world. The forces of emotional fixation have begun to move out of the old clan and family milieux on to the streets and the TV screen. The clamour of unbridled public information-as-propaganda in turn is forcing new fixations into the old spheres of personal intimacy, which were once no part of their proper awareness. The long-term outcome of this trend can only be guessed at, but the matter is discussed in my remaining chapters.

• FIVE •

SALVATION THROUGH STRUCTURES

They constantly try to escape
From the darkness outside and within
By dreaming of systems so perfect
That no-one will need to be good.

T. S. Eliot

One of the mental legacies of a civilisation originally shaped by the Judeo-Christian world view is a belief in the redeeming power of nominated structures. The Jewish passion for naming, or holy nomenclature, as a basis for meaning goes back to Genesis, when Yahweh named the elements and the flora and fauna of creation. Even the name of Yahweh himself — the Tetragrammaton, or Divine Name of almost unpronounceable consonants — became a source of connection between the Creator and his creation. The same notion was carried on into medieval and modern Europe. Naming led to recognition and recognition led to laying the slide rule of consistency and predictability over the features of the surrounding world. The distinction between the name of a thing and its deeper reality gradually became blurred. Yet, as contemporary physics has demonstrated, the world we see is in very large measure a construction of our own minds. It is the human intellect which puts 'edges' to things and carves up the continuous flow of the natural universe into that which is comprehensible and controllable. The function of a thing should never be confused with its true nature.

One of the prime features of the human thought process is the habit of trying to find descriptive general terms for every 'gestalt', or pattern of things which our senses discover. Thus we talk about 'beauty' when abstracting from beautiful things, 'decency' from our experience of rightness and order — which may not correspond with that of other people. Thus arose among bodies of intellectuals, rulers and codifiers of laws the conviction that the principle was higher than the individual *experience* to which it applied. This notion has become the basis of all morality, including the Ten Commandments laid down in Exodus. And it is true that no civilisation can conduct its affairs without broadly accepted canons of right and wrong, order and disorder, justice and injustice.

However, it is the Western love of elevating mere abstractions to virtues and detailed moral demands that turns civilising precepts into shackles. These can be broken even in secret only at the cost of crippling guilt and frequent paralysis of quite innocent forms of human experience. Just as Christians hanged, burned and tortured each other in the 16th century for rival notions of religious orthodoxy, so does modern popular ideology bully us mentally with concepts labelled 'racism', 'sexism', 'elitism', 'redistribution of wealth', and various other fashionable terms. There is nothing wrong with the compassionate and civilised sentiments behind such modern catalogues of sins and virtues provided citizens are not harassed by secular mandarins into the foolish view that virtuous behaviour and humane attitudes may be promoted by legislators and the coercive action of courts and tribunals. Standing above the new ideological demonologies, and replacing the old religious concepts of God, the Light and the Good, stands the most often invoked and potent abstract concept of our age — Democracy.

Democracy has always been more of an ideal in the world than a reality. It is a workable system for a small population of saints rather than the barely manageable mass populations of our century. The ancient and admired democratic model of Periclean Athens was merely that of a privileged citizenry of hundreds set upon the shoulders of helots — a slave-class of thousands. The model of democracy based upon a majority rule and a universal right to vote grew only very slowly in England. Even today, whether for better or worse, the political and legal equality of the British is still carefully hedged about by lingering tacit differences of class and status. The Westminster system of government has influenced the world far more, via the old British Empire, than the more radical French Republican model has done. Yet it is the American model of rule by the *demos* — of the people, by the people, for the people' — which has really mesmerised most of the Western

world, and has finally triumphed as the basis for an idealised form of
government since World War II.

The sentiments of the Pax Americana have filled the heads of social
reformers from Argentina to Nigeria, from Beijing to New Delhi.
Moreover, 'democracy' has assumed the aspect of a civil religion, as
powerful in its grave adoration of constitutional rights as any Christian
creed bowing down to Almighty God. Except for New England brahmins
and the fundamentalist sects of the Middle West, US citizens have
tacitly assumed that God must be a democrat, and this has led to what
American Jesuit thinker John Courtney Murray called the 'blind idolatry
of democracy'. The confusion of ideological notions of social equality
in secular life with the Christian concept of the equality of souls before
the Godhead has lately become almost complete. Even the Papacy
itself now speaks as if just and good government and a 'democratic'
political system are virtually the same things. By a supreme irony,
Voltaire and Rousseau, via Jefferson and Tom Paine, have become
ideological tutors to the Christian churches they once loathed and
dreamed of destroying. The incompetent cruelties of communism have
only contributed further to the headlong scramble for the democratic
millennium amid former Eastern bloc populations who barely understand as yet the high costs of liberalism.

THE FRANCO-AMERICAN POLITICAL MYTH

In the notion that 'all men are created equal' we encounter one of
the most insidious fallacies in modern politial thought. It is allied to
the presumption that the mere mind of man can plumb what the
Creator has decided in respect of 'human rights'. Let us examine in
more detail the Enlightenment-inspired Declaration of Independence,
largely written by Thomas Jefferson. First we encounter the reference
to 'life' in the Declaration. What sort of 'life' is being discussed, and
what the precise value of human life is, when humans freely take the
lives of others by means of crime, war, economic deprivation and
revolution, is not spelled out. Furthermore, we are still a long way from
understanding what the catchword 'liberty' in such documents really
implies, even when it is uttered by calm and logical people. As for the
'pursuit of happiness' in the Declaration, the answer of Viennese psychiatrist Viktor Frankl is retort enough: 'Happiness cannot be pursued.
It is a by-product which must be allowed to happen to a person'. There
are assuredly as many nuances of happiness as there are people to

experience them! How then can any system of government facilitate the attainment of all of them?

The United States is the greatest of all the 'democracies' in the Western world but still conducts its public affairs on the basis of unprovable generalisations about human nature — its fundamental equality and its inalienable rights, which science simply does not confirm, and which the founder of Christianity never taught. In fact the American Founding Fathers themselves were well aware of the problems implied in Thomas Jefferson's Declaration. Of Jefferson himself the conservative Gouverneur Morris from Pennsylvania noted: 'Mr Jefferson believes in the perfectability of man, the natural divinity of mediocrity and the wisdom of mobs'. A cruel thrust, but one showing that the Virginian sage was by no means unanimously accepted by his peers, even when he became President of the United States.

Denouncing the practical absurdity of many aspects of the Bill of Rights, American conservatives fought to prevent too much power being vested in a central government of the United States, much as States' rights supporters did in Australia over a hundred years later. Among the delegates to the First Philadelphia Convention, which led to the creation of the first Congress of the United States, there was a widespread conviction that 'democracy was a dangerous concept'. Arguing in favour of a life term for Senators, Alexander Hamilton claimed: 'All communities divide themselves into the few and the many. The first are rich and well-born; the other, the mass of the people, are those who seldom judge or determine rightly'. Even James Madison, a future President and a moderate, when talking of the perils of majority rule, claimed that his object was to 'secure the public good and private rights against the danger of a levelling faction; at the same time to preserve the spirit and form of popular government'.

Despite these misgivings, the Constitution of the United States has precariously stood the test of time, if only due to the fervent belief of most Americans in the great shibboleth of Liberty, and the flag that is its symbol. Alas, the American Republic has always been held together as much by symbol and abstraction as it has been by social reality. The *belief* that the American political system works is much more powerful than many practical evidences that it does not work very well, or even with conspicuous justice. The composition of Congress has been steadily ossified by the proprietors of local and State political machines, until American government has come to resemble an alternating oligarchy supported by a vast bureaucracy. Unfortunately the noble political declarations embodied in a constitution can form a legal straightjacket which later constantly works against change. This is extremely resistant to modification except by referendum or the decrees of constitutional lawyers.

The American legal system, as it has flowed from the Constitution, has become increasingly the property of lawyers and bureaucrats rather than the people it pretends to serve. One obvious example is the notorious absurdity, connived at by the US Supreme Court, that even a manifestly guilty and brutal mass murderer may go free if some minor technicality in the collection of evidence concerning his case is breached. Constitutional blocks against outlawing guns are another instance. Clearly, such nonsense has more to do with law than justice, with sterile ritual taking precedence over the violent realities of urban life.

The roots of Western quasi-democracy lie not in some abstraction of 'historical inevitability'; rather, the boasted 'open society' has evolved from the gradual shaping of a turbulent and often bloodthirsty rabble into orderly voting constituencies by middle-class oligarchs who never meant to extend the political franchise beyond their own class. This fact was as evident in the pre-Civil War United States as it was in post-Restoration England. Once the powerful myth of monarchy as a sacred office and the notion of an hereditary noble 'calling' was challenged, hereditary rulers were devalued in many nations to fading figureheads or symbols without mythic substance. After rejecting the 'Divine Right of Kings', there could be no logical restriction of voting power on the basis of property qualification, racial grouping or gender. Yet a universal franchise was won only by the steady erosion of the claim to legitimacy held by a succession of elite social groups. There has never been anything 'self-evident' about the strictly limited political rights given to ordinary folk by such groups. 'The people' achieved each extension of the vote by a combination of pressure and propaganda *on their behalf* by self-appointed spokespersons. Meanwhile the fragility of a democracy still lies, as Plato knew well, in the obviously unequal moral and spiritual qualities of its citizens. Worker and profligate, law-breaker and law-upholder, the wise person and the fool, all are given the vote in the quite mystic belief that there is some divinity in the Majority — and often a bare majority at that.

However, if the record of Western democracy is a patchwork of goodwill and absurdity, a much more alarming prospect is presented by a fixed oligarchy or a dictatorship shorn of any sense of 'noblesse oblige', or of a religious feeling that God may be watching. Despite such atypical figures as Robespierre, dictatorships normally do not need the support of grand abstractions beyond simple appeals to national sentiment, suspicion of foreigners or selfish material interest. This is particularly true if dictators efficiently deliver the kind of material prosperity that they have promised, as Hitler and Mussolini undoubtedly did in the early years of their rule.

Despotism can also apply the popular will or fancy in the service of an ideology which otherwise might seem too obscure or boring to appeal to a society on its own merits. Moreover, social anxiety and the personal immaturity that social anxiety fosters often supports a political obsession with purity and clarity in word and deed. This only a ruthless autocrat might provide. Dictators certainly 'get things done'. But the temptation for such rulers to practise paranoid cruelties and the denial of basic human aspirations is dangerously seductive, as Mussolini, Hitler, Stalin and Mao Tse Tung, Pol Pot, Ceaucescu and many Latin-American dictators have demonstrated. Nearly two centuries after Spanish colonial rule, much of Latin America has still not found a secure way to combine a stable system of representative government with the lingering feudal privileges of a moribund proprietorial class. Constitutional monarchy, on the other hand, works very well in all those nations where respect remains for the *symbols* of authority.

The truth about the 'free world', by contrast to authoritarian or totalitarian regimes, is that it consists of *representative* governments elected by all responsible adult citizens at intervals varying between three and seven years. 'The people' do not rule; their elected representatives actually do so, and with widely varying degrees of potency, efficiency, honesty or corruptibility. Elected rulers also owe all manner of debts to those party machines and organisations that helped to commend them to the mass of constituents, as the hired means of their presentation to the people can be immensely costly. Hence, ordinary people have no guarantee whatever that those parliamentary representatives to whom they have limited access will (or even could) reflect their current needs and desires. In every government that styles itself a democracy, representatives are divided between the quadruple demands of self-interest, the interests of their party, the interests of the nation as a whole, and not least, if they hold a Cabinet post, the interests of the permanent state bureaucracy of which they are temporarily in charge. In a modern state with a huge electorate, a political leader is responsible to vastly more than his or her own constituents. Moreover, the bureaucracies to whom he or she dictates policy and who deeply influence him or her in return tend to be responsible in theory to everyone, but in fact to no one. In fact, voters have virtually no day-to-day influence over the policies of the State. Winston Churchill once remarked that democracy is the best of all the bad forms of government with which the world must suffer from time to time. There is no evidence that parliamentary-style democracy suits all peoples. In a world too much governed by verbal abstractions, the tendency is to build structures of an incompetently visible kind to support the quite airy abstractions they claim to serve. In the end rampant bureaucracy threatens to prevail over the broader public interests it pretends to uphold as the troubled rulers of the former Soviet Union have recently discovered. The larger a public bureaucracy becomes, the more difficult it is to dismantle, or even change or limit its functions.

Examination of just two of the buzz-words and fond concepts of Western politics will demonstrate the gulf between what they are and what they are claimed to be.

Equal opportunity

The provision of universal primary education in most Western nations since about 1870 has assisted the belief that any newsvendor should have the opportunity to become a Nobel Prize winner, a prime minister or president. Yet it is still statistically recognised that there are insurmountable obstacles — genetic, environmental and motivational — to prevent more than a small number of people in any population from rising to the highest levels of excellence. Despite the mass media, the gap between the highly educated and the poorly educated is almost as wide as it was a century ago. That between the super wealthy and the ordinary wage-earner is equally as wide, even though the sufferings of the poor are greatly ameliorated by the intervention of State welfare agencies. The tendency of a few people in any nation to make the most of every available social opportunity and the tendency of the majority to fail to do so irritates obsessive reformers and envious lovers of structural manipulation. Hence, from a reasonable ideal of equal *opportunity*, the much more outlandish notion of 'equality of outcomes' has emerged. It is now one of the fashionable radical catchcries, particularly among American educators with racial obsessions, who believe that if there is any obvious disparity of attainment between Hispanics, blacks and whites, this *must* be remedied by governmental and bureaucratic manipulation. Hence the insidious notion of 'positive discrimination' which has crept into the thinking of social planners in several English-speaking societies. This means that, to secure 'equality of outcomes' in educational and industrial spheres, special aid should always be given to allegedly disadvantaged persons or groups. This provision violates the very principle of equal opportunity by giving special favours to one social group over another, though this is not admitted by reforming lobbies. The same sort of provision supports another popular socialist notion, namely the 'redistribution of wealth' by means of arbitrary political power. It is suggested that the State penalise the rich for their enterprise in order to support increasing numbers of the poor who may be poor for any number of reasons, from cruel and genuine misfortune to folly or indolence. In the last decade of the 20th century, Rousseau's original paradox — 'we must force people to be free' — has been taken a step further, to the socialist view that we must force people to *share*. It is remarkable how many leaders in the Christian churches ardently support this authoritarian solution, which has moved from a one-time plea to individual conscience to an outright moral demand upon the entire social order. The whole idea of 'equality of outcomes' not only goes against the facts of human nature, it denies the deeper right of most people to be *different*. Democracy should thrive upon diversity. In practice, however, too much diversity is always feared among us, even where it is not actually penalised.

'The right to know'

For unnumbered centuries, governments ranging from the despotic to the partly-representative have conducted their affairs with a measure of secrecy. Even the ancient Athenian model under Pericles frequently concealed its more private deliberations and decisions from the Delian Confederacy of which it was head. Indeed, the whole notion of 'open government' was largely the invention of late-19th-century newspaper proprietors who had their own particular interests to pursue. In the late 20th century the mania for sensational trivia about politicians and governmental processes has reached the point of a characteristic obsession. 'The right to know' presumes that citizens have a right to be informed about all the details of government — its trade-offs, diplomacies and commonplace deceptions — as well as the reasons for its major decisions or shifts in policy. In the case of Britain's notoriously irresponsible tabloid newspapers, the 'right to know' generally involves a process of 'digging up dirt' about politicians and Crown appointees (and lately, royalty itself). In a few instances this may serve a useful purpose; in most cases it is just newsworthy muckraking which only serves to impede the process of day-to-day administration.

In Britain and the United States sexual peccadilloes of Cabinet ministers are something of a press speciality, as the notorious Profumo/ Christine Keeler case or the sexual intrigues of US Senators and

Congressmen amply illustrate. The mock-puritanism lavished by the visual media and press upon these scandals is often more sordid than the facts of an affair itself. The idea that a minister of the Crown is somehow less efficient, trustworthy or 'decent' because of his private sexual weaknesses may once have had some relevance in a Christian confessional state, where manifest sinfulness in any area once disqualified a man to govern. But in a pluralistic age the idea amounts to little more than hypocrisy when it is argued by persons and agencies no less amoral than those public figures they denounce. Newspaper editors are not, after all, theologians or moral guardians. Once consensus about moral conduct in public life disappears, all that is left is an unsavoury appetite for profitable scandal, which is of little value to anybody but circulation managers.

Consider the Watergate Conspiracy which paralysed the Nixon Administration for months in 1972 and did great harm to the process of Cabinet government in America. It was later remarked by liberal Democrat senator Eugene McCarthy that the methods used by *Washington Post* reporters to uncover facts about the conspiracy were no less questionable than the conduct of the Administration itself. The quite peculiar combination of Calvinistic self-righteousness and cynical prurience with which Washington often pursues its fallen or fallible political heroes has long been a source of wonder to other nations. The point to be emphasised here is that the whole concept of the 'right to know' is primarily an obsession kept alive by the mass media, for whom politics vies with sex and sport as one of the three staples of mass interest and circulation building. In private, political journalists will scarcely deny this point.

With a nod again to Plato in *The Republic*, it is sometimes necessary for rulers to tell serviceable lies, such as in times of war or to prevent extreme disillusionment or panic. But as long as the obsession for complete political purity prevails in all those countries that have adopted the Anglo-American model of so-called open government, democracy is likely to be as hampered and destabilised by constant press and TV scrutiny of its smallest hesitancy as kept upon an honest daily path. In modern Cabinet government, there is a delicate equipoise between the public 'right to know' and an elected government's equal right to conduct its affairs in the way that it thinks best. This is usually done on the basis of information which can rarely be understood by other than those actually party to deliberations which always precede a legislative or cabinet decision. Public villainy or executive incompetence are always proper subjects for media exposure. However media campaigns dictated by political prejudice or venom are quite improper.

To understand the dangers of a political ideal once it becomes elevated to a deity for civil theology we need look no further than the United States of America, the nation where our conceptions of democracy, the universal franchise and majority rule began to take their modern form.

AMERICA — HOME OF THE BORN AGAIN

The United States represents the triumph of structural arrangement and political abstraction over natural reality. Yet even when making the criticism one feels somewhat guilty. Americans rank among the most generous, well-meaning, hospitable, hardworking, pious (though certainly not spiritual) people Western history has known. Since World War II they have been denounced by rancorous left-wing intellectuals of other nations for acts of economic imperialism, but with little gratitude for their costly resistance to social cruelty and political oppression in various parts of the world. The renaissance of Western Europe since World War II was made possible by tapping the ancient gifts of those restive peoples who had produced Aquinas, Dante, Napoleon, Da Vinci, Goethe, Mozart, Beethoven, Einstein, Mach, Victor Hugo and Churchill. However, without the largesse of America as principal victor the rebuilding of Western Europe could never have taken place so rapidly. If some Europeans had suffered unnecessarily from the well-meaning meddling of Woodrow Wilson after World War I, any error was more than atoned for by the generosity of the Marshall Plan, and the soldierly watchfulness toward Stalin and his successors of the Eisenhower Cabinet during the critical years of the Cold War. Apologists for the old Soviet Communist empire until very recent days now stand openly exposed for their double standards and their xenophobia towards all things American. Even the worst excesses of figures such as Joseph McCarthy, Al Capone, Huey Long and Warren Harding pale into insignificance when compared with the conduct of regimes whose wielding of naked power and peddling of murderous ideologies have brought death and misery to millions.

Yet the socio-political realism of Americans has rarely proved as vigorous and mature as their ways of fostering native economic and industrial genius. Were it not for the compulsive entrepreneurial energies of its puritan forebears and its vast resource base, the nation might not have prospered half so well. Moreover, the rich and balanced mix of migrant nationalities that provided the US with its strength in the late 19th century was always cemented by a traditional WASP core of citizenry which retained great power and competence over the government and finances of the nation. Piratical as they often were in practice, the Carnegies, the Rockefellers, the Vanderbilts, the Whitneys and the Morgans were rock-solid capitalists who not only considered their power and wealth God-given, but knew how to use it judiciously and with confidence. Today, it is otherwise. The WASP axis of power which once stretched between Wall Street and Washington has been terminally weakened if not yet wholly broken. Meanwhile young stock-and-bond conjurers have played havoc with whole economies.

For the first time in three centuries the fruitful equipoise of migrant racial forces that (apart from the evil of slavery) caused American institutions to work tolerably well threatens to tip over. A Hispanic movement of illegal migrants from the south of the United States has become uncontrollable and its poverty and high birthrate is providing a depressed under class on a scale hitherto unknown. As for the educated black population, it now more rarely pursues the worthy integrationist aims of its parents. Under the banners of black power, crude 'rap' music and enforced tokenism on film and TV, it demands ever more advantages to compensate for its ancient wrongs. The healing accents of Martin Luther King are heard less and less. There is frequent talk of overthrowing white majority institutions with, of course, an expected backlash from white supremacists. This rising clamour of racial, social and religious subgroups has led expatriate observer Robert Hughes to fear what he calls 'the Balkanising of America'. The 1992 Los Angeles riots represent the tip of a volcano. There is a warning here for a small nation like Australia which has adopted yet another intimidating abstraction called 'multiculturalism', chiefly at the expense of the mainstream heritage, which is too often intellectually deplored or brushed aside.

Even the mighty economic and industrial machinery of the US nation is no longer as confident or productive in output as it once was. Americans now buy Japanese cars because they know these to be better constructed and better value for money, while the domestic market for Japanese electrical goods has wiped out more than half of former US local production. As the grossly unequal balance of payments and the mind-boggling national debt of the US make clear, Americans are still consuming more industrial goods than they are producing, relying upon once-vast resources in timber, agriculture and mining to fill up some of the gap. While the corporate holdings of many old US families remain awesome, evidences of widespread foreign ownership are everywhere. Yet the nation increasingly defines personal wealth and individual significance by those who possess wealth as against those who do not. Paradoxically, the increasing suspicion with which American hegemony has been regarded elsewhere has rendered the rich and powerful of the United States increasingly uneasy and prone to new paranoid ruminations about the power of foreigners — especially the Japanese.

One of the great problems of America as she stands ever more precariously at the leading edge of purpose in the Western world is just where to go from here. The nation has built its wealth and extrovert optimism on a whole string of incantatory abstractions called 'Progress', 'Development', 'Change' and 'Innovation'. Meanwhile countless thoughtful American citizens have begun to doubt their utility and meaning. The coming of war in the Persian Gulf, for instance, found Americans ill-prepared for a confident moral commitment. Hence George Bush's failure of political nerve during the Gulf War in finally despatching Saddam Hussein, one of the world's most dangerous despots.

After the upheavals of the Vietnam era and the social turbulence of the late sixties and early seventies, a new American generation has arisen which is overanxious about its material and vocational future. In a time of international crisis it can no longer afford the luxury of navel contemplation or dalliance with frivolous lifestyles. An eerily earnest sense of conformity has recently descended over the university campuses of the United States after the painful discovery during the Reagan era that too much of American advanced education had closer ties to Disneyland, and the baseball World Series, than to Einstein, Edison or Walt Whitman. Overseas the states of the former empire of the Soviet Union are ready to sublet their own shops of troubles, while dictators rise up in the Middle East to threaten the future of the West. The American republic has to cope with smaller foreign enemies like Iraq and Iran that have shadowy and even violent messianic intentions. Yet on the ideological front, a necessity to counter and discredit those who torture and murder in the sacred name of Allah has been greeted with a notable degree of Western intellectual timidity and agnosticism. Modern scepticism gives no effective protection against fanatics. Indeed, the modern post-Christian vacuum offers little but impotent bleating for peace, without thought for how this is to be safeguarded.

A longstanding posture of extrovert, self-assertive helpfulness towards the world wears no better with nations than it does with individuals, because extroverts can only flourish with allies and admirers. They become querulous, suspicious and even hurt when their good intentions are doubted or their blunders criticised. This is why successive American Congresses since the fall of Lyndon Johnson have become increasingly defensive and inward-looking. Doubts about the trustworthiness of friends abroad and the sense of being assailed at home bring the urge toward defensive conspiracy. Had not the American media broken the back of the Johnson administration, it hardly seems likely that Richard Nixon would have surrounded himself with so many dangerous 'minders', and the Watergate affair would never have occurred.

While the freedom of the press in America is the envy of world journalists, it is seldom admitted that its effect upon the American socio-political process has become as much malign as helpful. Of the great American freedoms, it is the Fourth Freedom which has latterly been most abused. Again, this is linked to the obsession with 'right to know', even in situations where ferreting out such 'knowledge' can paralyse an administration and place the long-term cause of good government in peril. These difficulties always lead back to the fundamental American article of political faith conveyed zealously to half the world by means of international magazines, television and cinema. This is that democracy, *as romantically conceptualised*, is a quite sacred form of government: that 'Liberty' is so precious that it may be curtailed only at the greatest public harm, even when it is being outrageously abused by failed courtiers and malignant neurotics.

The Iran-Contra scandal, involving Colonel Oliver North and high-ranking members of the Reagan Administration, was transformed from a minor if sleazy administrative connivance, like Watergate, into a drama of international consequence so that political critics might be appeased and the media could regard themselves as an alternative arm of justice. Money derived from the holdings of a pathological Iranian regime was diverted for the support of central American rebels in Nicaragua. Those engaged in the enterprise certainly broke the law. But in any polled sample of the American people, the view emerges that no good was served by hounding such people as North and Poindexter through the US courts. These defendants obviously believed that they served and acted from patriotic motives. When Richard Nixon returned with honour to China not long after his fall from the Presidency, the protracted Watergate scandal was treated as a great mystery by the leaders in Beijing. Why the moralistic fuss, they pondered, since governments have been engaged in occasional administrative chicanery and bureaucratic espionage since time immemorial?

The zeal for superficial political purity in American public life is an ancient fixation that could have some ancestry among the witch-finders of late 17th-century Massachusetts. Today there seems something deeply immature about a great nation that airs its trivial political dirty linen on coast-to-coast video hook-up, as if this were the stuff of Greek tragedy. Alas, this masochistic pattern of the public 'beat-up' is being increasingly copied in other nations such as Australia, Britain and even South Africa, which can least afford its inflammatory consequences. The worth of a government should be measured less in the meticulousness of its constitutional observances, than in how decisively it moves in the interests of public order and the long-term welfare and security of its constituents. Rightness is not always on the side of the small battalions — as any victim of an IRA bombing or terrorist attack could testify.

To be fair, the contagious American belief in the sanctity of every detail of the representative political process and the right to maintain arms to defend it has had worthy as well as unfortunate political outcomes. The Berlin airlift of 1949 effectively checkmated Stalin's plans to end the Allied occupation of Berlin. The 1961 fiasco at the Bay of Pigs in Cuba was honourably atoned for by the courageous stand of the Kennedy administration in the 1962 Cuban missile crisis. Even the American armed defence of the non-Communist cause in South Vietnam had valid foundations in the outrage of the United States at the violation by Hanoi of the Geneva and Paris Accords.

Yet Vietnam too provided an embarrassing example of inconsistencies in policy. The Kennedy Administration wanted to save a large portion of Indo-China from Communist rule. Yet it connived ruinously at the murder of the tough South Vietnamese President Ngo Dinh Diem on the basis of some absurd scruple which had nothing to do with the reality of politics in the region.

As recently as 1989 the periodical bane of 'holier-than-thou' was shown in the Washington condemnation of the move by the British in Hong Kong to repatriate the thousands of boat people whom the tiny colony simply could not accommodate. The retort of a British MP that, if Americans were so concerned about the plight of thousands of fleeing Vietnamese, they should take a more substantial number of refugees into the United States, did not make for comfortable hearing in the purlieus of the US State Department.

The recent collapse of Communist regimes in Eastern Europe has laid bare the folly of political systems structurally based upon ideology rather than simple social transactions. Although the ideology of representive democracy is far closer to natural human aspirations than communism, *it remains an ideology nevertheless* and its rhetoric is always unfair to any alternative mode of government. Political arrangements should be pragmatic. They are not fundamental to human happiness but should only facilitate those civil conditions in which personal happiness might be found. Practical structures are needed for any nation to function — be these for the protection of life and property or merely to regulate the flow of automobiles at road intersections. The rest is propaganda masquerading as civil theology. Bismarck was right when he observed: 'Politics is the art of the possible'. It cannot be conducted on the basis of wishful magic.

The American zeal for elaborate political checks and balances forms a curious contrast with American *laissez-faire* economic practices. Britain has wisely retained some of her long suspicion of immutable structures and preferred the mystique of precedent and tradition. In this she has been assisted by the survival of a constitutional monarchy and the refusal to be shackled to a written constitution. Rousseau's delusion of the perfectibility of man never took firm root in the British Isles. There the profitable union between aristocracy and the merchant middle class, and a broad (if often resentful) acceptance by the populace of the inevitability of class stratification, produced a chronic scepticism about political strategies to erase human differences. Such an outlook enabled the British to govern an empire that evolved from the conquests of brilliant freebooters into an enlightened colonial system which, in the end, gave more in terms of order and a decent life to subject peoples than the radical posturings of many of today's British Commonwealth leaders would cause us to believe. This point is a reminder of other designated spectres summoned up by Western European political magic — 'Colonialism' and 'Racism'. These have led to the endless desire of every tiny principality to walk the world stage as an independent cockerel with complete disregard for the realities of an economically interdependent planet.

SHAPES OF SOCIAL MAGIC

The belief in structure for its own sake that has been so much part of Western-educated European thought since the Enlightenment is based upon the earnest conviction that social good must be *organised* rather than evolving through spontaneous human affinities and arrangements. In the economic and industrial spheres there must obviously be a real measure of organisation or else the great populations of the modern world could not be fed, housed, clothed or amused. But conviction that ancient forms of discrimination based upon race, family, sex, territory or even simple preference can be swept away by coercive legislation one by hectoring political and moral propaganda is an article of faith held mainly by intellectuals whose views of the right or good are rarely shared by the great majority of their fellow citizens. Here lies the fundamental inconsistency in those who ceaselessly proclaim the rights of the populace to full democracy.

A plebiscite held in almost all nations as to the fitness of capital punishment for the offence of premeditated murder would almost certainly result in an overwhelming majority vote of 'yes'. Hence, those very folk who are anxious to genuflect to the abstraction of majority opinion are willing to change their tune when this same majority is in favour of a public measure *they* think repellent. In respect of capital punishment, the argument goes than the average citizen is not 'expert enough' to decide an issue that should be settled by criminologists, lawyers, parliamentarians and sundry moralists. In this way the wishes of a person bereaved by the murderer are swept aside, as is the ancient conviction — well supported by most of the religious scriptures of the world — that he who wilfully takes a human life should justly forfeit his own.

Certainly, many public decisions are beyond the expertise of the average citizen, such as the appropriateness of a given drug to treat a given medical condition, the effects of the abuse of cigarettes and alcohol, and so on. But the issue of capital punishment (and many others like it) is not of that order. Those who campaign for its permanent abolition are suffering emotional revulsion backed up by flaky statistics which do not prove the case either way. Hence in vaunted 'open societies' we find privileged 'closures' by experts on every side who consider themselves better equipped to decide what citizens *should* want, were they enlightened enough to make the 'right' decision. The fact that such closures have always existed at every level of the social hierarchy — be they just or unjust — reduces Karl Popper's 'open society' to a mere seductive fantasy. It is hard enough to deal openly and justly with our next-door-neighbour and members of our own family without expecting an entire State apparatus to function along such Utopian lines.

Few fears concerning human intercourse now have to bear a heavier freight of obsessive thinking than questions of race and racial relations. Undoubtedly the worst legacy of the Nazi regime from 1933 to 1945 was the insistence by Hitler and his minions on a program or destroying or persecuting 'inferior' races under the domination of an imagined

Aryan master race. The ruthless slaughter of six million Jews subsequently made it impossible even to discuss the question of ethnic
differences without inviting reactions of repugnance, fear or hysteria.
As C. D. Darlington has pointed out, there has been so much
intermingling of ethnic strains, even in the 10 000 recorded years of
civilisation, that the whole theory of separate racial entities, let alone
of differences based upon mere colour, is thoroughly disreputable. Alas,
this does not make an end to discussion, since differences of *culture* and
conditioning between ethnic groups are real enough and cannot be
dismissed with a reflexive cry of 'racism'. In the case of phylogenetic
change over centuries, there are even some broad physical differences
between races, not based on colour, but upon the long response to
differing types of physical environment. Thus the Indians of the High
Andes developed large hearts and a more sturdy vascular system to
cope with the thin air at high altitudes, while many native Africans
and their modern American black descendants frequently show the
long ankles and high calves of people used for over a hundred generations
to running as hunters across the wide veldts and savannah lands of
central Africa.

As for differing emphases in intellectual style or 'intelligence' (very
loosely construed) there are also important distinctions to be made if
fears of racial discrimination can be quelled sufficiently to examine
them dispassionately. The academic outrage which greeted the assertions a decade ago of Arthur Jensen and H. J. Eysenck that there were
broad racial differences in 'intelligence' prevented both speakers from
delivering lectures and simple statements in many English-speaking
universities. Indeed, the whole concept of fully measurable intelligence
is open to question, including the methods of measurement used by
Jensen and Eysenck. Thus it was proper to greet such findings with
some scepticism, but certainly not with the arrogance and repressive
hysteria which denied such workers even a fair hearing. Moreover, as
demonstrated by the findings of the Minnesota Twins Study, reported
in 1991 by Dr Thomas Bouchard, the inheritance of elements in intelligence and even of personality is far more potent than radical politics
has permitted the intelligentsia of the West to accept. Geniuses appear
to be born, not made.

What cross-cultural studies do suggest, over and over, is that there
is a remarkable *variety* in ethnic response to different environments,
system of education (or lack of them) and in the type of religious,
cultural and social prejudices which tend to push the ethnic young in
one developmental direction as against another. That it has become

impossible to study this fascinating variety in more than the most general terms is a mark of the crushing disapproval visited upon any-one in Western society who now dares to suggest that one ethnic or cultural group may be better adapted in broad terms to one sort of function than another. The ideological determination to impose equality-cum-uniformity at the expense of important distinctions between individuals and environmental groups is as absurd as it is politically and culturally impoverishing. We concede the necessity for different provisions and environments for animal species, but politically deny the same variation in arrangements for human beings who are far more complex in their needs.

Nowhere are taboos upon discussion of racial differences more stringent than in discussions about the situation in South Africa. Fierce attacks on apartheid have not only ignored the harsh treatment tribal blacks mete out to one another; they helped obscure the fact that the practical question in South Africa is not whether the races should intermingle but rather, whether they should win equal access to edu-cation and, equal political and social rights. The chief sin of the white minority has been a determination to keep the black majority sub-jugated as a useful labour source from which that minority has been only too eager to profit. Only the extreme right wing of the Afrikaaner Broederband really believes in the ineffable superiority of the white races. For the majority of whites, economic expediency has clearly played a larger part than sub-fascist nationalism.

The ideological demand that races *shall* intermingle, *shall* be com-pelled to live hugger-mugger in the same neighbourhoods, belong to the same clubs, intermarry and so on would be just as arbitrary at one end of the scale of decree as a racist determination to see that they are kept separate by rule of law at the other. The right of a given ethnic, social or religious group to live within enclaves of its own has long been accepted throughout the Western world — not least in the United States, where ghettoes seem neither discouraged nor officially deplored. There are still real, if quite irrational, aversions to people of one colour marrying another, just as there are to people of different religions and social persuasions doing likewise. Such aversions are undesirable and they are contrary to the Judeo-Christian ethic. But they *exist* in *all* racial groupings and they cannot be expunged by decree or by militant advocacy of Christian clerics who are so distrustful of individual con-science that they prefer to demand coercive levelling legislation instead. The repugnance of the United Stated and various American administra-tions for apartheid is based in part upon the grim racial experience of

Americans. Yet the black population of South Africa is now composed of three-fifths first- and second-generation migrants who once *sought* jobs from the 'undeveloped' tribal lands to the north. Most whites are therefore the 'old' inhabitants. The fact that the United States originally imported her black minority as an impoverished slave class is easily overlooked.

A near-exclusive obsession by the West with former white sins as against black tribal blood-letting and corresponding infamies practised in several black African states is puzzling where it does not actually smack of hypocrisy. Consider the case of Uganda, which became virtually a ruined nation after the monstrosities wrought by Idi Amin and his successor, Milton Obote. Consider again the appalling Mengistu of Ethiopia, who was prepared to let millions starve while he pursued a brutal war against his enemies. Consider yet again the behaviour of even 'reasonable' states like Nigeria, which practised genocide upon the large minority of Biafran peoples under its sway with scarcely more than a mild protest from Western powers. Finally there is the more recent case of Doe's Liberia. Pop singer Bob Geldof's reference to many native African leaders as 'thugs' was hardly polite diplomatic language, but in behavioural terms it is all too accurate.

The distorting element in the race problem is that Western Europe has been plunged into too much understandable guilt over genocide wrought in such centres as Auschwitz, Belsen and Treblinka. Racial minorities of all kinds, with their own axes to grind, have not been slow to capitalise on this postwar guilt. The Christian churches too, hopeful of the kind of evangelical success in the Third World that has eluded them in developed countries, should confess their own dubious role in promoting such a guilt industry. To imply in a cringing fashion, as in often done, that racism is predominantly a *white* sin, is to promote a new sort of inverse racial bias.

The noted British economist Lord Peter Bauer has pointed out for years that the racial guilt borne by Europeans has been an enormously profitable source of financial aid for many Third-World countries, whose leaders and governments have proved thoroughly untrustworthy in organising for its honest disposal. Money sent to assist African agriculture and industry has been blatantly siphoned off into the private purses of black one-party rulers, or to pay the salaries of armies where tribal majorities prey upon their unfortunate minority neighbours. Bauer's repeated urging that the West should cut off lump-sum financial grants and supply the Third World only with food, industrial materials and skilled personnel has largely been ignored. Thus we encounter again the Western delight in building structures for foreign aid and reform that have no connection with common sense or actual local experience.

DESIGNS FOR A FLAT EARTH

The abstractions of modern politics lean almost to sanity and realism by comparison with those of economics — the arcane business of fuelling and guessing human needs and appetites. When the first stock exchange was set up in Antwerp in 1531, its Flemish founders could hardly have imagined a world which functioned largely on the basis of nods, winks and promissory notes and which had so little relationship to either real products or real consumers. Nor would they have understood forms of capitalism completely divorced from productive labour and so reliant on bank credit that entire nations can be placed under mortgage. If the central evil of the more dictatorial socialist economy has been its suppression of higher human ingenuity and incentive, that of the post-industrial capitalist economies has been that ego-enhancing means have been separated from practical ends. The constant obsession with 'growth' *for no defined purpose* has so encompassed the earth that it now threatens the very leviathans of the ocean depths and the regions of outer space. An idea of the lunacies of our post-industrial world can be gained from anecdotes such as the recent revelations that the once-pristine slopes of Mount Everest have become so cluttered with human junk that a clean-up had to be ordered; that the Aral Sea, one of the world's largest inland tracts of water, is dying because of human despoliation; and that a Concorde aircraft on take-off consumes as much oxygen as the entire Swiss population, including flora and fauna, needs in a week.

Perhaps the most disturbing belief held by economists is that, in reducing human beings to mere statistical units of consumption, they can broadly predict the real wealth or poverty of communities and nations. Psychology in itself is hardly an exact science, and when its predictions about the behaviour of persons and populations are borrowed for the purposes of marketing, the exercise amounts to little more than the old thimble-and-pea trick in which one guess in three is likely to be correct. The fact that product development and marketing strategies are built upon quite presumptuous and airy theories about consumer wants would have stood exposed decades ago were it not for the enormous expenditure devoted to artificially closing the gap between predicted consumption and natural behaviour. This is done by astutely debauching people through advertising into appetites and desires that would never otherwise have occurred to them. Historian Arnold Toynbee once acidly suggested that the destiny of Western civilisation turned more on the issue of our struggle with Madison Avenue than on the issue of our struggle with communism.

Since Toynbee wrote, communism has crumbled in most of its former citadels, but the power of advertising now seems almost without limit. Certainly, advertisers can stand above all conventional disciplinary criticism by citing as their defence the link between popular art and profit and by making much of a servile mass media dependent on them for survival. The enormous persuasive force of modern advertising, with its access to fantastic artistic and technical resources, tends to nullify many of the arguments of classical economic theorists. Adam Smith, for instance, taught that the consumer is the best judge of his own interests. But how free are consumers to judge or choose today when they are seduced and battered daily and hourly by dazzling advertising illusions unknown to Smith and indeed to every economist up to the young manhood of Keynes? As for the fashionable right-wing refurbishment of Smith's view that mainly unchecked 'market forces' best led to a balanced and prosperous economy, there is still a measure of demonstrable truth in the theory. But the principle is seriously undermined by the power of huge cartels and of multinational companies, whose dominance of resources seriously cripples or completely stifles real competition in many areas of marketing.

On the other hand, in state-run economies, socialists attempt to spread wealth by ruthlessly taxing the rich and ambitious and imposing curbs or bans upon the acquisition of private property and capital. As Communist countries found, this does not increase wealth, but encourages laziness, inefficiency and apathy, thereby spreading poverty more widely rather than alleviating it. Here too, economists simply cannot correlate complex human behaviour with their economic theories, because even the most cunning market research cannot wholly predict what *people* are likely to borrow, repay, buy or sell.

We come now to the principal economic iniquity of our time — that of the increasing distortion of economic endeavours by bankers and banking organisations. If an ordinary suburbanite were to lend a stranger or some club a substantial sum of money from his or her own savings without any collateral or real guarantee that it would be repaid, he or she would be dismissed as a fool. Yet this has been the standard international practice of banking organisations since the 1944 Bretton Woods Agreement and the creation of the International Monetary Fund. Countries such as Brazil, Mexico and even those with a middling reputation for economic responsibility such as Australia have been granted vast loans, both nationally and corporately, which it is doubtful they can ever repay. Brazil's repudiation of her national debt alone could cause an economic crisis throughout the Western Hemisphere and perhaps most of the developed world. Traditionally the most cautious and responsible of professions, banking has been likened lately to the conduct of a global casino in which the proprietors are only superficially responsible to their depositors and creditors, unless these entities threaten to send them broke. As a result, the world is awash with bank credit, with enormous sums of paper money that bear only the vaguest relationship to the concrete resources of individuals, industries and nations. Money that has no real relationship to either the movement of products or persons is ultimately worthless. Credit must have some relationship to wealth, either in human energy or natural resources, or it becomes a cancerous burden of debt. No person *or* corporation should ever be *encouraged* to live beyond their economic means.

As far back as 1954, Joseph Wood Krutch in *The Measure of Man* pointed out that much of modern industry and technology had approved quite disgraceful practices. Among these are planned obsolescence of materials, such as cars that wear out after about five years, the deliberate suppression of useful patents by powerful organisations and corporations that do not want to change their products or methods; dishonest, strident advertising by means of hard-sell techniques; the dumping of huge amounts of agricultural produce which could feed some of the world's hungry several times over; the encouragement of inflation by profiteering on scarce commodities; and not the least, subsidising farmers either to grow food that will never be used or *not* to grow food when there is really a basic need for it.

Behind all these unsavoury economic activities lies a prodigal waste and misapplication of materials of which the earth has only a limited supply. Notable among these exhaustible commodities are natural gas, forest products, coal, oil and some crustal metals. This observation carries no political judgement since former Iron Curtain countries have raped the environment even more callously than Western nations.

As for the wastage of forests and goods, this is an older story. Two-thirds of the oak forests of Britain not used on town buildings were lavished upon the creation of naval vessels from Tudor times onward. Precious walnut wood was used for rifle butts in the Peninsular War of 1814. The finest ash wood was used for carriage spokes in World War 1, valuable hardwoods are today being wasted upon trashy discardable office furniture, and in Japan upon subsequently destroyed frames for concrete buildings. It has been estimated that the equivalent of several hectares of woodland need to be cut to provide a single Sunday edition of the *New York Times*. The raping of the oceans is a tale unto itself, in which Japan's ruthless employment of vast driftnets for fishing provides only a single episode.

The fondly held belief that business is, or should be, concerned with the linear production of commodities to virtual infinity supports a doctrine increasingly under challenge by theologians, philosophers, earth scientists, biologists and environmentalists. Yet most ordinary Western men and women still construe poverty in terms of lack of money to buy products. In the collapsed Soviet Union the situation has been the reverse of this — there has been an adequate wage structure, but constant shortages of those necessities of life that wages can buy. A whole nation can be very poor in basic creature comforts, even while sending cosmonauts to the moon or building fleets of nuclear submarines. Yet the desire to be rich is not a main theme in *every* civilised country in the world. As Gunnar Myrdal's studies of India showed convincingly a generation ago, in so many discussions about wealth there is a confusion between needs and wants. In Australia or Britain, poverty could be defined as the inability to afford a television set, even upon rental. In large parts of Africa it could be better defined as the inability of a family to afford enough grain to make bread.

The limitless urge to produce and increase private material possessions has been a remarkable engine of economic enlargement in Western countries over the past four centuries. But unless it is underpinned by true cultural meaning and purpose, the constant hunger for wealth and consumer gimmicks becomes a self-perpetuating addiction. Once gratified, it gives pleasurable relief, or at least some temporary release from psychic tension in the person who gratifies it. Yet when an individual has more possessions and industrial holdings than he or she can possibly enjoy in several lifetimes, this individual is clearly no longer motivated by greed alone, or even the urge to be super-secure. He or she is driven by the lust for power and control over goods. Such insatiable craving for power lies behind a good deal of the feverish activity and long hours passed in corporate boardrooms, no less than in the offices of state mandarins, social engineers and civil-service commissars. There is something decidedly exhilarating in holding great power over the destinies of thousands or possibly millions of other people. Not for nothing did the Roman Senate provide for a soothsayer who stood in the chariot of an incoming Caesar to murmur in his ear as he rode to the throne: 'Remember that thou art only a man'. The possession of all power tempts ordinary people towards a denial of their own mortality and encourages pretensions to a super-adequacy that the frailty of our judgement and our physical organism belies. More subtly, it tends to persuade power-holders who have some vestige of altruism that their demi-divine mission is somehow indispensable to the welfare of the masses they dominate.

The chain of compulsion inside the head of the obsessive-puritan personality corresponds closely to that of the economic predator. Being is avoided for the sake of having and doing; the perils of self-questioning are submerged in ceaseless labour; labour leads to a measure of wealth; wealth in large enough amounts leads to the possession of great power. Finally the wielding of power becomes the most potent of all forms of counterfeit ecstasy for a person without poetic imagination. Most people work in terms of perceived usefulness and to provide the practical accoutrements of a contented life. Conversely, compulsives do not work to live, but live to work. In so doing they often miss the deeper significance of their life and work altogether. The benefits gained by others from their labour are partly nullified by the bad example they provide — since life needs no justification beyond itself as *fully lived*.

Moving from such deeper considerations back to the economy, one has to deal with the basic problem of a steady increase in the world's population. At the time the Domesday Book was written in 1086, the population of Britain was estimated to be something approximating one million. By the time of the Tudors it had increased to five million. By 1820 it was some fourteen million; in 1921, forty-two million; and in 1980, fifty-eight million. Due to birth control there has been a levelling off of Western population increase in the past decade. The population trend in Britain, as the first of modern industrialised countries, has been recently associated with the lowering of the birthrate and a corresponding raising of the mean age of death. Economists still anxiously debate whether population increase enhances consumption, and therefore wealth measured in the GNP, or whether the arrival of more people simply exhausts resources and only creates a greater burden on the State. But the Third World has hardly begun to address that quandary.

The most reactionary force against population control, the Catholic Church still refuses to face the issue at all. Its magisterium still clings to the teaching that chosen childless marriages are contrary to the moral and natural law. This stubbornly irrelevant Old Testament preference for 'increasing and multiplying' lies at the root of the Catholic procreative obsession, and not merely due to some sterile debate over natural versus chemical contraception. It has never been fully faced by the Vatican that the function of the married female extends considerably beyond procreation and child nurture. Its acceptance of women as equal holders of industrial and political power has always been grudging at best. It is not uncommon for conservative Catholic male theorists to express the belief that the planet could support ten billion people if the so-called 'green revolution' in scientifically enhanced agriculture were successful enough. Why the planet *need* or *should* support ten billion people in human terms is never explained. Nor is the curiously primitive biologism that the function of one human generation is to sacrifice itself unhesitatingly for the next, when it might have a true spiritual destiny of its own to fulfil.

By contrast with such medieval attitudes, one encounters increasing numbers of women in the developed world who are quite happy to use the wasteful and chilly practice of easy abortion as a remedy for failed contraception. This enables them to join their more promiscuous menfolk in the attitude that sex should be divorced from the question of procreation altogether. Even so, it seems likely that this amoral attitude to procreation is *partly* a reaction to centuries of the former treatment of women as mere breeding stock by religious moralists. The sheer helplessness of expanding metropolitan populations in the face of unexpected but possible termination of food supplies and services underlines a specially worrying aspect of population increase. It also brings into question (as did the late E. F. Schumacher) the essential folly of heaping up great masses of people into vast metropolitan centres in the first place.

In 1900 between 17 and 20 per cent of the population of the United States was involved in agricultural production. In 1990 most of the agricultural production of the US was produced by only 5 per cent of the population. This has been achieved by the use of automated machinery which has a deleterious effect upon soil adhesion, which promotes erosion by wind and water; and by the use of heavy applications of artificially applied fertilisers such as phosphates, whose grim side-consequences include creating poisonous algae deposits in lakes and water-catchments. Meanwhile, the devotion of vast territories to single-crop production such as wheat, single vegetables or corn completely belies the wisdom of our ancestors, who knew the value to the environment of crop rotation. In addition to this, natural flora and fauna are being progressively destroyed in order to provide more agricultural land for the feeding of hugely increasing populations. Behind all this 'smart' mass agriculture lies once more the obsessive salvationist principle of 'more' rather than 'better'. This is to serve urban populations increasingly absorbed in servicing and amusing one another rather than providing humanity with its basic nutritional and cultural supports.

By way of retort to this, American philosopher Michael Novak has accused environmentalists of making nature seem far more benign in her undisturbed form than is the case. He points to the ruthlessness of natural processes which once wiped out some primitive populations at an average age of 18 years, of the ravages of infectious disease, drought and tempest. There is little doubt that the dottier champions of a 'pure' environment have forgotten the darker aspect of nature when left unharnessed or unchecked. Yet in its prodigal daily waste of energy of all kinds, the United States consumes over a quarter of the world's resources, and it is hard to determine in such a case whether nature is being harnessed for improvement or merely raped for the sake of superficial comforts.

The consequences of the alienation of much of humanity from the natural and rural worlds can be seen in its cultural products — in public buildings that more closely resemble gladiatorial arenas or wheat silos than temples or cathedrals, in plays and novels that explore urban despair and degeneracy more zealously than they do heroism, high tragedy or joy, in abstract sculptures and bogus paintings that are as remote from human experience and feeling as possible and in which human beings completely vanish into mechanical labyrinths of asymmetrical structure. As a noted orthodox American artist once exclaimed in the New York Museum of Modern Art, 'I have seen rocks on the seashore more interesting than much of what I see around here. Perhaps evolution is really going backwards'.

SCIENCE AS A NEW RELIGION

Much of our Western belief that, despite all natural warnings, we *shall* be saved by our own intellectually devised structures is summed up in the hearty remark by Nobel Laureate Sir Peter Medawar, that most of humanity's problems can be solved by 'massive applications of technology'. There is not the slightest evidence in our more recent industrial history for such a piece of hubris. Such statements are almost as much an act of blind faith as the testament of any medieval theologian about who should be saved and who shall be damned at the day of judgement. This is hardly surprising, since one of my main themes has been that the more fundamentalist defenders of the Judeo-Christian religious world view and those who preside over official contemporary applied science are essentially similar people. They often possess the same kinds of personalities and share the same dedicated but narrow cognitive make up. Both camps still fervently believe we will be saved by structures, regardless of whether these structures be dogmatic or technological. The notion that scientists, because of their training, somehow are wiser, more powerful beings than their fellow citizens, has no more foundation in real-life experience than the once strongly held view that the clergy had a monopoly of knowledge about the ways of Almighty God.

Fortunately, there are enough dissenters and heretics within all the knowledge academies to give humanity some hope that the compulsive systems insisted upon by official science will not be allowed to prevail over either vision or commonsense. However, in every discipline, particularly those in technology and applied science, where a transformed nature is seen in such inflexible close-up, the longer view requires effort and is rarely possible. Also, the power of 'the establishment' to remain entrenched and to perpetuate its own methods and progeny should never be underrated. Far from being on the side of change, 'progress' and enlightenment, most scientific societies and establishments are extremely reluctant to depart from accepted ways of perceiving reality. They are horrified when it is suggested that the barnacle-encrusted conventions of scientific cognition and investigation themselves have become a frequent barrier to the acquisition of fresh knowledge and understanding — and that real genius ignores them anyway.

Lest this claim be doubted, one has only to look at the convention of preparing research papers for reputable scientific magazines. In an introduction to a typical paper there is a ponderous and tedious reiteration of the previous 'literature' in the research area, and an often obscure discussion of the methodology of investigation used. This is often hedged about by a whole series of quibbles, reservations and parentheses. After two or three pages of this preliminary throat-clearing, the actual findings of an investigation may amount to no more than a paragraph or two of print at best. This is usually followed by two or three other paragraphs of anxious speculation and discussion as to what the conclusions might or might not mean, so as to mollify the high priests of the official discipline. This is customarily followed by a long bibliography. Many of these academic pieces are submitted on a basis of 'publish or perish' so that the worker can advance in his or her profession. Most conventional effusions are scanned by the merest sprinkling of workers in a discipline. Remarkably few of them contribute anything to real knowledge within the scientific community and most 'findings' are never heard of again. Once more, the bureaucratic structure of a given activity has grown so encrusted with obsessively irrelevant rituals that it is difficult for any gifted radical innovator to find an audience.

Much scientific caution has little to do with protecting the reputation of a discipline, and a lot more to do with buttressing the preconceptions and prejudices of those who preside over the sciences in a given epoch. The case of Ignaz Semmelweiss, one of the great pioneers in bacteriology, represents one of the most shameful cases in the history of medicine. Because he saw hundreds of women and children dying in childbirth because of inadequately sterile ward conditions, Semmelweiss loudly (and perhaps tactlessly) condemned his conservative opponents. Scientific objectivity vanished as Semmelweiss was seen as a threat to the medical profession, and his powerful peers closed ranks against him. Anticipating Lord Lister in antiseptics by a full fifteen years, Semmelweiss died broken in health and insane in 1865 because he had been ostracised and his findings ignored. They did not fit in with the 'accepted theory' of his time.

In a brilliant essay published in 1962 entitled *The Structure of Scientific Revolutions*, Thomas Kuhn demolished the popular view that science advances carefully and majestically by logical steps. Indeed, it moves jerkily by erection of paradigms or theoretical models to which scientists become attached and which generate most of the questions they prefer to ask. There is nothing inevitable or even rational in the selection of a paradigm. It can hang around obstructively for years before experiment, experience or sheer banality finally confirms or banishes it. Then another paradigm is proposed in its place. If a scientist is well placed or influential, the new paradigm will gain attention. If he or she is not, gaining attention can be remarkably difficult and sometimes impossible. And the outworn paradigm may linger on by default.

In the social sciences most paradigms are borrowed from 'hard' physical science. They are usually weak and poorly constructed and hence professorial autocracy and academic myopia can reign virtually unchallenged. Entire generations of students can be directed away from exploring areas and questions of which their teachers disapprove. It was in this way that, after World War II, psychology ceased to be a broad study of both subjective and objective mental processes and was reduced to the measurement of scattered bits of external behaviour — the sum of which has never amounted to a satisfactory picture of what human beings are actually like.

Official science can be just as remorseless as political parties in pursuing former heroes once they have fallen from grace. Consider the notorious case of Sir Cyril Burt, one of the pioneers in the testing of human abilities. Because, after the end of his career, Burt had been discovered by some bright workers to have faked some of his statistical evidence, he was sent into posthumous disgrace. The fact that Burt had spent nearly thirty years previously performing a great deal of quite respectable and useful research has been ignored. Having been caught out in one heinous sin, most of Burt's contributions have been consigned to the scientific limbo reserved for all those otherwise-eminent figures who are unlucky enough to get caught on a bad day. Since all professional scientific structures tend to be either usefully or uselessly erected by obsessive persons and later guarded by like-minded successors, even a minor evidence of wickedness must be greeted by hue-and-cry or quiet excommunication.

William Broad and Nicholas Wade summarise the present social situation of formal science:

> If science is worshipped in Western societies, it is not merely because of the toys and technological comforts it may produce. . .Science seems to represent an ideal, a set of values, an ethical example of human affairs of what could *or should* be [my italics], were reason to be man's guide. In the secular world. . .science performs part of the inspirational function that myths and religions play in less developed societies. It is perhaps because of this inspirational role that it is so difficult to see science as it really is. . .Does the scientific method really exist? And if it does, do scientists always follow it?[1]

If science plays the same role in a god-barren myth-starved Western society that religion once did for our ancestors, the technology that comes from the application of scientific discovery plays the same role for the masses that ceremonial magic did in ancient days. If pure scientists have become our new metaphysicians, engineers and accountants are likewise our revered witchdoctors. Because their applied endeavours are more powerful and much better organised than those of old magi, they can produce visible and even strident miracles. Thus the person in the street believes that surely the various cloistered vaticans of 'pure' science must present a far better gamble for humanity than counting on an invisible God or even than thinking and choosing for oneself. In this way, fallible human structures take on the aspect of partly adored engines for our salvation.

But all of these structures *in the long run* provide only for a kind of flat earth of the human spirit beyond which people plagued with anxieties (which seem to multiply in proportion to their inventions and possessions) dare not venture. Amid the pomps of the modern world with all its technological and bureaucratic power lies the potential and actual reality of bluff and guesswork committed every day by prominent people who hide their counterfeits of personality behind the shelter of their accomplishments. Meanwhile the human soul remains the true *terra incognita* of the modern world.

• SIX •

COUNTERFEITS OF LIFE

I t seems as if the rulers of our time sought only to use men to make things great: I wish they would try a little more to make great men; that they would set less value on the work and more on the workman; that they would never forget that a nation cannot be strong when so many belonging to it are individually weak.

Alexis de Tocqueville

When English speakers speak of self, they usually mean little else but ego. As the old metaphysicians and psychologists have properly under-stood it, the ego-soul relates merely to that assembly of psychic elements which we have built upon a biological base from human influences and cognitive impressions since babyhood. It has been confusing but commonplace in Western countries to identify the personal ego with the individual soul. As distinct from this, the spirit is believed by all the great religious teachers to be the deathless and imperishable spark at the heart of each human creature and independent of space and time. The ego-soul is more the middle term of our being. It arises out of a developing matrix of sensations, memory, experience, imagining, desire and will.

The notion that *we make* our own soul has been taken up repeatedly by the noted archetypal psychologist James Hillman, who was formerly director of research at the Jung Institute in Zurich. He reminds us that the young doomed genius John Keats long ago seized upon inspired hints from William Blake about the nature of our earthly task — which was to become like artists in the fashioning of our own individualities.

'Call the world, if you please, the vale of Soul-making', Keats once wrote, 'then you will find out the use of the world'. Indeed, he believed that the richer the soul-life, the brighter the light of Spirit burns at its heart.

THE SELF AS SENSORY-PHYSICAL

Some years ago, bodybuilder film star Arnold Schwarzenegger visited Australia at the same time as a leader of the Hare Krishna sect. The guru warned the 'Austrian Oak' not to become too identified with his body. 'But I am this body' retorted Schwarzenegger: surely the most succinct summing-up of the unreflecting view held by most Western citizens. 'Quality of life' has been one of the stock clichés of business and self-improvement seminars, but it is usually *quantity* of life that is meant and constantly craved; for quality is a matter of soul-life and of being richly aware of existence rather than having a set of well-designed arrangements for living. Despite the gradual ageing of contemporary Anglo-American populations, middle-class society still worships youth and, before the coming of the ill-omened Wall Street yuppie, endowed it with every benefit save real politico-economic power. At a juncture where spiritual immortality is most doubted — even by those who consult 'channellers', Tarot-readers and sundry clerical carpetbaggers to persuade themselves of it — the plastic surgeon, the cardiologist, the naturopath and the cancer expert promise an extension of the sensory-physical self beyond the limits of the old hopes. But since it is the nature of obsession to be insatiable, we do not give thanks for the gradual discovery of aids to rude longevity but constantly demand new instant miracles, such as the unnatural dosage of age-retarding hormones, whose reported cost is $20 000 per person per year.

The most paradoxical aspect of the passion to extend life, or at least postpone death, is the gruesomely vulgar fascination of film and TV producers with the images of human deformity, violence and decay. Tod Browning's 1931 MGM film *Freaks* was banned in several countries for up to forty years because its use of genuinely handicapped people with chilling disabilities was considered too shocking for ordinary cinema patrons. Today television audiences may be treated to the spectacle of a woman with a face half shot away so that the ingenuity of her plastic surgeon may be better exposed. Armless and legless thalidomide children are displayed for our combined admiration and compassion; and the victims of murder and road trauma are frequently flashed across the screen as proof of media daring and veracity. Have the recent images of bloody war and the horrors of Auschwitz and Bergen-Belsen irretrievably coarsened public sensibility? Even this would hardly explain the apparent 'success' of the nauseous imagery of 'splatter' movies such as *The Evil Dead* and *The Thing*. A more likely explanation is that these *frissons* seem the more titillating for a visually numbed population because their sanitised lives are insulated from the *real* stench of death and decay our ancestors endured — rather like viewing a stuffed cobra in a glass case and knowing it can no longer strike.

The Western yearning for extended fleshly life and pleasure is only half of the bargain made by Faust with Mephistopheles. The other half of the compact — to place for a time the cunning and pinched wisdom of the philosopher-egoist into the handsome head of youth — seems less important in today's consumer environment. Yet without intelligence, the elderly unspiritual man or woman has only the golf-and-cribbage banalities of the retirement village. Compared to these, even earthly vainglory might seem better than no glory at all. Who, when contemplating even the wretched aspects in the lives of the consumptive Keats — dead at 26, Schubert — gone at 31 from typhus, or Mozart — dead at 35 from kidney failure, would not feel that the brief glory of human moments like these might not be preferable to the fate of thousands of querulous elderly nuisances whose empty hold upon life has outlasted even the guilty loyalties of their offspring. Not the least of the problems of a culture that immerses itself in the body is the economic vampirism the young and the old must practise upon each other for survival. Physical immortality requires a near-perfect world and that is why both the wisely fulfilled person and the suffering person die willingly. As the Hindu sage put it long ago, 'without the breath of Brahman, what art thou but fat, skin, hair and excrement!' Even the body-worshipping Greeks knew that the beauty of the flesh was most exquisite when one accepted its impermanence.

The core of the self construed as sensual must be sexuality. Eros has long been the god of our time, but we do not even remember the art of worshipping him. True eroticism too demands a soul-life, and a right blend of emotional discrimination and the moral freedom to experience it splendidly. Western culture suffocates itself with mere sexiness instead. Sexiness can only be heightened by the still-remembered stings of taboo and regret, while eroticism knows its true role in the human and divine order and plays it honestly.

The remarkable tartiness of some adored female media stars such as Cher, Madonna and Bette Midler and the swivel-hipped narcissism, projected by male icons such as Tom Cruise, Richard Gere and Eddie

Murphy make it clear that, in modern English-speaking societies, doomed Tristan and Isolde are way out of style and that, far from being in touch, Eros and Psyche have been divorced for some time. The media's image of sex supplies to the jaded world only an endless montage of heaving loins, with the penis rampant wielded against the uterus redundant — all thoroughly deodorised and cleansed by industries producing various toiletries to the tune of many millions of dollars a year. One is never sure whether such plastic passion is intended to be athletic or cosmetic.

Before the shadow of AIDS fell across the primrose path of hedonism, affluent society in the seventies often saw erotic fulfilment as a booming multiple orgasm with a hearty therapeutic aim. Masters and Johnson in *The Human Sexual Response* contrived to produce surely one of the dullest and most turgid books since Marx penned *Das Kapital*, but for a brief period its consequences seemed no less revolutionary. So emerged countless 'sex therapists' proclaiming the garbled doctrine of Wilhelm Reich that what the jaded urban masses needed was the full emancipation of the groin. The chaste Judeo-Christian sneeze in the loins, too long haunted by clock-watching mechanomorphism and male chauvinism, might now become a convulsive cosmic event — for women even more than men. Alas, a cult of Dionysian liberation was not to be revived so naturally, least of all in the antiseptically earnest bedrooms of middle America. Before the afterthought of proper *personal counselling* dawned upon impetuous sexologists, the initiatives of Masters and Johnson often amounted to little more than a humourless surrogacy or solemn varieties of organ-tuning. From being yesterday's forbidden fruit, promiscuity for many became a duty and, of course, yet another renovated compulsion.

The almost neurotic preoccupation with health issues in Western societies has been mentioned in Chapter 5. 'Health', loosely understood, is a thriving industry in which all manner of recommendations to citizens, ranging from the grimly conservative condemnation of 'drugs', through prudent self-medications to dieting, jogging and vitamin swallowing jostle impartially in the media for our attention. Many of the alternative aids to health have some merit and they at least help to loosen the bonds of the love-hate relationship Western people have long had with their doctors. But we still live in communities where nothing is believed to succeed like excess. Thus jogging soon became a 'turn-on' like speedway racing, while the warnings of the orthopaedic surgeons about traumatised hearts, knees and ankles were ignored.

The cult of exercising in various gymnasia with programs varying from vigorous aerobic leaping performed against deafening disco music to 'super-set' muscle building with weights and furtively popped steroids also proceeds apace. Certainly there is nothing wrong with the regular gym 'workout' in crowded cities where millions normally sit upon spreading backsides in driving seats. But the balanced, smoothly Grecian bulking-out of male bodies, fashionable in the days of bodybuilding idols such as Steve Reeves and Gordon Scott, has given way to straining, fleshless monsters with ugly knotted and veined torsos, suggesting nothing so much as flayed animals in an abattoir; and female bodybuilders whose breasts are reduced by steroids to mere extruded nipples. How remote such Western grotesqueries seem from the classical ideal of 'a sound mind in a sound body'!

In Eastern Europe and large parts of the Third World, even daily labour or walking along a city pavement can be a real health risk. And in two Romanian towns, citizens are literally blackened and choking from clouds of petro-carbon atmospheric emissions and slowly poisoned by toxic gases and heavy metals. Yet in parts of the United States, Australia and Canada, public hysteria explodes at the suggestion that a few fibres of white asbestos may be hidden behind a safely sealed schoolroom wall or ceiling; the antismoking lobby in several countries is turning into a bullying vigilante group, with US Surgeon-General Everett C. Koop sounding more like an Inquisitor-General than a health advocate; and panic occurs over the most flimsy of suggestions that radiation from overhead power lines could cause muscular dystrophy or cancer. The difficulty with so many inappropriate 'beaten-up' health obsessions is that they distract both media and public from vastly more important *global* environmental issues such as the steady disappearance of species and rainforests and the rape of oceans and river systems. As for the contemporary mania for dieting and debates about every minor issue from the significance of blood cholesterol to the relative merits of cooked and uncooked fibre, even doctors now grow weary of the appetite of their patients for nosing out anxiety-evoking trivia.

Because of their tendency to be locked into an active 'instrumental' mode, men emphasise their physicality more in act than appearance. Hence competitive sport becomes their badge of potency and main basis of sensate excitement. Running, jumping, hitting, grappling are traits more commonly rooted in the biological inheritance of the male, with his heavier musculature and different hormonal emphasis, and it can be seen in most small boys from an early age. Yet even here Western sex stereotyping loads the dice in favour of sex difference. During the Vietnam War many Americans marvelled at (and feared) the speed and efficiency of female Viet Cong partisans in the business of entrapment and killing. In Europe, working women in medieval times were expected to labour as long and vigorously as men. The macho cult of largeness and muscular force in Western nations seems to have grown in emphasis with sex-role specialisation only over the past two or three centuries.

On the other hand, Anglo-Saxon-Celtic Western European women have become the special target of a fashion and health industry that has emphasised the slim, boyish figure rather than the ample contours accepted by our ancestors. Lately this has reached the point of downright pathology as the psychosomatic disorders of anorexia and bulimia (or voluntary vomiting) have lately swept through groups of teenage girls. High school girls in developed countries report in increasing numbers how they hate their bodies and strive to strip themselves of even a normal amount of flesh so as to approximate to the bony androgyny of French mannequins, themselves often none too healthy.

For over two thousand years Western folk have either adored or scourged the flesh — and often practised both together. Today we start at the opposite extremity to the early desert Fathers who mortified their bodies only to be tormented the more. Our reactive wallow in the flesh is little different, in essence, from their hatred of it. The body is indeed the temple of the Spirit, as the early Christians taught. We will only make peace with it when we accept it as neither palace nor pigsty, but the wholesome home of a wholesome soul.

THE SELF AS ACHIEVER AND CONSUMER

When Edmund Hillary was quizzed about why he climbed Mount Everest in 1953, his reply was: 'because it was there' — surely the ultimate expression of the passion for achievement for achievement's sake. From one viewpoint Hillary's reply represents the ethos that has shaped the most ingenious aids to Western civilisation; from another it could be regarded as the reply of a brave but restless yokel with little better to do but assault a mountain which Indian and Nepalese folk, who have lived with it for centuries, have preferred to simply worship and admire. For it is the mark of the compulsive male achiever in particular that he cannot bear to let things alone. Thus he constantly meddles and destroys beautiful things in the very act of new creation. So, of course, does Nature, but her space-time scale is vaster and she works her marvels with a patience which is utterly alien to mountain-botherers and the breakers of records and necks everywhere. Indeed, the *Guinness Book of Records* effectively represents little more than a calendar of human compulsions and obsessions.

The achievement ethic has been a peculiarly male phenomenon and even Far Eastern cultures have shown definite elements of it. This is because men as former hunter-gatherers traditionally have achieved the feat of separating the universe from their perceived self with greater success and emphasis than women. The female is usually more in harmony with nature and more a hostage to its rhythms. Nobody has yet succeeded in radically shortening or substituting a human pregnancy or hastening or enhancing the psychophysical development of the child in more than a marginal way. As witness and harbinger to such biological realities, women seem almost instinctively aware that the rigid separation practised between person and thing by European men in particular is an essential error. One of the saddest features of many aspects of militant feminism since the days of Kate Millett and the younger Susan Brownmiller is the rage of so many intelligent women to pull up their biological and uterine roots and to indulge in the kind of brittle power games that sterile menfolk have so morbidly equipped themselves to play.

For those who can never be prime ministers, film idols or Nobel Prize winners, sport played, rehearsed or avidly watched becomes the most obsessive mode of male achievement. The reported sentiment of Demosthenes in the 3rd century BC: 'The men of Hellas know that they most please the gods when they celebrate the beauty of contest and leave pride in victory for time of war', finds little resonance in an epoch which accepts the slogan: 'Winning is not everything. It is the *only* thing'. Even the modern Olympic Games, which was an attempt by its founders to recapture the old Greek ideal, has become distorted by greed, ambition, national chauvinism and the endless manic chantings of media commentators about 'winning gold'. The international row over the taking of anabolic steroids by Olympic competitors in recent years obscures consideration of the dishonesty and egoistic stupidity which prompts athletes to use them. When a prominent athlete was asked whether if, by taking dangerous levels of androgens, he could win an Olympic gold medal, even if it shortened his life expectancy to merely another five years, he promptly replied 'Yes'.

Such an outlook in countries such as the US, Canada, Australia and Britain is more common than most sports people will admit. The issue is made more pointed by the fact that apart from pop music, sport is almost the only means by which a quite young person can become an international success. But is the acclaim of the world's masses such a blessing? Many an idol has been psychologically devoured by the mob whose favours he or she has courted.

The worship of the winner in sporting circles is truly the most well-marketed of obsessions among the less fastidious masses. The gentleman and ruffian may now jostle impartially on the sporting fields. Boxing, has long been regarded as a brutish relic of bare-knuckled gladiatorial days by sensitive people, and any honest afficionado of the 'fight game' will admit that blood and violence rather than pretty balletics is the reason why it lingers in the affections of the box office. Since the fifties, however, *all* sports seem to be increasingly promoted as forms of ritual combat with language to match. Thus even in the hallowed precincts of Wimbledon, players from Jimmy Connors through John McEnroe to Pat Cash have cursed at the crowd, smashed racquets or shaken their genitalia to applause, on the principle that athletic talent can excuse not only crude manners but glaring weaknesses of personality.

The growing phenomenon of violence at soccer matches, mostly perpetrated by the new rootless under class of Britain's industrial cities, tends to be rationalised as due to the tension-evoking absurdities of a game where most of a match may pass without a single goal being kicked. But soccer has been played as it is now for over a century without hosting anything like the horrors of the Brussels massacre of 1985. The likely truth is that the role of team sports in urban life is changing because sport is increasingly promoted as the peacetime equivalent of war in bored, distracted industrial societies. In such communities, social determinists in criminology and social work are slowly eroding the punitive, curbing aspects of the law. Violence is increasingly deplored but still permitted, and explained away when committed by almost anyone but officers of the state who must try to curb it. An extreme example of this is when political terrorists may kill innocent citizens at random while demanding all the privileges of a democratic judicial system devoid of capital punishment for themselves.

Those who have achieved little — in their own eyes at least — frequently erect covert or overt mental shrines to hollow media celebrities where, in earlier days, the cults of saints, military heroes, explorers and true artists were more commonly celebrated. Moreover, those who find little loving rapport with closely-living role models frequently practise a fashionable necrophilia by plastering their walls with pictures of the dead, such as James Dean, who were little more than projected mirages of the mass media, even when they were alive. A writer like Norman Mailer can sell a million copies of a book celebrating Marilyn Monroe, whose physical beauty was the one untarnished and obviously real thing about her. As for Elvis Presley, there is something quite macabre about the long queues of middle-aged tear-stained devotees who gather to peer at his gaudy personal artefacts at Graceland, while older folk in the music industry know that Presley was as much a tragic fabricated media icon in life as he was to become in death. The drive for achievement as a celebrity seems to be as easily transposed from the image of Hero as Predator to that of Hero as Victim. The two images can often be sado-masochistically linked. A culture of winners will also celebrate its eminent losers just as gladly if they are 'packaged' with sufficient commercial cunning and cynicism.

In the end the champagne of the compulsive achiever is the unceasing pursuit of financial gain and the brittle power that money confers. Gordon Gekko's motto, 'Greed is good,' in the 1988 movie *Wall Street*, has gone down in history. Yet whenever avidity for wealth is challenged by a more powerful political or religious idea, its barrenness of inspiration is laid bare — as shown by the impotence of the fabulously rich ruling families of Kuwait in the face of Saddam Hussein's self-justified invasion in 1990. The power derived from financial gain must always be a dynamic thing and its devotees constant attention to its enlargement or maintenance eventually makes them its captives. The late American oil billionare Jean Paul Getty was forced to live like an over-guarded and gilded hermit so that his costly dwelling with its art treasures would not be invaded. Numerous other magnates live in daily dread of being robbed, having their children kidnapped or of having their holdings taken over by entrepreneurs more predatory than themselves.

On the other hand, the brash and conspicuous consumption of wealth creates its own cohorts of the ideologically hate-filled or bitterly envious. The very rich are envied by most but admired by few. The uneasy ambivalence of the capitalist West towards its own money and wealth would provide a study unto itself. With the puritan Christian superego still weaving its hidden grey thread through the entrepreneurial mind, it is still only rarely possible for the grossly rich Western industrialist to emulate the Indian rajahs or Chinese mandarins by treating wealth and power as his or her simple karmic right. Thus the obsession with wealth becomes the more febrile since so few people in the West can luxuriate brazenly in its fruits without incurring private guilt or public disapproval. Yet, however poisoned the chalice, few who seek the exhilaration that vast wealth confers are not prepared to drink it and be damned. As Christ and the Buddha alike taught, wealth can never define the worth of self. Neither, despite recent secular-socialist distortions of Christ's scriptural message, should poverty, as such, confer any contrasting sanctity. As a character in the Fritz Lang movie *The Big Heat* notes: 'I've been rich and I've been poor, but rich is better'. What matters most about wealth is the spiritual price one is prepared to pay for it.

THE POLITICAL SELF

Often in the 20th century politics has been not so much a vocation as a necessary affliction. Over the past 150 years, ideology has steadily obliterated religion as the opium of the intellectual classes. Latterly, a pugnacious political construction has been placed on every conceivable human relationship — male with female, child with parent, citizen with bureaucrat, even priest with lay person. But politics is not about human affinity, or even justice, but about power. Thus we have the contemporary jargon of the politician and social worker who no longer talk about lovelessness or loneliness among the masses, but 'powerlessness' — most absurdly, when the peoples of Western nations and of the United States in particular have never enjoyed greater political leverage in world history. Also, despite the essentially bloated and entrenched character of the modern bureaucratic process, it flourishes because the masses find it as useful as it is enslaving. However the majority of citizens may grumble about the shortcomings of their elected political masters, they are unwilling to rebel against the intrusive bureaucratic machinery of Western government. It protects them all too well against the risks of independent enterprise and having to make provision for their own socio-economic welfare.

An illustration of the seductiveness of benevolent bureaucracy is the illusion of 'free' medicine as it operates in the United Kingdom. The 'National Health' is the largest employer in Great Britain, and its operations are now so vast and its habits so entrenched that even the redoubtable Margaret Thatcher was unable to put so much as a dent in its command over the public purse. At no improvement in quality of service or public choice of doctor, British National Health Service spending rose from £9 billion in 1979 to £29 billion in 1989. Yet the NHS remains unassailable, not because it presents a more efficient system for the population than privately insured medical care, but because it suits the ideological outlook and self-interest of those who run it and those numberless hypochondriacs who exploit it. The same situation is developing with the operation of the Medicare systems of Australia and Canada. Health and education systems together with large sections of the mass media, in fact, remain the most secure public shelters for those with the left-wing radical view of public life, while even the most hardened of capitalist entrepreneurs have no choice but to accept these structures and be taxed for their operations.

As the great scholar of myth and culture Joseph Campbell has reminded us, the modern state has become less a living organism composed of its many constituents then a vast demythologised machine, working under its own fundamentally inhuman momentum. According-ingly, the 'professional politician' (a dangerous and contradictory latter-day designation) has arisen, not so much to serve the people as to work the countless wheels and levers of an increasingly abstract system. The fact that he or she almost never succeeds in doing so with much competence is what provided, some years back, the hilarious but bleakly perceptive substance for the BBC TV series 'Yes, Minister'. Only the humane conservative relatively free from obsessive fixations under-stands the truth that it is the *evolution* of governmental processes that best assists useful change; whereas revolutions merely replace old brahmins with new ones — breeding extra bureaucrats by the thousand to serve the latest innovations. Politics is too dangerous a profession for 'professional' politicians. Yet, unfortunately, it is becoming almost unmanageable for all but the most gifted amateurs. This means that the roots of public order must strike more deeply into the souls of a sufficient number of reflecting citizens or the various lumbering commonweals we have created may finally serve to bury us. Sane political activity is undoubtedly rooted not in cabinets or parliaments but in the nursery and at the dinner table. Ultimately, though, it should not be permitted to invade, via the corruption of language and ideology, the sphere of private relationships. When politics bursts the boundaries of the public order and encroaches upon our estimation of wives, husbands, friends and neighbours, it invariably assumes a malignant face.

THE CULTURE OF ADDICTION

One of the major deficiencies of urban life in this century has been the progressive disappearance of the opportunity for real solitude and a neurotic fear of being left alone. Part of it is due to the development of what Oswald Spengler in 1918 prophetically called 'the megalopolitan civilisation' in which the wishes and cravings of people in crowded cities dictate most of the affairs of our planet. Some of the most useful and enriching civilised recreations require a measure of solitariness for their enjoyment — reading, listening to serious music, writing letters, reflecting upon events and tasks, even savouring in retrospect one social encounter before going on to the next. Modern younger folk, by contrast, are encouraged by the mass entertainment industries to regard life as not a matter of personal experience but as an endless series of 'happenings', any shortage of which may produce boredom, anxiety, restlessness or a regularly reported feeling of emptiness.

To be almost *wholly* dependent upon external stimuli for one's satis-faction or distraction is simply to surrender to increasing varieties of addiction. And what is an addiction but a social stimulus that we have so absorbed into our minds and bodies that it becomes a compulsion? Indeed, the contemporary peer group constitutes a new culture of com-pulsion against which even the older demands of blood and kinship may be powerless.

In former centuries those ordinary people lucky enough to enjoy a few hours of leisured existence which rose above the stringencies of poverty were glad to seize upon them as a means of delight, self-expression and group recreation. Today, most of the instruments of leisure are thrust upon mass populations in prefabricated forms. By pressing a button or flicking a switch we can summon up the whole world, or what the media choose to offer as denoting the world. Only the sturdiest and most resolute folk are prepared to use their own mental resources or exert themselves by using their time as a space for reading, genuine communication, quiet fantasy or self-expression. In the late 20th century *passive*, compelling recreations are everywhere, while the electronic media offer little more than instant chewing gum for our eyes and ears. That far-seeing eccentric, the late Marshall McLuhan saw something of the problem when he prophesied: 'Just as we now try to control atomic fallout, so we will one day try to control media fall-out'.

THE STRUGGLE BETWEEN AMUSEMENT
AND AWARENESS

If one were to cite the three most powerful instruments of social com-pulsion since 1900, these would inevitably be the automobile, the gramo-phone and the television set. So pervasive has their influence become that it is almost impossible for anybody today to imagine what the social and sensory experience of a citizen in 1900 would have been like. Since 1960 television has become the most potent transmitter of behavioural mores since the days of the pre-urban tribe. Its hold over mass imagination has been pungently criticised by Neil Postman, a professor at New York University. Postman first came to the public attention with the publication of his book *The Disappearance of Childhood*, in which he outlined the role of television as the transmitter of information which was once restricted to parents, families and teachers. He argued that the mass media are producing millions of children who have lost any pretension to innocence and wonder about the external world by the age of 6 or 7, and two-dimensional adults who never really evolve beyond the tastes formed in their mid-adolescence. In 1986 he broadened the scope of his attack in a work entitled *Amusing Ourselves to Death*. The nub of his argument is summed up in the following comment:

> When a population becomes distracted by trivia, when a cultural life is defined as a perpetual round of entertainments, when serious public conversation becomes a form of baby-talk, when, in short, a people become an audience and their public business a vaudeville act. . .then a nation finds itself at risk, Culture-death is a clear possibility.[1]

He later continues:

> I am not very optimistic about. . .proposals to improve the quality of television programs. Television serves us most usefully when presenting junk-entertainment; it serves us most ill when it co-opts serious modes of discourse — news, politics, science, education, commerce, religion — and turns them into entertainment packages. We would all be better off if television got worse, not better.[2]

Postman's arguments are only a more sharply focused, more experienced expression of the warnings of Aldous Huxley in his book *Brave New World*. Huxley was a far more accurate prophet than George Orwell about the future forms of social compulsion. He prophesied a culture where there would be no precious secrets left to reveal, where every serious dimension of human life would be reduced to a nickelodeon. The instruments of tyranny over the mind and heart would become amusements of such addictive fatuity that whole cultures might giggle, twitch or dance their way towards an entranced form of barbarism. Indeed, speaking of Huxley, Postman himself observed:

> In the end he was trying to tell us that what afflicted the people in *Brave New World* was not that they were laughing instead of thinking, but that they did not know what they were laughing about, or why they had stopped thinking.[3]

Television is only trailing after the technological ingenuity of a restless civilisation — a culture that confuses 'more' with better, that construes its hectic images of perfection in terms of excess rather than moderation. Instead of being merely a source of amusement for *occasional* use, television has been converted into a childminder, a superficial educator, an endless supermarket for the objects of advertising and, worst of all, a conveyor of the notions that the image of a public person and his or her true *character* are interchangeable and that knowledge can be reduced to selected snippets of information.

There is no doubt that a constant diet of television and video hiremovies of poorer quality poses not so much a threat to the rough and ready literacy which enables people to flick through automobile and fashion magazines or skim through Mills and Boon bosom-heavers, but to any *sustained* examination of all but the most trivial concepts and ideas. The results of such a constant TV diet are well known. The portents were already there when the American CBS Network conducted a detailed survey in Britain on the effects of television half a generation ago. Attention spans narrow, deeper interest in public issues quickly wanes and people tend to watch and identify with pictures and situations rather than absorbing discussions. Violence and grosser sensuality in particular invite weaker citizens to accept these elements as social norms. Grammar and syntax constantly splinter under the onslaught of sports and entertainment compères, while politicians mouth platitudes out of carefully staged images or repeat sonorous clichés on the principle that the medium, not the message, provides the meaning.

Since the Americans have always led the way in media innovation, it is fascinating to reflect that in 1860 the populace of the United States enjoyed the highest level of average literacy in the Western world. The reference to the farm boy bearing a book while following the plough was hardly a piece of hyperbole. Abraham Lincoln's famous debate with Stephen Douglas in the presidential campaign of that year lasted four hours! The large public audience was sufficiently acquainted with the issues, the arguments and the language of the spokesmen to understand every point they made and participate with gusto. Whether we concede it or not, it is in detailed *verbal* exposition that aspiring democracies must build a well-briefed involvement in social and political processes, and not in the manner of an ephemeral peepshow. If and when a truth is transferred from word to image, the image should be our own.

Politics may be boring, devious, inspiring or merely repetitive, but when it is used as mass televised entertainment, any nation stands in risk of being governed by cosmeticians instead of statesmen. Issues such as abortion, apartheid, disarmament, equal sex opportunity and the powers of bureaucracy can never be effectively dealt with by a medium whose principal reason for existence has become to please and titillate.

There are countless examples of the way television exposure in the Western world debauches public sentiment and trivialises important issues. During the 1989 San Francisco earthquake audiences were harangued by television commentators who were irate that the World Series baseball match in Candlestick Park would be postponed. At all costs, even a stricken city must not be deprived of its circuses — even when bread supplies might be in doubt. Public welfare provides countless notorious cases of the misuse of TV. A weeping Australian mother is presented on prime-time television to complain that no money is available to allow her child to have a very chancy heart-liver transplant in New York. It is never suggested that such touting for money represents a most undesirable precedent and gross favouritism in the use of both money and the TV medium. For even the contemporary newspaper, let alone TV, to pose a contrast between the pop-odyssey of one tear-stained Western mother and handicapped child against the fate of hundreds of thousands of children who die from starvation and disease in the Third World, or even of the countless thousands of human foetuses that are surrendered in pregnancy terminations, would take real media courage. Our forebears might not have shrunk from drawing such a parallel, but television does shrink from it because such comparisons are uncomfortable. Discomfiture is the stuff of waning control over public imagination and therefore of falling ratings. Indignant compassion concerning some injustice is good sometimes for TV news and documentaries, but it is wise not to give viewers too much of it. In the US, even religious programs must 'rate'. That corn-fed style of Christian evangelism which was once the staple of backwoods preaching has infected mainstream religious discourse and mostly drained it of reverence and intelligence.

One of the most dismaying aspects of global television is the extent to which expertly groomed media personalities with autocues at the ready can cause great private corporations or elected persons and governments to tremble at criticism or a disparaging frown. An indication of the political power of television near the end of the Vietnam War occurred when a distraught President Lyndon Johnson was reported to have exclaimed in the face of criticism by veteran newsreader/commentator Walter Cronkite: 'If I have lost Walter. . .I have lost the people'. In this way did an audiovisual medium, drenched with nostalgia for J. F. Kennedy's illusory Camelot, hasten the departure of one of the most able of American Presidents.

Far from providing genuine alternatives in entertainment as they did up to 1970, television and the cinema now bear an incestuous relationship by an exchange of talents and through the widespread availability of programs on videocassette. Cable TV, at least, gives more affluent viewers an opportunity to switch off from the imperialism of the networks and their rating-fixated style of self-promotion. Furthermore, few can fail to marvel at the extravagance of more than forty regular channels available to US citizens in the larger cities. Alas, the tendency to rely upon the vast news sources of the major networks and the national syndication of past and present on-screen icons such as Walter Cronkite and Dan Rather tends to ensure that even forty channels cannot give viewers other than a carefully filtered appraisal of global life.

In England during the sway of Lord Reith over the BBC, there was a consensus that basic British institutions would be supported and that events would otherwise be dealt with without undue coloring or political bias. Failing that, it was better not to deal with them at all. Although this policy had its own stodgy 'establishment' limitations it was far superior to the view apparently common on BBC TV today: that the medium should frequently take an adversary or irritant attitude to the power elites of the day regardless of its original mandate to seek objectivity. Throughout the Thatcher decade the BBC supported a veritable wasp's nest of xenophobic talk with programs such as that run by Australian expatriate Clive James. James frequently invited guests such as Anthony Burgess and Dennis Potter, whose view of authority and indeed of most of their fellow Britons was certain to be either hostile, snobbish or contemptuous. Potter was allowed to say of international press magnate Rupert Murdoch: 'Next time he comes to Britain he should be publicly hanged', adding that Murdoch would have to be cut down while still alive because Potter was opposed to capital punishment. Genteel laughter followed. Similar attitudes are often aired by the Australian Broadcasting Corporation. Trial of prominent persons by media, once considered a deplorable exercise, has now become standard TV fare.

Occasionally, as in the revelation of the brutality of the old men of Beijing and the 1989 Tiananmen Square massacre, the Western world can get an unplanned front-row TV view of how totalitarian governments conduct their business. But for the most part, the US and British media tend to engage in highly selective, capriciously edited commentary which reflects the local cultural prejudices and political fixations of TV journalists rather than offering a several-faceted picture. After the spectacular collapse of several Warsaw Pact governments, the unwritten policy of major TV networks in the US and Britain was to continue to treat episodically authoritarian governments such as those of South Africa and Chile as still being equivalent to totalitarian regimes in China, Iraq, Ethiopia and the former Eastern Bloc. This has blurred the vital distinction between an inconsistently thuggish paternalism which is still subject to the pressure of world opinion, and unheeding totalitarian rule by starvation, torture and murder. Sadly, a viewing audience among whom less than 40 per cent could locate most global situations on a map has neither the sophistication nor the involvement to realise that the problem of most current-affairs television is not what little it records but what it chooses to ignore.

Television orthodoxy contributes mightily to our cultural obsessions on two counts: (i) its ceaseless rapacity and its hunger for material which must, in some instances, fill screens for twenty-four hours a day for TV-dependent watchers: and (ii) its dread of not being regularly viewed. The latter possibility seems to fill even semi-autonomous broadcasters such as the BBC with almost as much apprehension as it does the commercial mandarins of the CBS and NBC. The circular thinking typical of obsessive rumination fills the minds of TV executives to an unusual degree. Does the TV medium create the tastes it claims to satisfy? 'Yes, *and* No' is an answer that has long caused dyspepsia to the linear thinkers of the entrepreneurial world. That public media tastes *can* be created everybody knows. But nobody can predict whether a given personality, or given comedy or drama series, will catch public fancy. Television can always hope to win and hold viewers through the exploitation of the more primitive human emotions of envy, curiosity, fear, aggression, sensuality, snobbery, empathic sentimentality and avarice. Yet nobody can predict which combination of these elements is likely to retain public fancy beyond a 'pilot' program.

American TV in particular is dominated not by quality or content of programs but by chasing audience numbers and longevity in ratings. In some programs, such as 'L.A. Law' or 'Hill Street Blues', there has been occasionally a happy coincidence of quality and popularity. But in the case of 'Eyewitness News', and 'Sale of the Century', and such saccharine or tasteless sitcoms as 'Roseanne' and 'The Golden Girls', it is hardly excellence which matters. Sometimes an off-beat conception such as that behind 'Beauty and the Beast' can unexpectedly capture public mythic imaginings. Yet it is rapidly shaped to the inevitable formula situations that tap into the same identifications and compulsions as every other series, from Pacific island idylls to cops-and-criminal melodramas.

Thus the public has become addicted to TV and TV has become addicted to its public in turn. Cultural addiction always thrives on such artificially contrived symbiotic or parasitic relationships. These relationships inevitably damage, or at least limit, our open communication with peers and the natural world, vindicating Plato's warning that art sometimes could be a danger to the soul because it was at a second remove from the real.

THE COMING OF COMPUTER SHAMANISM

If a *passive* symbiosis between person and device is encouraged by the indiscriminate watching of TV, an even more persuasive link of an *active* sort is encouraged by our growing dependence upon the computer and its supporting software. The air of contemporary applied science lately seems full of facile chatter about 'artificial intelligence'. 'Intelligence' is something for which psychologists over the last seventy years of investigation have not managed to provide any satisfactory comprehension or definition. Intelligence is certainly more than the sum of our abilities and functions. It starts as signals from the neurones of the cerebral cortex and ends up as a quality as evanescent as morning mist. What the new fanatics of the computer world really mean when they talk about 'artificial intelligence' is a machine that will replicate and enlarge a variety of human functions or *abilities*. Yet when even all the known abilities of the human species are listed and combined, we are still no closer to the full meaning and ramifications of human intelligence. Our cognitive-emotional make up is, at the least, an extraordinary blend of memory desire, intention, intuition, curiosity, synthesis and exposition. No computer can lead us to beauty; yet we are all struck by beauty when we enounter it. No computer can tell us why we are impressed by one person and disquieted by another; nor can it even begin to interpret what we mean when we speak of concepts such as love, God, peace, justice, mercy or even 'good health'.

The weird notion that a computer can become in some way more wise, more reliable and more meaningful than the near-miraculous human mind which created it requires a new term which I shall coin as *mechanomorphism*. And the mechanomorphism of today is no less a blasphemy against the ineffable than the anthropomorphism of the medieval era. Not content with having the computer as his newest servant, modern Westerners' infatuation with the mechanical and predictable has led them to adore its freedom from fantasy, emotion and mathematical limitation because they doubt the worth of those very qualities which make us human and vulnerable. The computer is vulnerable only to error during input, or to mechanical breakdown. Yet, as Ilya Prigogine, 1977 Nobel prize winner in Chemistry, has pointed out, it is precisely the quirky vulnerability of organic beings, their flexibility and frequent instability, that lays the ground for that quantum leap toward reorganisation at a higher level of intelligence and awareness than before. The mechanomorphic worshippers of the new computer-god either do not understand this proposition or do not wish to recognise it.

Not for nothing has Joseph Weizenbaum, himself a professor of Computer Science at MIT, described some of the more ardent disciples of artificial intelligence as propagators of a new idolatry. At least the pagans of pre-Christian times, when they set up images of stone and metal to represent gods ranging from Ptah to Baal and Ishtar, realised, that the power of the god rested not in the image but in those unseen resonances which the images evoke. The new idolators of the late 20th century adore the mechanical products of their own hands and often lavish more care upon them than they do their spouses, lovers and children. Across nearly six centuries one again hears murmurs of Bishop D'Oresme's Clockmaker-God, with mechanised man as his enthusiastic sorcerer's apprentice.

The computer and its recent links with the TV cathode-ray tube represents one of the leading edges of a technology that has taken on board all the domineering compulsions of its priesthood. The computer is an ingenious and helpful vehicle for the storage, arrangement, synthesis and retrieval of *information* which has been permitted to assume dangerous pretensions to fundamental *knowledge*. The mentality of its more extreme devotees has been summed up in the words of professor John McCarthy of Stanford University: 'The only reason why we have not yet succeeded in formalising every aspect of the real world is that we have been lacking a sufficiently powerful logical calculus'.

Such arrogantly obsessive talk is a far cry from the view which once prevailed in the West from Homer to Sir Isaac Newton, that intelligence, at its roots, is a mysterious gift of grace. As Michael Shallis has retorted against the view of computer enthusiasts like McCarthy and Marvin Minsky of MIT:

The notion that the real world can be formalised by a 'calculus' is part of the general fallacy widely found in the sciences. Because the behaviour of some physical phenomena can be approximated by mathematical expressions (as in the computer) it is ridiculously assumed that the whole world is underlaid by one powerful formula, whereas the world is complex and unique beyond description.[4]

The challenge posed by the video-computer screen at a purely psychological level is its ability to enslave the imagination of the young and so codify and over-structure the operations of speculative intellect that there is no room for the random, the poetic, the ambiguous or even the beautiful. Most disquieting of all is boastful propaganda put out by such troubling American disciples of the computer as Marvin Minsky, who about twenty years ago remarked with a certain measure of seriousness that computers would be one day in a position to 'decide to keep us as pets'. The extraordinary aspect of such statements is that those who make them are in no way socially ridiculed or rebuked. This is because of the arcane nature of computer programming. At such a frontier few lay people have the necessary skill or courage to brand such publicists as subversive monomaniacs. The ivory-tower behaviour of many programmers shows that once a compulsive pursuit of a single objective gets out of control amid the priesthood of the microchip, Dr Frankenstein might not be long in coming! Moreover, as Theodore Roszak has pointed out in his critical book *The Cult of Information*, an enormous amount of money is involved in selling ever more sophisticated computers to business, industry and the defence forces of the Western world. . .and such devices are often programmed by people dangerously isolated from common educated understanding or control.

A generation that has never known anything but near-continuous watching of television, that has a notoriously short attention span when it comes to the detailed culture of the magazine or the book, that can no longer hold a sustained argument or experience elevated feelings, presents an ideal target for educationists who are willing to use the computer not only as a teaching aid, but as a substitute childminder and adolescent entertainer. It is well adapted to those children of limited creative and verbal resources who would soon be bored by the more personalised routine of talk, encounter and chalk. Meanwhile our judgement of the relative importance of various items of stored data tends to falter when such an aid is employed, even in schools, as a high-level form of Trivial Pursuit. Contributions that have enriched humanity incomparably, from the sayings of Christ to the formulations of Einstein, are matched impartially with revelations as to who hit the largest number of home runs in the last American World Series or who won the English Grand National Steeplechase in 1933.

The common reply to all this is that the computer is neither good nor bad but 'powerful'. The same description can be applied to the motor car with an unnecessary V-8 engine or a high-powered rifle, but this hardly reassures anybody concerned about their overuse or misuse. *The world is not shaped by our access to limitless data. It is shaped by the wise and parsimonious use of that selected information which can help us enrich ourselves and our social environment.* Such use requires a large measure of individual reflection and discrimination — best exercised when the computer screen is switched off.

THE DECIBEL CULTURE

If our contemporary culture of sensory addiction has been intensified by the pervasive presence of television and the computer screen in the visual mode, surely rock/pop music (which now engulfs the radio frequencies of the whole planet) can be regarded as its *aural* equivalent. It seems fair to claim that rock music and its derivatives present only the most noisy, coarse extension of a non-stop Muzak which lately seems to seep like treacle, wanted or unwanted, into every corner of contemporary life. For this we must thank another misapplied electronic boon — the invention of electrical sound recording in the late twenties. One wonders how Beethoven would have reacted had he realised that the 'Ode to Joy' from his Ninth Symphony would be listened to by people seated on their toilets, or whether Stravinsky would have been edified by the news that his 'Rite of Spring' was being used as an obligato to having sex or chopping vegetables. From one aspect this indulgence reflects the problem of people in sensately 'hooked' societies who never seem to be able to attend to one thing at a time in a healthy absorbed way. Hence the appeal of rock music with its endlessly reiterated rhythmic joggings.

George Steiner, one of the most eminent culture critics of the Western world, is deeply concerned about this rampant form of musical imperialism. He writes:

> The hammering of rock or pop creates an enveloping space. Activities such as reading, writing, private communication, learning previously framed with silence, now takes place in a field of strident vibrato. . .the tune is last month's or last week's Top of the Pops; already it has the whole of society for its echo-chamber. The economics of this musical esperanto are staggering. Rock and pop breed

concentric worlds of fashion, setting and lifestyle. Popular music has brought with it sociologies of private and public manner, of group solidarity. The politics of Eden come loud.[5]

About this problem of loudness alone there is much to say. A musical sound barrier at parties, gatherings and even in shops and restaurants seems almost subconsciously welcomed for its very impediment to communication. It relieves us of the necessity for self-revelation. Above the level of a 100-watt amplifier it barely matters whether one is revealing one's sex-life or reciting the multiplication table.

Research has been reporting for some years on the damaging psychological and physiological effects of loudly amplified pop music upon people who listen to it constantly. A teenage fad some years ago was to take raw eggs to rock concerts and place them at the edge of the music stage. Midway through the concerts the eggs could be eaten as hard-boiled, as a result of the sonic impact! Rock devotees never seem to have considered what the same music might be doing to their brains and bodily tissues. A three-year study of university students by investigators at Germany's Max Planck Institute showed that more than seventy decibels of noise caused vascular and arterial constriction, particularly dangerous if the coronary arteries are already narrowed by arteriosclerosis. The evidence that excessive resort to loud pop music produces harmful *physical* effects is clear.

Since the pop-music industry earns somewhere between $4 and $6 billion a year in the United States alone, it has become a sacred cow with hired protectors ranging from babbling jukebox illiterates on television to elitist commentators in quality magazines. All of them impart the idea that what is happening in the pop-music scene is quite as important as that occurring in politics, science and educational endeavour. Pop music has become part of the very furniture of modern life. Yet it is dismally easy to point to casualties of the rock/pop culture, which tends to devour all but the most ruthlessly exploitative of its own heroes and heroines. Jimi Hendrix died of an overdose of drugs in 1970; Jim Morrison of the Doors came to a similarly unfortunate end; Janis Joplin killed herself with heroin, as did Brian Epstein, the manager of the Beatles, and Brian Jones of the Rolling Stones. Early in 1979 Sid Vicious was released from prison after having murdered his girlfriend only to kill himself with a heroin overdose. To this mortuary line-up one could also add Buddy Holly, Jim Croce, Mike Furber, Terry Kath, Keith Moon and many others. Not long before he was killed by a crazed fan, John Lennon, a member of the most talented quartet of popular musicians in the latter half of this century, was quoted as saying that:

> . . .for sensitive people in the rock scene it can be a way of death. The masses all want pieces of you, and one day you have no more pieces to give. Sure, we have become rich. But if the kids have nobody bigger to believe in than people like us, then there is not much hope for them.

One of the reasons for the apparent untouchability of the rock/pop music scene has been its foundation in a potent alliance between profit and radical-chic politics. Daniel Henninger, writing about the sixties in the *Wall Street Journal* in 1978 observed:

> For the first time in recent history the important parts of the prevailing American culture — the Anti-War Movement, the Civil Rights Movement, campus turmoil and the enormous transformation of personal behaviour that spilled over into politics — were kept in motion (and to a certain extent were caused) by a popular art form, rock-and-roll music.

As the late, doomed rock star Jim Morrison was reported as saying: 'Erotic politicians — that's what we are. Interested in everything about revolt, disorder and all activity which has no meaning'. And if we notice the increasing loudness and arrogance of music since Morrison's time, particularly Heavy Metal, this is alarmingly frank comment, if anybody cared to be dismayed.

It will be objected, of course, that not all popular music is either bad or overloud. Nevertheless, few inquiries have really taken the trouble to examine relationships between the perpetual use of the snare drum and electronic guitar, and the restless, confused and distracted lifestyle of so many young people in Western cities. Research indicates that scarcely a single psychophysical function cannot be affected, either favourably or unfavourably, by musical tones or a rhythmic pulse. This is as much as the Chinese, Hindus and Greeks taught over two millennia ago. Used *occasionally* at times of defined celebration, rock music may enliven and create feelings of visceral pleasure. Its potent orgiastic effects may help to release many tensions which sedentary people have built up during the day and could not discharge physically in other ways. Unfortunately, vast numbers of younger people no longer dance to such music; they merely 'plug in', submit to it passively and pull it over their heads.

Ancient high cultures were confident of the music espoused by communities as an indication of the level of their civilisation. Music was seen as an important way of influencing the soul and human behaviour. Confucius believed that good music could help to perfect a man's character. He remarked:

> The music of the noble-minded man is mild and delicate, keeps a uniform mood, enlivens and moves. Such a man does not harbour pain or mourn in his heart; the violent and coarser movements are foreign to him.[6]

The ancient Greeks thought similarly and both Plato and Aristotle expressed the view that espousal of violent and ugly music could cause social and personal disorder. They would have agreed with Confucius that: 'If one would desire to know if a kingdom is well-governed, if its morals are good or bad, the quality of its music will furnish the answer'.

It was the *sound* of music and the arrangements of its tones and ground rhythm that most preoccupied the philosophers of the ancient world. They considered them even more important than the actual verbal content of songs and chants. In China by the time of the T'ang Dynasty, the Emperor himself paid special attention to the music performed in his kingdom and often travelled about regulating tonal scales and performances. The Dynasty kept no less than fourteen court orchestras, often consisting of from 500 to 700 performers! It was believed that the energy invoked by the 'divinely attuned' tone patterns of these orchestras had a profound effect upon the affairs of the nation.

Such views would be scoffed at by the commercial know-alls of our time as antique superstition. But there is abundant case evidence about the negative behavioural change possible in a person who listens too avidly to rock music without sufficient silence or correctives from other sources. Henry Lai of Washington University, Seattle, has found that experimental animals exposed at length to high levels of neutral 'white' noise as well as loud or harsh music show lasting changes in behaviour and brain chemistry. On the other hand, gentle or grandly inspiring music with low percussion content is being used in hospitals to calm patients and promote moods of well-being. Far more than jazz, rock/pop music is recognisably African in its intervals and rhythmic basis. In its departure from the sophisticated tune-spinning in the previous age of Gershwin, Cole Porter and Irving Berlin, rock/disco music shows a definite regression to a primitive, pounding, unvarying tempo, usually overlaid with inanely repetitive and undeveloped three- to four-bar melodic fragments. The bashing *ostinato* of the bass pulse is often un-related to the forgettable short-winded theme intoned above it. Yet this pounding pulse must *always* be present: its percussive beat is intended to override everything else, hour after hour, until stupefaction sets in.

Far from constituting some 'chosen' escape from the obsessive pres-sures of urban industrial life, pop music often imposes new primitive commercial compulsions in place of what is left of the high artistic rituals which took European peoples a thousand years to evolve. The minimal savage musical figurations which served the cultures of the African continent long before its invasion by the whites are no more appropriate for our jittery effete civilisation than would be a revival of the drunken frenzy of a 9th-century Viking banquet or a mock rape in the village Bacchanals of preclassical Greece. In this instance it is *culture* rather than colour that maintains most Afro-European tensions and to cluck piously about 'racism' is to completely miss the point.

Finally, there are the messages, the lyrics, of so many popular songs. Parents object to these, perhaps excessively, wihout realising that it is the overwhelming *sound* in pop music that disorients the young, more than its fatuous messages. However, in a book written some years ago called *The Coming Parent Revolution*, Jean Westin described the situa-tion long faced by even the most tolerant of Western parents. Some of the lyrics of pop songs in the late seventies and early eighties would never have been broadcast a generation ago. Typical titles were 'Bad Girls' (a tribute to prostitution), 'Cold Ethel' (about necrophilia), 'Glad to Be Gay', 'Wild Love', 'Part-Time Love', 'Good Girls Don't — But I Do', 'Baby Talks Dirty' and 'Cocaine'. An American study showed that of all pop records sold in 1979, 70 per cent had some kind of sexual statement or innuendo. By 1985 this had risen to over 80 per cent of lyric content — with suggestions of violence and alienation increasingly added.

It could be objected at this point that modern mass culture is surely of one inescapable piece despite its parts. Harsh and steamy music arguably matches the psychological foreboding of the post-atomic world. Films, books and documentaries all convey similar messages of anxious striving, of desperation and dislocated sensuality. This is true enough. But people of sensibility do not have to live with a book which spits violence, crudity and alienation from between its covers. It speaks to nobody until they are disposed to pick it up. One can avoid an ugly or boring film, a bad painting or a silly TV soap opera. However the Muzak environment, whether regarded as a sonic pleasure or purgatory, is only as close as the nearest neighbourhood radio or the nearest backyard rockfest. The old sonic privacies are now no longer predictable, and even to ask for them is to be condemned as antisocial. Such compulsory musical togetherness makes it possible to be superficially communal and yet far more isolated and anonymous than any bookworm in a silent library. Two generations of English-speaking youth, in particular, have grown up in an entire aural climate of this sort of prefabricated electronic pseudo-music. They have rarely sampled the splendour of real ceremonial dance, of folk music, played a traditional instrument or heard the sound of a straight ballad. And if there is one thing that now disturbs most younger Western folk even more than serious music, it is silence.

THE GREAT GOD AUTOMOBILE

Having dealt with the main visual and aural forms of entertainment in popular culture, we must now turn to the oldest and most powerful technological aid to modern living — the automobile. What once emerged as a valuable utility enabling people to travel easily to work or holiday resorts had already become, by 1950, what Marshall McLuhan dubbed 'the Mechanical Bride'. Indeed, I have known many car-obsessed young men in my practice who have displayed more concern for the health, appearance and functioning of their motor cars than for the welfare of their girlfriends, wives or, for that matter, their own longevity and safety. The automobile represents a fourth key element in a grand quartet of technological marvels that now tend to ensnare or enslave people as much as serving their innocent desires. In its compelling enlistment of our *tactile* sense, the motor car can become an engine of gut-moving power and suberotic excitement. It provides the kind of 'hands-on' thrills that an otherwise passive, sedentary spectator civilisation rarely provides outside of its spasmodically played sports.

Following an ancient primitive imperative, the motor vehicle has become both an engine of flight and the disposition to fight. Such elements in combination provide a sense that one rides a multi-horse-power steed many times swifter and stronger than oneself. Within its deceptively protective womb of metal and glass one feels secure in a manner which would never be possible while walking exposed upon city pavements. With road surfaces, buildings and geographical reference points whizzing by, the car often provides a type of hyperstimulation which causes diminished ego-control, particularly when younger people show off to one another when driving at high speed. Indeed, thousands of young men throughout the developed world rarely think of the automobile as merely a valuable utility or a mundane carrier. Their view is close to a perception of it as a gladiatorial extension of their own personalities. Meanwhile, all the advertising propaganda of car manufacturers lends its guile to vaunting the automobile as an engine of escape, beauty, power and status. In a windscreen vision of the world, quite small and petty people can wax very large in their own fantasies.

The automobile is commonly the most expensive object most Western people own outside their own houses. So it has become clear that psychological fitness to drive such a powerful piece of machinery rarely has anything to do with the actual psychomotor reflex or skills tested before one is granted a licence. More people have been killed and injured upon the roads of the Western world than died in military service in World War II and the Korean and Vietnam Wars combined. In some countries where there are wide-open spaces and low populations this abuse of the automobile borders on national pathology. The head-injury rate in Australia, for example, is almost three times that of the US, and Britain, most of it brought about through automobile casualities. Nearly 5000 people in Australia, out of a population of about 17 million, suffer serious and permanent brain damage every year as a result of head trauma. To pander to all the signs of blatant addiction in this area, Australia also publishes the highest number of motoring magazines per head of population in the Western world.

Australia is merely at the leading edge of a worldwide phenomenon, especially in the United States, where it is assumed by the population that the privilege of owning one automobile or several is tantamount to a *right* — a kind of Fifth Freedom — which no red-blooded American male in particular would willingly surrender. Thanks to the innumerable car chases, incredible stunts and thoroughly irresponsible images of automobile misuse provided by Hollywood crime films, the younger generation has no trouble in identifying the automobile as an instrument of lethal entertainment and moronic risk-taking. The power of the automobile and petroleum lobbies throughout the developed world, has lead to the overproduction and contrived obsolescence of automobiles, causing one of the largest wastes of rubber, metal and other natural resources on the planet. Furthermore, the use of automobiles in central London or Manhattan in preference to the subway, has nothing to do with simple convenience or the speed of arrival at one's destination. Here, the car is a badge of both conformity and status.

It is now recognised that about 56 per cent of atmospheric pollution in the Western world is caused by the exhausts from the internal combustion engine. There is very little inclination on the part of nations to limit automobile registration or to make licences more difficult to obtain. The automobile is believed by the leaders of several nations to provide an *indispensable* basis for the economy and an essential form of mobility for workers. Petrochemical interests make every effort to ensure that there are as many vehicles as possible using their fuels. Governments reap rich rewards in taxes, sales and registration fees. An entire wing of the legal profession in several English-speaking nations is supported by the outcomes of automobile accidents, injury, misdemeanour and theft.

In recent decades many European nations, particularly France, have striven to make public transport more attractive by providing superb railways and bus networks. Such nations have done everything they can to get pedestrians back into circulation and with a modest measure of success. Unfortunately the United States, Britain and Australia show few signs of following suit. Railways are carrying fewer passengers and deal with less and less freight. Authorities make little effort to regulate the use of trucks, lorries and trailers, whose polluting juggernaut approach destabilises the foundations of roads, homes and public buildings. Irreplaceable monuments, such as the Parthenon and the Roman Forum, to say nothing of innumerable medieval cathedrals, have had their fabric seriously damaged, eroded or weakened by neverending floods of heavy automotive traffic. Honking motorists are a constant annoyance to tourists who would prefer to walk.

In less than a century since Henry Ford produced his T-Model car the automobile has moved from becoming a useful and rapid means of transport to becoming a universal fetish. 'Power under the bonnet' is the most often reiterated theme of automobile advertising, followed closely by appeals to luxuriousness and snobbery. The contribution of the automobile to environmental pollution is constantly played down when matched against other factors. In a 1989 visit to Australia, environmentalist David Suzuki managed to give a whole public lecture on environmental dangers without once mentioning the motor car. Even those zealous for the welfare of rainforests and delicately poised natural environments see no incongruity in driving headlong into them in heavy four wheel drive vehicles which damage the very terrain they are trying to conserve.

The automobile has also had an impact on the family and our sense of community. When it became widely available to lower-income families after World War II, it was argued by writers and publicists that the automobile would keep the family together, making it possible for

members to travel great distances to resorts and have vacations together, which would not have been possible in former decades. In fact,
the automobile and the easy access of late teenagers to the ignition
key has had a more divisive and disruptive effect on family life than
any other invention in this century. Restless mobility has taken the
place of convenient travel to definite destinations. 'Going for a spin',
or 'driving around' have become ends in themselves. In a household
where every adult member has access to a separate automobile, it does
not require much imagination to realise the damage done to their
shared experiences. In such matters, the home becomes a kind of bus
depot — a mere point of eating, sleeping, arrival and departure. The
same could be said about community life and local gathering places.
Not so long ago it was possible for urban and suburban communities to
know each other in a friendly way. There were useful solidarities of
street and neighbourhood which helped to preserve the pedestrian
principle of self-help — to say nothing of law and order. Today, many
metropolises have become jungles where only the poor and disadvantaged — who do not have motor vehicles — seem to have any sort
of community relationship that goes beyond a nod or a fixed smile as
a household member passes into the driveway. Just as higher barriers
toward our recognising and taking trouble to understand one another
have been raised by television, and an unending diet of rock/pop music
has made so much of sustained listening and conversation the first
casualty, so has the motor car frequently promoted the *final* escape from
community: that of removing one's physical self from domestic roots
and numbing any deep sense of physical belonging.

ANODYNES AGAINST THE WORLD

I have pointed to the automobile, the gramophone, television and the
computer as representing the seemingly benign yet corrupting edge of
a public passion for entertainment and diversion, not so much as an
adjunct to life in its fullness as a substitute for it. This contributes to a
culture of sleep-moving, sleep-listening and sleep-talking, promoting a
climate with diminished awareness of soul and neighbour. Compared
to these massive central distractions, drug addiction, alcoholism and
various forms of bodily and mental abuse do not affect the majority of
the population. Moreover, such abuses are deplored, not uncritically
celebrated or embraced like the automobile and the audiovisual culture.
Yet something should be said about drugs and alcohol as a means of
blurring awareness of daily pressures which would otherwise seem intolerable. Alcoholism and drug addiction begin as a partly unconscious

protest against, or evasion of, a civilisation which is terrified by ageing, failure and death — the usual melancholy backdrop to an obsessive life. Far from representing a 'death wish' in terms of pop psychology, drugs are resorted to as new addictions/compulsions on one's *own* terms, however destructive the long-range consequences might be.

As Stan Peele and Archie Brodsky pointed out in their book *Love and Addiction*, drug and alcohol abusers feel that many of the sobrieties of contemporary culture are institutionalised forms of oppression from which there are only two escapes. One is to find the solace of genuine love. But, since love's absence or its counterfeits are *far* more common, quick pharmacological transformation of the consciousness of everyday life is seen as the only alternative. William James, one of the fathers of experimental psychology, stated this clearly when he wrote nearly a century ago of strong drink:

> The sway of alcohol over mankind is unquestionably due to its power to stimulate the mystical faculties of human nature usually crushed to earth by the cold facts and dry criticism of the sober hour.[7]

Yet the 'skid-row' abuser of drugs and alcohol would hardly feel him or herself to be searching for mystical awareness. And the poor have always resorted to cheap alcoholic beverages in particular as a means of muffling the miseries and deprivations of their existence. In the case of the middle class, which can afford a range of such dubious delights as cannabis, heroin, amphetamines and cocaine, the situation is rather different. Already swamped by the sensory overload of contemporary society with its noise, Muzak, aimless mobility and ceaseless search for unattainable goals, many judge that dope provides a means of liberation. For the sensitive, disturbed (and yet often strangely aware) folk of bourgeois communities, these dangerous delights can provide a short-term glimpse of a better, more expanded conscious life. Yet, given this culture's obsessive awareness of time and its passing, the 'fix' must be a *quick* one, and lasting contentment remains as elusive as before.

When the uses of inebriating substances like alcohol are contained within a tight framework of accepted ethical norms or group etiquette, flagrant abuse is not only rare but can also be greeted with tough reprisal, even against oneself. When intoxicants are limited within religious ritual and group sanction, abuse is again unlikely. In the south-west of the United States there are about 300 000 legal users of mescaline — the so-called peyote culture — which has sustained tribes of Indians who would otherwise have been condemned to a life of alcoholism. Even so, drug-taking exists only in the side-alleys of religious affirmation, and rarely along the highways travelled by the great teachers. Alas, all such highways are less and less travelled in developed societies. For the idealistic seeker there seems little to choose between a highly materialistic market-oriented culture and those fringe cults which deal in the search for pleasure, ecstasy or private enlightenment.

Without some benevolent ritual norms which do not suffocate people, contemporary society can be a frightening place. It is so easy to seek flight with a series of 'joints', a dose of hashish, a snort of cocaine or 'crack'. Thus the drugged peer group which supplies a pleasurable refuge from a situation where the sufferer cannot cope with his or her community becomes a kind of pseudo-family. Here all the characteristics of the aggrieved, dogmatic, paranoid subculture can come into play. I have listened to dozens of young, moderate users of narcotics, amphetamines and cannabis who have argued the almost sacramental uses of their practice: that it enhances their empathy with each other, their social and natural awareness and so on. Alas, much of this boasted enlightenment is mainly due to an induced absence of stress and the social comradeship is mostly a matter of cupboard love.

Yet we must also be fair to drug-takers themselves. When they point to the madness inherent in the acquisitive, overdriven mainstream community, they are partly right, even if their own solutions prove to be pathetically inadequate, when not actually self-destructive. Thus we have had a sharply polarised stand-off between what one might call the Doped Dionysians and the Drugless Apollonians. On one side we frequently hear cut-rate humanism, cheap religion or bad metaphysics; on the other, tough-minded, myopic science with little social insight and almost no imagination.

In truth, there is no such thing as a drug of addiction; there are only people who become addicted to drugs. A signal example is the case of suppression of LSD and other psychedelic drugs in the seventies because of the overreaction of the medical and scientific establishment to the misuse of psychedelic drugs by the hippie subculture. This has meant that an often valuable adjunct to deep psychiatric therapy is now unavailable for legal, professional use. The LSD controversy is thus one of the great litmus tests of ideological orthodoxy over the last thirty years. Any sort of expansion of human consciousness, whether this be benign or malign, is not something which appeals to linear thinkers at one extreme of the mainstream culture who prefer their safe, staid compulsions. Representing the other extreme are the absurd antics of Dr Timothy Leary whose followers posed as bombastic shamans promising a psychedelic heaven on earth, and who merely changed their tune when the next 'new age' fad happened along.

Rollo May has remarked on the feeling of helplessness that motivates many drug abusers. He points to drug addiction as the sufferers' gesture of nonconformity to the cultural demands and customs over which they have no control and which take no account of their experienced needs. In the grip of his or her favourite substance, the addict gains a magical sense of power and the illusory freedom to use it. Others have also questioned whether the drug-using dropout may not in this respect be merely in the vanguard of much of metropolitan mankind, which threatens to strangle itself by ceaselessly multiplying formal structures and inflaming new commercial appetites.

Drug abuse, of course, is not confined to illicit drugs — it extends to an almost limitless consumption of prescription drugs. Whilst in the Third World and in subsistence communities doctors combat diseases borne of deprivation and economic hardship, in our world, medicine and pharmacology are increasingly required to remedy those diseases borne of surfeit and excess, or even prolong physical life in those cases where the sufferer is trying to nullify the consequences of a grossly dissipated existence.

With the decline of the Christian belief in the soul's survival of death, the craving for physical immortality grows apace. Yet the overdose and misapplication of potent drugs, even by some doctors who ought to know better, frequently subverts the alertness and vigour of the short life that drugs are claimed to preserve. Boredom, tension and overstimulation now increasingly invade middle-class life and people turn increasingly to tranquillisers and analgesics as pacifiers. Anglo-Saxon-Celtic women, in particular, consume a higher proportion of analgesics than any racial subgrouping in the world, with Australia once more topping the list, per capita. The abuse of a single psychoactive drug, diazepam, assumed the proportions of an international scandal in the 1970s.

The mechanomorphic way of life pervading Western societies (with nations like Japan and South Korea as rapt converts) now extends to our perception of our anatomy and physiology. Our bodies can be as subject to renovation or dismantling as our domestic devices or automobiles. The consumer middle class has become a voyeur at a costly supermarket called Health — or is it disease? In *The Loved One*, written two generations ago, Evelyn Waugh mocked the American way of death whereby the titivated dead were made to look healthier than their mourners. Cadavers were treated as 'departed', 'resting', or even waiting for some fundamentalist trump to vanquish the conquering worm.

Despite the cost of the professional skill and equipment involved in what could be called the human spare-parts industry, the organ transplant has become the high-fashion area of modern surgery. No well-disposed taxpayer could object to a transplant for a young person otherwise in life's prime. But when children scarcely out of the maternal womb are given surgical procedures with a less-than-average chance of success, and ageing reprobates clutch like ghouls at a new heart to replace their self-ravaged original, one must question the priorities of much of the gee-whiz surgery practised at the scientific frontier. There is assuredly too much surgery for surgery's sake. Yet at the other end of the spectrum of bias, much 'alternative' medicine, diet and natural healing is treated as quackery by a suspicious establishment which often uses the wrong criteria of testing and proof. Just one example was the sweeping 1990 recommendation of an autocratic Australian health establishment that numerous items used in Chinese herbal medicine be banned from sale.

For a culture which is as afraid of succumbing to death and decay as any other before it, the officially licensed doctor has replaced the priest as a final source of consolation. Yet it is never explained why the prolongation of physical life and health is of such importance, if that life is experienced by oneself and others as spiritually and emotionally sterile. In Nature's ruthless view the termination of an individual life has no tragedy beyond that which we as human creatures confer upon it. Developed societies dispose of tens of thousands of human foetuses every year. Yet a coast-to-coast television hook-up concerning one crippled athlete lays bare obsession with physical disability, *once it has become visible*, as something about which to simper and sentimentalise. In a ward full of young male paraplegics, nobody dares to make the slightest distinction between those patients who have irresponsibly caused the injury themselves, and those who are others' victims.

THE SELF AS PATIENT

At this point the wheel of the argument I began in the Prologue turns full circle — back to officially defined pathology: those who suffer it and those who treat it. If, as I have contended, the only difference between obsessive-compulsive neurosis and the grindingly meticulous transactions of the everyday world is of degree rather than kind, it must follow that the psychiatrist and the clinical psychologist assume an ever-burgeoning importance in our lives. This has led, in the United

States at least, to what sociologist-critic Phillip Reiff referred to as 'the triumph of the therapeutic'. But what are the aims of therapy in our time? In his book *The Triumph of the Therapeutic*, Reiff comments on a few of them:

> A tolerance of ambiguities is the key to what Freud (and his successors) considered the most difficult of all personal accomplishments; a genuinely stable character in an unstable time. . .To help distinguish between guilt on the one hand and the sense of guilt on the other, between responsibility for an offence committed and fantasies about offences intended or merely imagined, seems a moral or therapeutic aim. . .A man can be made healthier without being made better — or morally worse. . .Not the good life, but better living, is the therapeutic standard. It is a popular standard, not difficult to follow for Americans, despite Freud's wish to make it difficult . . . Freud proclaimed the superior wisdom of choosing second best. With no place to go, and for lessons in the conduct of contemporary life, every man must learn, as Freud teaches, to make himself at home in his own grim and gay little Vienna.[8]

Of course Reiff's remarks concerning Freud are relevant to many other wings of therapeutic counselling and self-help. The late Carl Rogers taught both therapist and client alike the post-Protestant religion of what he called 'unconditional positive regard'. This was a lot less difficult than the old Christian or Buddhist precept of loving the divine spark in your neighbour as readily as that within yourself. But at least it seemed an achievable ideal for ordinary people.

Assertive himself and teaching assertion, often of the bluntest kind, Albert Ellis and his Rational-Emotive system teaches people a doctrine useful for obsessives as far as it goes. He has pointed out that it is our own restrictive pedantic thought patterns that create so many of our needless burdens and commitments. It is we, therefore, who must find the guts to challenge these intellectual patterns when they become unbearable. The behaviourists too have taught us not to worry too much about abstract factors. They also have something to say to the obsessive, to the effect that he or she is controlled by theoretical fixations rather than reality, and that explaining and conceptualising one's pain is sometimes less important than dealing with its symptoms.

One of the salutary uses of good psychotherapy and psychiatry is to teach people that their personalities, habits and attachments are not immutable and that the 'self', as vulgarly clung to, is less a solid edifice than a ramshackle collection of egoistic annexes under continual change and renovation. Such a realisation is a wonderful antidote to stubbornness and fanaticism, but it cannot find us any way of faith or altruism. Nor does it say much about our origins and destiny or our capacity to live life well. However, it can remit a lot of guilt and allow the enjoyment of life's fluctuating pleasures less ambivalently and half-heartedly. Embracing second best is at least an improvement on a compulsive quest for earthly perfection which will never be realised.

Before about 1950, much of the serious work of therapy and healing of the ills of the mind was the monopoly of psychiatrists. Despite the fact that Freud had declared in his monograph *The Question of Lay Analysis* in 1922 that it was not at all necessary for a psychoanalyst to be medically trained, psychoanalysis rapidly became an enclave of psychiatry, even within the founder's lifetime. It says something for the deeply ingrained, almost conspiratorial, fellowship of medicine over the last 200 years that the average psychiatrist still learns far too much medicine and far too little psychology. In the British Commonwealth in particular it has created an intractable organic and biochemical bias to the healing of personality disorders, increasingly reinforced by medications as the principal weapon. The famous 'talking cure' of the depth psychologists is quite disregarded by a great many psychiatrists who merely enquire about symptoms, cultivate an aloof psychophobia and industriously write out prescriptions, telling the patient to return in two to four weeks.

Even the nosology (or clinical classification) of psychiatric disorders has created a pattern of self-fulfilling prophecy where one is never sure whether the syndrome is describing the patient or whether the patient is being conveniently fitted to the syndrome. The development of the diagnostic manual known as the D.S.M.3. in the United States has meant that clinical entities are multiplied and numerically listed. Radical psychiatrist the late R. D. Laing attacked this enlarging manual as the perfect instrument in the hands of a totalitarian authority, where a refractory citizen could be hospitalised by any group of psychiatrists in agreement merely by reference to a list of often phantom categories. While Laing's criticism was too extreme, it contained enough truth to lend force to the old sceptical complaint that 'all labels are libels'.

Obsessive-compulsive neurosis, however, is rather more clearly defined than most neurotic disorders, and neither its symptoms nor its onset can be held to be constructed. Moreover, as remarked before, many physicians who take up psychiatry tend to have obsessive traits of their own. Indeed many other medical specialties such as neurosurgery and microsurgery seem to find the hypermeticulous traits of the obsessive-compulsive outlook a positive advantage. The narrow margin for error in many delicate medical and surgical specialties means that obsessive traits in the medical practitioner can often work to the patient's benefit. However, in psychiatry it can lead to an unhealthy love of classification and categorisation which can 'type' a hapless patient, marking him or her unfairly for years to come. The days when patients were arbitrarily consigned to asylums because they expressed seditious or unusual views, or because scheming outsiders wanted their property, are thankfully past in Western countries, though it is only a few years since unwelcome ideological opinions were one of the reasons for consigning Russian citizens to mental hospitals. The employment of psychiatric diagnosis as a basis for incarcerating those who have offended against little more than culturally defined norms is apt to make even a moderate human rights defender nervous, particularly when it is remembered how tenuous the boundaries between officially and unofficially defined sanity often are.

Unlike clinical psychologists who use fairly rigorous testing, psychiatrists frequently offer very subjective diagnoses. The fact that psychiatry is still the most inexact of all medical sciences has helped swell the fortunes of many less reputable mental physicians or clinical psychologists who attend courts of law to give evidence on behalf of either the State or patient with unfailing regularity and confident certainty. Writer J. B. Priestley was somewhat caustic about forensic psychiatrists and psychologists who peddle their professional opinions in this unselective fashion: 'They are whores — tarts with degrees, selling their opinions for profit'. This is not to say that there are not some very fine forensic physicians, psychiatrists and psychologists operating in the Western world. It is merely that professionals who make claims for near-certitude about human behaviour that cannot be sustained by detailed day-to-day experience deserve no credibility, and they harm their reputation along with that of their more scrupulous colleagues.

The increasing reliance by psychiatrists upon medication and psychoactive drugs to achieve some kind of tranquillity or happy pacification in their patients has become another of the drawbacks in the obsessive approach to psychiatric illness. Prior to 1950 the major kinds of behaviour-pacifying drugs in use were substances like chloral hydrate and the barbiturates. Dipping into the treasure trove of botanical substances from the New World, the French finally came up with the first phenothiazine drug known as promazine. Thousands of patients walking the streets of our cities today would have been permanently incarcerated in mental institutions had it not been for the discovery of the phenothiazine group of drugs. Their use in the treatment of psychotic disorders, particularly of schizophrenia, has been invaluable.

The success of such medication, alas, went to the heads of many organically biased psychiatrists, particularly in Britain, and this has led to the familiar reductionist belief that all serious mental disorders will be found to be of biochemical origin. This belief has been accelerated by the increasing development by clinical psychologists of therapeutic, strategies which do not employ drugs, thus encroaching with increasing regularity on the older territory of talk which was thought to be the proper preserve of the doctor. This has led to the increasing abuse by doctor and patient alike of calming substances such as diazepam and the minor tranquillisers of the benzodiazepine group. These substances are quite safe and relatively harmless when used in the short-term and in properly prescribed doses. However, people's tendency to become habituated to them is increasingly apparent, and they have now become almost as great a problem in terms of addiction as the equally effective but more toxic barbiturates they were designed to replace.

Occasionally there is a brilliant biochemical breakthrough, such as the case of lithium treatment of manic-depressive psychosis by the Australian psychiatrist John Cade, but such breakthroughs are few and far between. Most of the disorders in the schizophrenic group, for example, have mainly responded to medication as a behavioural suppressant only. Yet claims for almost exclusively biochemical causation have persisted. In the case of obsessive-compulsive disorders, many psychiatric workers are increasingly refusing to recognise the essentially *cultural* base of this disorder, and the fact that its culturally deviant incidence in Western developed nations is significantly greater than than in Asia and the Third World.

Disease or cultural malaise?

In the *New England Journal of Medicine* Dr Michael Jenike of the Massachusetts General Hospital refers to obsessive-compulsive and related disorders as 'a hidden epidemic'.[9] He speculates, as others have done over many years in respect of schizophrenia, that the biochemical substance in the brain known as serotonin may be intimately involved in obsessive-compulsive disorders. Yet Jenike admits that no special differences have ever been discovered in brain activity of obsessive-compulsive patients as distinct from untroubled ones. Psychosurgery, for many years relatively discredited, is again being suggested in a 'low-risk' operation known as bilateral stereotactic anterior internal capsulotomy (though even the length of the name seems terrifying enough!). Moreover, although the development of new forms of psycho-active medication have been helpful in partly suppressing compulsive rituals in some patients, medication to suppress obsessive thought patterns has proved inconclusive to disappointing. Yet still the stubborn urge to find solutions in an essentially reductionist, anti-cultural manner persists. This kind of medical behaviour is what I might term 'the Nelson error', whereby the gallant admiral put the telescope to his blind eye at the Battle of Trafalgar.

By way of counterattack to treating so many mentally disturbed people in a social vacuum, Professor Robert Spillane of Australia's Macquarie University argues that we are becoming ever more inclined to attribute behaviour that is offensive, illegal or morally upsetting for others to illnesses for which there is no real *medical* diagnosis. He cites as an example the epidemic of repetitive strain injury, or RSI, which occurred in Australia during the latter years of the 1980s. It seems certain that Australia, with its generous endowments for work injury lay-offs was leading the world for claims in this sometimes valid but sometimes completely illusory disease. Spillane also points out the obsessive habit of multiplying various psychiatric syndromes to create new categories of illness which have a very tenuous basis in reality. Speaking of the rather tenuous claims for off-work entitlements based upon designated 'anxiety neurosis', he comments:

> It's a game. I don't use that in a frivolous sense or in the sense that people are deliberately malingering. . .Anxiety neurosis is a symbolic communication. In one person it could be translated as being unable to cope. Symbolic communications can be serious and important, but they are not medical. They are about. . .people unable to be authentic about what they want and disguising it behind illness.[10]

Spillane argues that many of the conflicts in modern Western people (and this would certainly apply to obsessive disorders) are of moral and social origin, and the habit of 'medicalising' them is costing taxpayers in Western communities literally billions of dollars worldwide. It also subsidises thousands of psychiatrists, who might be very trustworthy physicians, but who are often very poor psychotherapists. As long as the reference-frame of contemporary psychiatry, particularly in British Commonwealth countries, remains essentially materialistic and almost psychophobic, the medicalising of diseases which are of broadly environmental, familial and social origin is likely to continue. This is not to argue for a thoroughgoing social determinism, which could lead one from the extreme polarity of believing that every disturbance of behaviour is an illness to the opposite aberration, that of believing that every social disorder is the fault of *somebody else*! This latter view is one of the stock themes of left-wing sociology, and cannot be entertained seriously in any post-Marxist society. But as long as Western society considers economic productivity more important than human affinities, there will be a tendency for medical and social agencies to multiply diseases which are nothing more than socially generated obsessions and compulsions.

Westerners' fundamental personal conflict lies not in the physical-sexual-aggressive nature of the human creature, as organic psychiatry, Freudian psychoanalysis and Christian theology in their different ways have supposed, but *the overestimation of intellect* and its enthronement as a tyrant rather than a gifted servant. Surely this is the very core of obsessionality. If we were purely vegetative, socially heedless beings, the cleverly argued hypothesis of Arthur Koestler that our sufferings lie in a chemical argument between our primitive 'old' brain and the modern neocortex might well be true. A magic tablet, some genetic manipulation and even psychosurgery would resolve our boredom, self-hatred, envy and hostility and finally return us to a new Eden. Sigmund Freud and his successors were hardly as naive as that. The father of psychoanalysis believed that high civilisation and full human content-ment were incompatible. Only mankind at its primordial, preconscious level could have been consistently happy, because it was free from meas-ure, time and reflection upon the coming of death — a true insight, as far as it goes.

For their part, the theologians of the West made the fatal error of devaluing spiritual experience and simple identification with nature in favour of over-intellectualised systems complete with laws and dogmas. The pagan gods were banished because only Yahweh and his Son could be held up as both divine and real. But all religion, Christianity in-cluded, must inevitably partake of myth and metaphor. Because of our excessive ego-consciousness, the partly true and partly false sense of separateness from the universe forces us to live only by *analogies* of divinity. Our false consciousness and distorted perception mistakes the radiance of concrete things upon which the sun shines for the sun itself. As all the mystics have taught, spiritual bliss begins only when the questioning mind is awed, aghast or stilled. Small wonder, then, that the most frequent report of the acute obsessional neurotic is that he or she does not know how to 'switch off' his or her endless ratiocinations. When the atheist Freud dismissed religion as a form of obsessional neurosis, he had the truth reversed. Rather, obsessional neurosis is a parody of religion in its minutest and maddest forms of observance. Psychiatry is of small help because it too is a discipline often divided against itself.

When Carl Jung stated mysteriously that the gods had become diseases, he was referring to the damage that both Christian and post-Christian technocratic civilisation had done to the vital connections between human beings and the planet of which they were unquestionably a part. Lesser divinities no longer whispered amid the trees, the mountains and rivers about the great spiritual Mystery of which they were agents. Apollo no longer spoke through the Oracle of Delphi, the Great Mother no longer blessed fertility in her sacred grove, Amon-Ra no longer sailed across the sunlit heavens in his sacred barque. Jealous Yahweh/God/Allah had destroyed them all. Ironically, contrary to any likely teaching of the living Christ, the earth lay dead of spiritual meaning, ready for the axe, the excavator and the plough.

To carry the weight of a dead universe, even one transformed into power, light and activity by the mind of humanity, eventually becomes an insupportable exercise. There are no more presences to warn, heal and guide. Divinity is now the lonely province of people themselves; and they must eventually grow sick and die upon the earth that they have treated so irreverently — their greatest sin being that egoic pride by which legend tells the Lord Lucifer fell. Organised religion is lately of little avail because its function in society has become so stereotyped and morally formalised that the spiritual sap which once gave it vigour flows more sluggishly with each passing decade. The Church, which once unwittingly desacralised the world and laid upon it the glorious weight of her sanctuaries, has become at last desacralised herself. Secular obsession is now the master, and what passes for spontaneity is mostly media-inspired frenzy. Is there an escape from the terror of our own ruminations, and the darker side of our own creations? My last chapter will consider the alternatives.

SEVEN

BEYOND OBSESSION

E ndless invention, endless experiment
Brings knowledge of motion but not of stillness;
Knowledge of speech, but not of silence. . .
Where is the Life we have lost in living,
Where is the Wisdom we have lost in knowledge,
Where is the Knowledge we have lost in information?

T. S. Eliot

The developed world has latterly been prone to embrace all kinds of cut-rate mysticism as a bulwark against the confused hedonism, getting and spending of the contemporary world. In the United States especially, this has led to fringe preoccupations such as 'channelling', crystal gazing, amateur Tarot reading, pop-astrology, watered-down Yoga and Zen, to say nothing of those perennial Yankee favourites, revivalism, pentecostalism and 'born-again' Christianity. It is fashionable in smart journalism to treat these uneasy outcomes of social god-death with an almost despairing mockery and cynicism.

Worst of all, as in the case of militant sceptics like A. J. Ayer, Martin Gardner and Carl Sagan, is the attempt to take refuge in the most hard-nosed of intellectual paradigms and to measure all such inspired eccentricities against the pattern of establishment science, which itself offers no hope of ego-transcendence. Indeed, how could it, because our science too is the most wonderful product of the ego-intellect and cannot get beyond it. There is a likely grain of benefit in most 'New Age' cultic absurdities if only from those positive energies that people invest in them. Recall the striking observation of Porphyry quoted in Chapter 1: 'The object is to make those who draw near to [images and temples of the gods] think of aspects of God thereby, or to enable them. . .to address their prayers and vows to the seen representing the Unseen'. Most people are not capable of responding easily to any reality that goes beyond their five senses. If there is a supersensory world (and contemporary physics plainly indicates there is) then sensory/physical representations, even at their most primitive, must still be the starting point of our efforts to reach it. And if there is a God, it is an utter absurdity to believe, as Catholics recently did and as orthodox Muslims still do, that there is only one structured set of ways to partake of God's healing grace.

Those who lately scoff at 'New Age' philosophical beliefs and occult subgroups see only the more gullible and regressive aspects of such involvements. In fact these are all downpayments by the anxious ego on the hope of immortality. It is seldom accepted that life and death are merely two forms of the same temporal reality. The wisest of the ancients knew that neither life nor death as *we* mundanely experience them constitute a final statement about reality or existence as a whole. The physicist and the mystic, from their quite differing viewpoints, are still in broad agreement about that much.

If using astrology as one of several frameworks to daily conduct appears ridiculous to the sceptic, so is using an accumulation of a million dollars as a symbolic hedge against ageing or eventual decrepitude. Even a cure for cancer is important only in proportion to the value we attach to our lives as healthy animals, free from pain. The Italian peasant woman who prays before a statue of the Virgin, or the Hindu devotee who honours the god Shiva, are still making unwitting symbolic statements about the problems and meaning of their own existence. The office-worker who gulps down a recommended new tablet for backache without realising that it is only a placebo of sugar or salt is repeating an ancient gesture of faith and hope which our remote ancestors once attached to spells and incantations. So too are the tormenting rituals of compulsive neurotics, part-survivals of an attempt to placate some archaic 'god' long departed from civilisation but still threatening sufferers from the depths of their archetypal unconscious. The very rigidity of their almost ferocious rationalisations and their sterile worship of linear structures are reactions from the deeper fact that they have not yet freed themselves from the reflexive superstitions of the pre-intellectual and animistic world. As with the Bellman in

The Hunting of the Snark, saying or doing something 'thrice' makes them feel true and safe.

Mention of this pre-intellectual world, which was part of the useful experience of the ancient Vedic Hindus and the Egyptians and Greeks of the Homeric age, warns us that we have some reason for lamenting its passing. It is no longer desirable or even possible in evolutionary terms to return to that world. Herein lies the error of many 'New Age' cults, which dabble in witchcraft, demonology and nature worship and the lower forms of occultism. Apart from being an unpalatable pill which Biblical fundamentalists have refused to swallow since Darwin's time, evolution is both a human and cosmic fact. Regardless of whether the space–time continuum which carries us from age to age travels in a straight line or a circle, the truth is that there is no such thing as a static universe, and as living entities we are all *moving somewhere*.

It is possible that all consciousness and energy quanta in the universe will move back to their inscrutable origins after a period so vast that it is meaningless to attempt to measure it. The proper message of evolution is that life may be *enriched* as it evolves, however ruthlessly Nature, as a divine agent, changes, transforms and 'purifies' all species through each cycle of birth and death. With the materialism typical of the late 19th and early 20th centuries, biological scientists have merely confined themselves to the physical dimension of evolution. Yet the Hermetic philosophers of Alexandria in the 1st century before Christ were already teaching that soul and spirit are evolving too. What Darwin discovered was merely the transformation of the infinite variety of biological apparel in which the spiritual energy of the universe is dressed. All the great religious teachings and myths of the world are told and occur *in time*, for our intellect was not designed to grapple with timeless conditions. That spark of divinity within still pricks at us beneath the multitudinous trivialities of suburban life, but mostly makes us hunger for the wrong kind of immortality. Nietzsche undertood this in his famous verse:

The world is deep!
And deeper than the day has thought!. . .
But joy doth seek eternity! Profound eternity!

Unfortunately the limitations of everyday consciousness and of our language have led Western philosophers and monotheistic religions since early medieval times to mistake eternity for a kind of linear everlastingness. Over the past six or seven centuries this has only reinforced the human mind's bondage to time, space and history. Eternity is about that perpetual Nowness that post-Einsteinian physics has lately discovered to be perhaps the first and last of realities. It was this Nowness or Immanence the ancient Hindu metaphysics identified with Brahman or the universal divine Essence. In the words of Shankara, the Vedantist master, Brahman 'is not the object of anything but its own self, and out of it, as the Unmanifest, come all manifest things. Therefore it cannot be defined by word or idea. . .it is the One before whom all words recoil'.

Such a numbing concept offers little consolation to the Western ego-mind which plays out its anxious futurism against the backdrop of that Omnipresence from which it has long felt divorced. One of the most piercing thinkers of our generation on these problems is the American writer Ken Wilber.[1] Perhaps better than any other writer on psychology and metaphysics he has suggested the present position of the spiritual evolution of humanity in its long journey from the mythical Garden of Eden. This journey is toward a possible form of superconsciousness that might liberate us from the obstinacies and the torments of the human intellect. This might be done while still preserving some of its finest creations within a much vaster paradigm. Wilber argues that, for all the value of their contribution, depth psychologists, notably Freud and Jung, confused those elements of mind which are 'below' normal rational consciousness and those which are 'above' it. Thus, the diffuse and dim perceptions of true divinity in the archaic 'time of the gods' have been confused by depth psychologists with the future expansion of consciousness beyond the prison of egoistic thinking.

Freud dismissed superconscious awareness of divinity, referred to in the Hindu Upanishads as merely an echo of the 'oceanic' feeling a child experiences within the amniotic fluid of the womb. Meanwhile it was only at the end of his life that Carl Jung realised that the enlightenment talked about by the great spiritual masters was not a regression to the ancient archetypal world but a real transcendence of the worlds of both myth *and* reason to something much vaster than them both. To use Wilber's words, Freud reduced the trans-rational to the pre-rational, whereas those who thought as Jung did elevated some elements of the pre-rational to the trans-rational. Wilber refers to this confusion as the Pre/Trans Fallacy. It is useful to reproduce his diagram to make the position clear.[2]

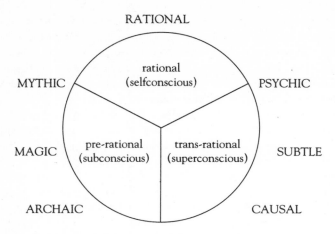

The three major realms of consciousness (Ken Wilber)

Significantly, Wilber's diagram is circular rather than linear. It suggests an evolutionary process that is cyclic and can vary in both individuals and groups. After his work in East Africa, palaeontologist Louis Leakey suggested in 1964 that primitive hominids are likely to have existed for a long period on earth along with the newer species that we find recognisably human: apeman and *homo habilis* living in coexistence.

THE TYRANNY OF THE RATIONAL EGO

The real problem of Western culture since the 18th-century Enlightenment is that it has become locked too tightly into the Rational-selfconscious segment of Wilber's circle of progression, ignoring the *continuing* existence of the mythic, magic and archaic elements in human make up and the ever-present possibility of regression to these levels under stress or flashes of high imagination. Schizophrenia in some forms shows definite signs of a regression to the magic and archaic realm. This can be discerned sometimes in entire societies, such as those created by the Nazis in Germany where a whole modern nation could be rooted for a time in the mythic and magic modes. Here there can be even deeper regressions to a type of archaic brutality, as witnessed by the horrors of the SS death camps and in the cruel mentality of a Saddam Hussein. In the sub-rational realms, regressions can occur in either a benign or a malign form, because law and dogma can only have effect and meaning at the rational level.

By the same token, the belt of consciousness just above rationality represented by the Psychic makes it possible for glimpses of reality beyond the everyday space–time continuum. It is at this point that certain gifted people may be able to give glimpses of a world that exists beyond the five senses. Intuitive flashes, clairvoyance and so on are not uncommon in people who partake momentarily of this level of consciousness. This is also a zone where creativity and inspiration seem to function more readily, especially in poetry, music and other arts.

As for Wilber's Subtle and Causal levels, one needs to refer to the metaphysics of the East in order to understand what these might be like, since Judeo-Christian eschatology is often too primitive and literal-minded to promote much awareness of them. These levels are where the 'self-transcendence needs' described by psychologist Abraham Maslow have their origin and arise partly as a result of rigorous contemplative and meditative practices. Saints and mystics who experienced these worlds struggled in the language of the various orthodox philosophies and religions to convey them to us. But since such realms are beyond verbal categories, mystically elevated experiences have to utilise distorting forms of imagery. The same thing may occur when the more responsive rational mind is fractured for a period by doses of mind-expanding substances such as lysergic acid. This can sometimes promote a powerful biochemical glimpse of the subtle and causal realms in the case of sensitive and intelligent subjects. Unfortunately this sort of imperfect perception often appears to be cluttered by material from the personal, mythic, magic and archaic regions as well.

One of the chief advantages of briefly pushing beyond the rational segment of consciousness which so holds Western civilisation in thrall is that it can promote enhanced awareness of the body no less than that of possible regions beyond the ego-mind. Despite the stubborn belief of materialists that mind is a mere epiphenomenon of the body, most men and women in the street imagine that they live primarily in that area between their ears which they equate with the head and brain. In cultures with deep access to the mythic and psychic sides of consciousness, such as the ancient Greeks and the Hindus, everyday consciousness was thought to be more centred in the region of the *heart*. The body–mind symbology of most ordinary Western people is still the rather wretched model of René Descartes — that of a spirit dwelling in the cranium and working the body as a machine. Yet even a rudimentary knowledge of neurology shows that large areas of the body are controlled at the vagal and spinal levels, and are not directly responsive to cerebral action at all. It is this unfortunate dualistic amalgam of body and intellect created by Aristotelian philosophy and perpetrated by both Christian and post-Christian thought that has helped to create an everyday culture where proper fusion of body and spirit in moments of natural ecstasy seems confined almost exclusively to rare moments of sexual orgasm, drug-induced states or rare moments of pleasure in natural surroundings such as standing on mountain tops, being submerged in warm water and so on. The reality is, that in the useful term coined by Wilber, human beings are essentially 'centaurs', or half-spirit and half-beast. Thus excessive ego-consciousness is as unkind to the body as it is to the spirit, crippling a free awareness of both.

Where, then, does obsession lie in Wilber's hypothetical cycle of consciousness? One would have to place it in that uncomfortable borderland between the mythic and the rational. Rational consciousness tends to exercise an extreme structuring tyranny over the elements of the mythic and the magical, primarily because these are becoming so insistent at subconscious levels. Obsessive and compulsive defences are desperate attempts to be *super-rational* in order to prevent elements of the mythic and magical from overwhelming the sufferer. This explains the terrible tension that exists in obsessive-compulsive conflicts, in which all dilemmas appear to be polarised at states of extremity. Here the 'centaur' has been torn in two, the beast becoming most savage because it has not been fully 'baptised' or integrated into the individual's self-concept. Meanwhile the rationalising side of the perceived self becomes more desperate, more strained and more rigid in doing battle with it. Therefore anything that is not rational is feared, and the *non*-rational is constantly confused with the irrational. Our education systems, until recent times, have taught children to distrust every kind of experience we cannot rationally formulate or at least describe. Educational conservatives and radicals alike equally distrust unstructured situations because there is always an obsessive fear that the beast, which only the mind itself has alienated, will somehow gain the upper hand.

Having located the obsessive style of living at the 'bottom' end of the rational phase of human development where reason meets with the magical and mythical realms, we might see where the contradictory split in the behaviour of so many modern folk arises. Instead of honouring, embracing and incorporating the archaic, magical and mythical aspects of his evolved nature into the 'higher' rational dimension, the obsessive-compulsive feels emotionally threatened, since much of his or her stereotyped, arid behaviour is unconsciously designed to exorcise these very aspects. The woman who is compelled to return to her household six times to assure herself that the gas taps are turned off knows the wearying excessiveness of her compulsion, but would never dream of linking such behaviour by analogy to that of a primitive native of the Amazon rainforest who must repeatedly perform some sacred gesture to placate the forest spirit before felling a tree. The business executive who is forever worrying whether he or she 'measures up' to peers in the matter of sales-performance would rarely connect such behaviour with that of an early anchorite who felt obliged to rise in dead of night to examine some personal worthiness in the sight of God and the angels. Yet the subterranean links are still there. The gods have mostly departed, but their great footprints still mark the pathways of the secular life. The paradox is that people are rarely more unreasonable than when they are taking refuge in arbitrary rationalisation.

Modern academic and learned life shows that the rational dimension of our nature has become not merely a valuing and ordering element but an intolerant and bullying overseer standing sentry to the preconscious world that the ancient philosophers knew, and often barring all doorways to spiritual, superconscious life. Borrowing from Plotinus and neo-Platonic philosophy the notion of human beings as essentially tripartite creations rather than bundles of dualistic conflict, that maimed but far-seeing genius St Augustine wrote: 'Every person has three lives, the life of the soul in the body, the life of the soul in the soul, and the life of the soul in God'.

It is to that life of the soul in the soul, not only in its rational core, but also in its possible communion with many lesser 'gods', its multiplicities, fantasies, hopes and fears, that true psychologists must address themselves. The three great segments of Wilber's circular diagram cannot be fenced off from one another. The healthy rational soul — the middle term of human existence — must be quickened by both animal and spiritual powers. Without this quickening there can be no real religion, no art, no poetry, no true musical inspiration, only the perpetual weighing, measuring and exploiting of the world. He who is driven by a dominating urge for rationality at all times, James Hillman has described as 'monotheistic Reformational man' — the enemy of images. Hillman points out that the word 'idea' comes from the ancient Greek word *eidos* which originally meant an image. Rationality is forever preoccupied with abstract symbols, words and semantics, forgetting that most ideas that arise in the rational dimension are pictured before they are verbalised.

THE NEED FOR MYTHIC IMAGINATION

There have been feeble attempts over the past half century to rescue the preconscious, magic-mythic elements in human life by means of orgiastic pop music, sporting carnivals, car races, beauty contests and all the neon-lit din of an energy-greedy world. Always these attempts are subverted by the commercial, basically mass-produced means by which they are realised and staged. Instead of welling up from the dialogue between imagination and reason inside ourselves and between ourselves and nature, such escapes are imposed artificially through the arbitrary structures of profitable entertainment. Almost always now-adays our fantasies are *somebody else's*. Also they are *bought* and invariably shared. There is no private chapel of the self whereby the mythic dreaming of childhood (and of adulthood too) can be cherished and preserved. Dionysiac frenzy is artificially created with lasers, trans-ducers, microphones and maximum decibels. The consciousness-expansion of speeding over the earth has been transformed from galloping horses and the thrust of human hearts and thighs into the roar and stink of piston engines. Dislocated sexuality seems to go marauding in the public domain while becoming stale and divorced from tenderness in private life.

As James Hillman has pointed out, the last significant attempt of Western civilisation to put the tripartite nature of the human creature — preconscious, conscious and superconscious — body, soul and spirit — into some kind of interacting harmony occurred during the Italian Renaissance. From the time of the great poet Petrarch the concern of Renaissance scholars was considered to be the 'care of the soul'. This soul was thought to be better formed by looking right back to the mind of antiquity rather than to the late medieval world in which Scholas-tics debated endlessly about obsessive theological details, such as whether Christ actually sanctioned the use of money among his disciples or whether angels occupied physical space. Instead, *imagination* informed by the intellect was enthroned by the Renaissance artists and human-ists, whether this was exercised through the study of science, magic, love, art or geographical voyaging.

Renaissance thinkers discovered that the Greek philosophers had no proper conception of the Christian notion of 'the love of God'. After all, 'love' of a disembodied and formless spirit was considered by Aristotle to be impossible. Divinity could only be loved and adored through its manifestations and reflections. The elevation of the soul, therefore, was best managed through imagery and the use of active imagination. But after the coming of the Protestant Reformation, the Catholic Counter-Reformation and the Industrial Revolution, the claims of sovereign rationalism were reasserted. There was a further move away from God (and gods) reflected through worshipful imagination, back to a world of heroic but short-sighted reason where divinity could have very little to do with the motives and dealings of everyday life. In this way the concept of purely mental man, stripped of mythic imagination or superconscious longings, came into being to produce the distracted, spiritually enfeebled creature that so often appears before us today.

Without imagination, without the idea as *eidos* or image, faith withers and hope is not long in following after. When some Renaissance philosophers went so far as to put on the robes of the ancients, restore their shrines and record imaginary conversations and debates with them, they were recognising the role of *vision* and the structured waking dream as a means of escaping from the narrow historical prison of so-called pure rationality. Today it is mostly children who are permitted to construct imaginary companions, speculate about fairies at the bottom of the garden, or address imaginary conversations to Santa Claus. Indeed, even this sacred area of child-imagining and fantasy is being encroached upon by misguided and pushy parents whose only conception of a child's talent seems coded in terms of the greed-filled social world which *they* inhabit. For an adult to admit to dialogues with the unseen constructions and projections of the soul would be to invite social suspicion that he or she should be consulting a psychiatrist. Yet without this deliberate '*holographing*' type of imagination, with image projection into the external world, that concretisation of fantasy which we know as artistic creation cannot happen.

A constant constriction of imagination is the reason why obsessive-compulsive neurotics are mostly uncreative. Their dialogue is always with the rational ego and is always circular. They permit themselves to be conscious of no gods and very few therapeutic images or ideas. Outside the arid canons of 'proof' or blind faith, they allow themselves no really private form of worship. Since most people are not saints or possessed of some special grace or superconscious intimation which is given only to one in a million souls, they cannot leap up suddenly to the Subtle or Causal realms of enlightenment from the purely rational platform of the ego. There must always be an apprenticeship, with 'dreaming' and some immersion in myth and creative imagination.

For the hyper-rational, educated citizens of the modern Western world a rise to the realms of the spirit can only begin, as a rule, by some measure of backward detour through the subtlest experience of the body and some celebration of nature through the senses, but in the most focused way. This us why the extreme ascetics of all religions have been so mistaken in believing that the heights of spiritual religion must be attained at the cost of *denying* all the ancient 'calls of the blood' which come from our preconscious life. The personal soul is largely the sum of its body–mind experiences and its connections with collective or archetypal history. It is only by presently exercising as many of these as possible that we can ever hope to supersede them. The obsessive hopes to find peace through stasis, by filtering or excluding things, whereas true liberation must *include* everything of importance — even when some of our experiences might seem socially shocking or ridiculous.

Such reflections lead one to confront the essentially dichotomous world of binaries and opposites on which all educated conventional daily thought has been based. It was one of the best insights of the teachers of Hellenistic Alexandria and ancient China that the Supreme Being had ordained that the chief function of evolving human-kind was to work at *the bridging of all binaries* and the reconciliation of all contending opposites. This was because the world of true spiritual freedom knew neither plus nor minus, male nor female, good nor bad, light nor dark, heaven nor hell but only a comprehensive Unity containing an infinite plurality of worthy things between which no real conflict was possible.

To accept this anti-binary doctrine, which was more than once hinted at by early Church fathers such as Origen, was to renounce all theologising about a God or a universe in which some intellectualised 'supreme good' was the final aim. The very notions of goodness and badness, however useful in social terms, are only meaningful to the ego-mind and intended for the life of human beings at a particular phase in the evolution of consciousness. The truth of the universe is that it is ultimately neither 'good' nor 'bad' but evolving mysteriously towards some timeless unnameable state of completion. This has nothing to do with moral good, as popularly conceived, and therefore cannot be other than a *tragic* process during one limited human incarnation. Tragedy is confused in the popular mind with hopelessness and despair. In fact, it merely means that because human beings are still labouring as spiritual mutants, they must inevitably suffer the pains and disappointments of their imperfect state. How such afflictions are accepted and surmounted determines the pace of one's movement towards that final enlightenment, where there is suffering no longer, only bliss. This

Table 3: The Great Cycle of Consciousness
(developed from suggestions by Ken Wilber)

	Mode of awareness		Worldly function
The Trans-Rational Super-Conscious World	The Realm of Essence Without Manifestation (The 'subtle' plane.)	Nirvana, the Kingdom of Heaven, Samadhi, the Beatific Vision, et al. The end of individual life and all real distinctions. The Many in the One.	No function except to be the Ground of existence, the Holy Spirit or Brahman. To be the Mystery which underlies all mysteries. The 'Ain-Soph' or intellectually unknowable.
	The Realm of Causation and Personal Deity	God the Father, Jesus Christ as Saviour, Buddha as the Awakened One. Krishna as Lord. The personification of Essence which has no real properties except those special to itself.	To call humans back to the divine soul, to aid enlightenment as to ultimate reality. To make saints, sages and saviours 'in the image of God.' To abolish binary questions and dichotomies.
	The Psychic Belt	The world of great dreams and Archetypes (Jung) Intuition, Clairvoyancy, Telepathy, Telekinesis, Divination etc.	To integrate reason with intuitive activity and imagination. To warn, foretell, discriminate as seers and forerunners of the divine.
The Rational Ego-Conscious World	The Realm of Reason, Analysis and Measure	To see the world of nature as a separate object of cognition, as other than oneself. To 'put edges' to things and to ponder practical means for material means for material aid and political organisation. The realm of morals and ethics.	To create and govern all the organisations of the modern world, its thought, politics, pragmatic standards, material aids, structures, armies, clergy, bureaucrats, educators and law enforcers. To create and pursue formal scientific endeavour.
	The Realm of Compulsion and Obsession	Subsistence in notions of concrete perfection through the ideal political order, the flawless economy, the absolute moral structure, the 'true' religion, the 'final' scientific answer or solution.	In rare cases to help fashion works of genius. In most cases to create rigid moral and social standards in those who might doubt them. To accept the dichotomies of a binary, adversarial world as being final. To convert others to a self-conceived 'truth'.
The Pre-Rational Semi-Conscious World	The Mythic Belt	'The Gods' of antiquity and legend. Man as hero/saviour, woman as earth-personification and lifegiver.	To transform the energies of nature in nature and nature in humankind and to guard and govern phenomena. To make semi-divine forces palpable in the form of legends and stories.

Table 3:   (Cont.)

The Realm of Magic	The sense of the planet as a living organism whose powers may be invoked, harnessed, honoured and replenished. Black magic to do harm; white magic to celebrate normal gifts.	To use vital powers to control the natural instincts of people. To help and heal by worship, ritual, symbols, sacraments and enchantments. To change 'base metal into gold' in the world and in human conduct.
The Archaic Realm of Nature	Animistic, pantheistic consciousness. Sense of oneness with animals, plants and the landscape. No separation of human consciousness from general earth consciousness. The amoral realm.	To abolish ego demands by regressing into a natural orgiastic mode. Sometimes, in modern people, regression into psychosis. To strengthen and serve nature by fusing with its energies. In malign cases, the world of evil and dissolution with which debased people collaborate.

state is what the Buddhists refer to as Nirvana, and Christians as the Kingdom of Heaven.

One of the primary aims, therefore, of a life lived according to this understanding is that one must live out all given things fully and well but try not to harm any creature in doing so. This is not only the 'will of God', as the theologians have conceived it, but an imperative handed down from our higher spiritual nature which has always partaken of the Godhead from the beginning. The final realisation of the metaphysic which emerges is that there can be no transcendental Deity outside the universe, but only Immanence. As the Sufi mystic Rumi remarked: 'He is closer to us than our own breath'.

At this point we have moved a little distance from the obsessive dilemma. I have mentioned something about our likely spiritual destination, but nothing of how we might travel toward it. Yet even to talk of travel and of journeys is to make a mere metaphor in terms of the Ultimate. From the divine perspective, there is ultimately no journey and no 'person' to travel it, because the causes of things lie outside the space–time continuum known by our mundane personality. Thus it may be helpful, following the suggestions of Ken Wilber, to convert his cycle of human development into a 'ladder' (as shown above), including the tormented and divided zone inhabited by the obsessive subject.

This rendering of what is cyclic in vertical form should not be interpreted in terms of 'lower' or 'higher' forms of consciousness except in a purely evolutionary sense, since a Now Universe must embrace all stages in the cycle simultaneously. Moreover, the enlightened or fully realised person in spiritual terms does not shed all the 'lower' experiences in human awareness, as a snake does its skin, but encompasses them all as a totality. As the *philosophia perennis* has always taught, each person is a microcosm of the Macrocosm which contains all the universal elements and possibilities within him or herself. Nevertheless, it can be seen from this scheme that the realm of obsession or compulsion is mainly a 'lower' form of the egoic realm of reason, analysis and measure. It represents a kind of degeneration of even the limited possibilities of rationality, denying it even its *own* flexibility and dynamism. Otherwise as rational beings we could not properly perceive extreme obsessionality as a sickness. There was an ancient hint of this decline from reason into compulsion in religious rather than psychological terms when St Paul wrote in the Epistle to the Romans 7:15–20:

> I cannot understand my own behaviour. I fail to do many things I want to do and I find myself doing the very things I hate. . .the fact is I know nothing of good being in me; that lies in my unspiritual self — for though the will to do what is good is in me, the performance is not. . .

In this famous Pauline passage we are again reminded of two points: the originally religious basis of the obsessional problem in the West and the origin of the Christian struggle *against* nature, instead of seeking wisely to harmonise with its imperatives. If the concept of sin in the Judeo-Christian tradition has any proper meaning, this can only be seen by contrast with the parallel concept of virtue. Both concepts have importance in the social-rational-moral 'bands' of consciousness, but in a superconscious world without binary dilemmas, they are simply irrelevant.

But here is the rub. The overwhelming majority of human beings cannot or do not wish to enter any level of superconscious life. Even those brief episodes arrived at by a few people who still pray, meditate or practise introverting techniques such as yoga, zen or even psychedelic drug-taking cannot be sustained beyond a brief period. Even those folk who can push beyond the ego-conscious dimension into the Psychic Belt often lack the prudence, commonsense and experience to be able to distinguish its higher traits and faculties from those found in the darker Magical-Archaic realms 'below'. Hence the frequent outbreaks of cultism founded on such dangerous hybrid groups as the Moonies,

'channellers', 'rebirthers' and so on — all founded on the longing for
some guru or teacher to show one way out of the labyrinth of modern
ratiocination.

Alas, the understandable refusal of genuinely enlightened teachers
to found socially distorted cults and organisations makes them difficult
to find. Perhaps one of the most significant exceptions to this in the
last half century was the unfairly caricatured though still outrageous
Indian sage, Sri Rajneesh, who permitted every relatively harmless
form of hedonism to luxuriate about him in the hope that a large
enough net might catch a few genuinely enlightened fish.

THE CONDITIONS OF A POST-
OBSESSIONAL CULTURE

The Western world has already developed the basic intellectual and
technical means for rescuing the planet Earth and promoting the relative safety of its occupants. But it can find no agreed way of endeav-
ouring to stand outside the rational-egoic trap of limited conscious life
from which these brilliant means have been devised. Yet where the
heart is paramount, a sufficient spiritual thrust cannot be far behind.
When a world emerges where poets are as read and honoured as economists (as in Ming Dynasty China), where personal meditation is thought
far more important than social agitation, a favourable climate for a
post-obsessional culture will have come about. Action there must be,
and the genius of the West lies in its practical skills. But this action
must be followed against a backdrop of transcendent values and higher
intimations. This means recognising daily that we are in the process of
dying as well as living, and, in the face of that death, every day must
be lived as richly as possible. How strange that this fact was known in
ancient Egypt and yet is barely faced in our time. True genius and true
sanctity have always included an awareness that if we do not live for
the day thereof, there can be no future worth caring about. Mozart
realised this not long before his untimely death at the age of 35 when
he wrote in one of his last letters:

> Since Death, strictly speaking, is the true end-purpose of our life, for
> several years I have made myself so familiar with this true, best
> friend of men that his image holds nothing frightening for me any
> more. . .I never go to bed without considering that perhaps, as young
> as I am, I may not see the next day dawn. And, no-one of all the
> people who knew me would be able to say that I was sullen or sad
> in my relationship toward anyone. . .For this supreme joy, I thank

my Creator every day and wish it to every one of my fellow men from the bottom of my heart.[3]

There is something inherent in a confinement of thinking to the rational-egoic mode that tends to develop toward fixed ideas and a continual preoccupation with the future. This creates the constant peril of a slide into some obsessive-compulsive groove which brings one to the bleakness of a future where there is future no longer, only a series of past challenges ignored or missed.

The rescue of the body

Towards the end of the presidency of Abraham Lincoln, the leader remarked of a high official in his government that he did not like the look of the man's face. Stanton, the Secretary of War, is reported to have protested: 'But Mr President, the poor man cannot help his facial appearance'. Lincoln is reported to have replied wryly: 'Everybody over 40 is responsible for the appearance of his face'.

One of the best clinical discoveries of the unbalanced but brilliant late Freudian Wilhelm Reich was that the ethic of worldly striving and over-achievement could be hostile to both bodily well-being and psychosexual adequacy. While this dictum was later carried to extremes by many of his followers, who preached a cult of perfect orgasm, it is a commonplace discovery in the consulting room that anxious, futuristic patients usually have organic blocks or functional derangements in one or more parts of the body. This merely echoes the insight of Chinese Taoist medicine nearly two millennia ago that misdirected psychic energies can cause a similar serious imbalance of energies in the physical body. Even Western doctors are fully aware that strained, foolish life-modes grouped under the bland euphemism of 'stress' can disrupt digestion, cardiac function, breathing, proper function of joints and sexual satisfaction. In such instances the body is regularly abused yet inordinately worried about, since it is easier to accept a malfunctioning physical organism than accept that one's lifestyle and values are absurd and health threatening.

People who treat their body alternately as a vehicle for excessive desire or the inhibition of desire after the crippled Patristic Christian ethic, or abuse it as a workhorse after the fashion of modern executive capitalism, are hardly likely to rejoice in or celebrate its energies and functions. Also, ethical prejudices and taboos have decreed throughout the Christian centuries that, while a woman's body may be considered either chastely beautiful or an object of lust, a sensuous celebration of the equivalent beauty of the male body, as by classical civilisation, is thought a perverted exercise.

Yet, human skin and fleshly contours in both sexes may seem beautiful to the eye and also a source of great tactile delight to those who touch and are touched. As a variety of psychophysical therapists ranging from Wilhelm Reich to Fritz Perls have pointed out, most Western men in particular are either partly or wholly switched off from the epidermal body as a source of delight. The macho cult of masculine hardness often causes a restriction of tactile pleasure to the genital area alone — a situation foreign to nature. Indeed, Western culture is more agitated by the sexual aspects of male rather than female nudity. Only in hard-core pornography is full-frontal male nudity usually permissible, whereas in respect of the female, the audiovisual media have lately abandoned almost all taboos.

We live in a period in Occidental culture when, prior to AIDS, the more despairingly promiscuous types of homosexual adventure among men were increasing, while women complained that they could rarely find male companions who were not either rigid chauvinists or womanising weaklings. So it seems timely to reject the old required Biblical dichotomy between absolute masculine and absolute feminine as an outworn form of repression that has caused suffering to millions. In its place a healthy measure of androgyny in sex relationships, where strong men can *consciously* accommodate their psychobiological feminine *anima* and confident woman their masculine *animus*, may occur without distorting the assertive and receptive elements in either sex. As for a fundamentally homosexual or bisexual condition, which appears in every known society, there must be a way of accommodating into Western understanding that there is indeed a minority condition of 'intermediate' sexuality that should be subject to no more and no less than the social sanctions that heterosexuals are required to observe. Thus both the significant sexual mythology of the androgyne and its correspondence in modern biology can be accepted without theological taboos. Reproductive function certainly represents something of our sexual destiny, but mere anatomy does not.

Robert Lawlor, an American writer living in Australia, points out that the abuse of new hormonal technology has contributed to the decay of erotic fulfilment even while freeing couples from the burdens of unnecessary reproduction. He notes with anthropologist Lionel Tiger that women who abuse the contraceptive pill walk about in a continual state of virtual pseudo-pregnancy. The consequences for their male partners have rarely been evaluated. But one clue as to what happens when men no longer feel responsible or valued for their sexual potency is the galloping increase in premature ejaculation throughout Western communities. This problem now occurs in about half of all middle-class men from time to time and it shows the pernicious effects of hasty compulsion and self-observation in a culture of *sex à la carte*. Here the sexual event is as haunted by time and the achievement mystique as any other encounter.

Granted his rather overstated bias against Christian culture, Lawlor shrewdly notes that when 'the Christian church repressed and diminished female sexuality, male sexuality diminished with it'. He notes that the drive of men to control and dominate women (reaching a near-psychotic intensity in writers like Norman Mailer) comes from an inner weakness and role-confusion. Male sexual chauvinism is mostly a mask for concealing emotional frigidity and powerlessness. Lawlor's analysis goes far to explain why over-competitive politicised feminism has not so much civilised male sexual conduct as accentuated its primitive anxieties. Men or women who use the conjugal bed for social control rather than private ecstasy play a dangerous game in which mutual delight and respect are the first casualties. Men's remedy for this common situation is to assume full responsibility for *their own* erotic and orgiastic activity, to practise prolongation of sexual feeling in discriminating ways and with far less dependence upon exploiting the female or demanding her endorsement as 'proof' of their masculinity.

All psychophysical therapists have pointed out that most energy blocks in the body are muscular and that the blockage of energy flow caused by muscular tension frequently gives rise to organic disease over time. This is one of the themes of the bioenergetic form of therapy developed by Alexander Lowen. Frequently the location of the bodily tension areas shows a symbolic connection with a particular psychological problem. We recognise this even in our casual language with comments such as 'He makes me sick', or 'She makes my blood boil'. To *get back into* the body, as distinct from identifying cerebrally with its difficulties, is part of the process of freeing ourselves from psychosomatic ailments. Before doing this it is necessary to understand that though we *have* a pain, the pain is not really 'about' us in any essential fashion, that we *have* a disease or malfunction but that the malfunction is not intrinsic to us. It is only when we accept the proposition that our consciousness fully participates in the entire body's energies and is not merely imprisoned in the skull that we can really begin to enjoy the body. Neither to reject or over-identify with our physical self is the fundamental basis of healthy living at the 'centaur' level.

A RETURN OF THE GODS?

One can learn a lot about people in developed communities by the state and content of their homes. Some are pallid, overdelicate pastel places in which nothing stands out and everything is nebulously neat and hygienic; other homes are garish, cluttered and over-coloured environments which thrust their walls at the visitor in aggressive primary colours; others are full of posters, junk objects and fuzzy, squashed furnishings. Another kind of home carries the individuality of the more sensitive tenant in every room — each having the relaxed, lived-in yet tastefully individual character of a whole person. This is a home where every valued possession *means* something, where most things have significance as well as utility. This is a place where the 'gods' might be happy to have a shrine. Does this mean we should once again take up obeisance of household idols and images, as did our remote ancestors? Assuredly not, though it is hardly pagan to say that a beautiful reproduction of a statue of Apollo or Aphrodite might be less jarring than a necrophilic poster of James Dean or Marilyn Monroe or even a poorly executed red-carbuncled picture of a pretty-boy Jesus displaying a Sacred Heart. Also, we must understand how 'the gods', or even the symbols of astrology, can be a type of shorthand for dominant or stunted forces within ourselves.

Having 'the gods' as guests also means a capacity to project our desires outward to cherish and commune with those mythic and symbolic figures which express our noblest and best yearnings. These can include art objects, scenes, books and even good videotapes which prompt that elevation of soul which is so lacking from our loud and gaudy civilisation. One might ask: Would not a baseball star, a film idol or pop-music phenomenon suffice as well? Not if their only function were to do one thing superlatively well, while the rest of the life pattern displayed by this chosen idol is cheaper and even more foolish than our own. The stuff of mythic heroes and heroines of old — Perseus, Theseus, Eurydice, Arthur and Lancelot, Joan of Arc — was much larger than life. All their attributes and lineaments were cut according to noble mythic contours; even their faults had something of the stuff of a demigod or goddess. A freakishly skilled sportsman separating from his third wife, a pop-music star who has recently killed himself by driving too fast under the influence of drugs, or a tragic film star who has debauched herself with alcohol, are often just tragic zanies, even to themselves. So why celebrate or identify with such fallen and corrupted figures? By contrast, perhaps some courageous, meditative space traveller could be our new Icarus, the founder of a great hospital another Demeter, a great and worshipful scientist a modern Parsifal.

The mythology of heroes and heroines in every age is still worth teaching in classrooms and holding up to youth — even if we must sometimes put this in the wrappings of science fiction and swaddle it in the shining armour of elegantly simple apparel. But somehow we *must* have them. Such mythologies are far more nourishing to the soul than the views of debunkers and petty demythologisers who have turned the modern world into a mental desert with their sceptical derision.

In the nineties the home and the private room seem about the only remaining refuges for the mementoes and tokens of demigods of the more potent sort, be they pre-Christian, Christian or merely post-religious. The dismal post-Bauhaus gravestone architecture typical of the new cities of Europe, North America and Australia provides little room for meditation or communion with myth or our own mythic levels. Indeed there seems more variety in the trash-filled vacant lots such clinical architecture has come to replace. In order to recover, let alone understand, something of its mythic heritage, the deprived youth of the West is forced to revisit remaining old buildings, cathedrals or museums. Language scholar George Steiner has dubbed much of the trade of the humanities in North America as 'a museum culture'. Here, Western artifacts and books are lovingly preserved and computer cross-indexed, but they bear very few inspired modern progeny. As classicist Allan Bloom commented plaintively a few years ago, the campuses of the US in particular are plentifully populated with quite nice young people who know a lot of slick worldly-wise things but nothing about Western culture in any depth.

Without a sounder appreciation of the psychological and 'soul' importance of honouring god-figures and heroic examplars, the intelligent modern young will find it very difficult to chart a healing path through the maze of peer-group fads, cut-rate media cults and embryo scientisms which daily clamour for their allegiance. When young people are eventually disillusioned by these influences and when their propagators turn out to be cheats or neurotics, it is unlikely that they will turn back easily to Homer, Dante, Arthurian legend, the great poets or even the New Testament. Without a soul-map they will turn again to the brittle dichotomies of power-politics as did their fathers and mothers, losing their way amid the same structural totems and abstractions which give no nourishment for the world's hunger for love and light. The desperate time is not far off when any small room stocked with a few great books and images of great souls and epic deeds, any quiet space where a mat or a cushion can be unrolled for silent communion with the self or a beloved friend, will become a temple no less important than that of churches where one partakes of communion and hears the words of the Christ.

Part of soul-making in the mythic mode is also deeply connected to our relationship with the natural world. When Westerners turn to nature it is too often with the alienated gapings and camera-clicking of tourism (ironically caricatured by visiting Japanese detached from the deep natural awareness held by their ancestors) or under the macho delusion that sweating, skydiving and canoeing could represent a deep communion with the subtleties of mountain, field or forest. Even today when Japanese attempt to join with the spirits of nature and their ancestors, it is often amid the great forests of inland Nippon where the most cherished Shinto-Buddhist shrines have long been situated. Human connections with nature are best attained in a receptive mood and approached in personal stillness or companionable quietude. Painters and poets do not deal with nature from an automobile or with a portable CD player but pause to let the face of nature unite with their inward eye. Thus objective and subjective can briefly fuse into a single heightened awareness. For a time, at least, the unhappy amputations of consciousness in our world can be healed.

How can high mythic imagining be therapeutic? Simply because what we *identify* with, we tend imperceptibly to become *like* — not merely a copy, but perhaps partly *become*. Much as the pregnant woman in ancient Athens was taught to look upon beautiful images and contemplate godly things in the hope that her child might be born with the same beauty, so, in a far more real way, does strong heroic envisioning make a possibility of a heroic enlargement of ourselves. Similarly, identification with the great images of 'the gods' and of great folk and deeds — be they historical or legendary — helps us to push back ever so marginally the banal boundaries set by ego-consciousness. None of this should be dismissed as idle daydreaming. We must constantly remind ourselves that there are no boundaries to consciousness but those mental conditioning and custom have set for us. Only the iron clamps of our supine ego-habits hold us back from a whole view.

Perhaps some future manned expedition to Mars may create the beginning of a new mythology built upon an enlarged consciousness of our role as a tiny microcosm of a great universe. As Captain Edgar

Mitchell, one of the first astronauts, was reported to have remarked: 'There are no atheists on the moon'. It is surely not too much to hope that an extraterrestrial loosening of the purely *physical* bonds which hold us so tightly to our social institutions and prejudices might help to push back the frontiers of consciousness itself.

TOWARDS MINIMAL STRUCTURES

Has our so-called global village become too overbuilt and crowded for any human intimacy beyond that of the kitchen or the bedroom? If so, the dictum of E. F. Schumacher that 'small is beautiful' needs a respectful second hearing. It is worth examining each major societal process in turn.

Politics

The world has grown weary of a century and a half of ideologies — communism, socialism, fascism and liberalism. The means of their departure should be hastened. The nation-state simply needs competent government from wise people and the form that this takes is irrelevant. Even so, constitutional monarchy, as it operates in countries as disparate as Britain, Spain and Thailand, offers the best compromise between tradition and innovation that an imperfect world can offer. The compulsion to set up the Franco-American variety of 'democratic' republicanism in every emerging nation should be abandoned, as should the accompanying fallacy that *any* kind of political machinery can hope to guarantee social equality. The best form of government is the one that allows the best and noblest executive talents to exercise authority, as long as the possibilities of those who have little talent or spiritual stature are not smothered by those who have much. Preparation of well-seasoned social elites for government upon modified Platonic lines seems ultimately inescapable if future societies are to enjoy a large measure of external order and contentment. Democracy is noble only when worthily attained. Otherwise it becomes another abstraction hindering acceptance of reality.

Politics must cease to be a form of therapy for unhappy or alienated citizens. The world has already suffered appallingly from the failure of communities to heal such people or suppress their mischief. If citizens are to develop spiritually and mature emotionally they will need a stable public framework in which to promote the opportunity. Political change will occur from time to time, though change has no intrinsic value. There is already ample change in life, nature and social intercourse without worshipping it as an abstract political principle. For the rest, a humane conservatism that accepts the natural occurrence of hierarchy in human affairs is worth respectful recognition. This is certainly better than putting up with the concealed conventions of rationalised envy and obsessive ambition which are used to energise political activity in most Western nations.

Economic life

Economic theory and practice is generally weakened by a sad deficiency in psychological understanding. In all modern discussions of production, income and wealth there is a tendency to reduce living people to units of consumption. The successors of Adam Smith, the father of the untrammelled free market, seem either social Darwinists or secular Calvinists at heart, the accumulation of wealth and power providing them with its *own* vindication, sometimes completely ignoring how this is achieved. In an age of amoral advertising and mass media saturation 'the unseen hand' of the market does not function naturally, but *forces* countless consumers toward a preconceived goal. Meanwhile the complicity of financial systems in promoting wealth based upon pyramids of debt encourages an economy where money as a medium of exchange has less and less real relationship to the goods or labour it represents.

At the other extreme the State in socialist systems has failed to fill any valid or competent role as an entrepreneur, however useful its role might be as an economic *regulator*. The State arguably still has a role as a watchdog, lest the limitless greed of a few threatens the welfare of all. But for all its lumbering starts and halts, the capitalist economy, with the state and the international community acting as watchful sentinels, seems the best compromise available. Economic theorists from Smith to Marx and Keynes, Friedman and Hayek to Galbraith have all made useful criticisms and recommendations for the conduct and regulation of economic activity. The economic practices of the future should be pragmatic rather than dogmatic.

Economics still awaits its grand synthesiser of allegedly irreconcilable views. Nevertheless, the belief in production and consumption to virtual infinity, regardless of population and environmental factors, has had its day. A 'steady state' economy is practically unattainable in the long term, but there may have to be a measure of international consensus as to its short-term enforcement in times of human and ecological crisis. Waste, redundance and pollution as economic byproducts are rapidly becoming handicaps the world can no longer afford to tolerate.

Ethics and the law

One of the consequences of the turning of conventional representative government into a type of civil-cum-moral theology over the past 200 years has been to create a clamour about what are too loosely termed 'human rights'. Such 'rights' are essentially about what is permissible in *external* social conduct. As will be noted from earlier chapters, once basic liberties of thought, expression, trade and worship are granted in any community, any increase in demand for 'human rights' is likely to be a social projection of human bondage to the ego. By contrast, family life, education and other institutions in their well-meaning way, have all conspired to implant guilts rooted in some egotistic failure to *achieve* as the chief controlling agent in human conduct — whether such achievement be seen as moral or merely material. Thus, even in a post-Christian epoch we still labour under the burdens of a guilt-culture rather than a shame-culture. Shame arises from a deed or a specific violation of a social norm. Guilt is tied to the less understood notion of *remission*, the inner liberation of the soul from the lingering psychological consequences of having been disposed to do wrong — that which theology once defined as 'original sin'. In dispensing with the Catholic confessional, Protestantism dispensed in large measure with the remission of guilt for this propensity to do wrong. The secular world had to find an antidote, or rather a distraction, from the sense of *not* having its sins remitted with a permissive fever for material, political and social achievement.

The long-term effect of a confusion between remission and permission in human affairs has led to a quasi-democratic society where citizens are often punished too leniently for serious criminal acts but still writhe in torments of guilt or social inadequacy over deficiencies that have nothing to do with courts of law or serious wrongdoing. Unfortunately an ever-present sense of guilt puts an almost permanent brake upon any move into higher consciousness. A man who is constantly preoccupied with his deficiencies, be they secular or religious, is not likely to look very high towards the light. The West has lately created consumption-compelled communities that support a culture of greed and vulgarity which could well evoke some measure of shame but instead are treated as a subject for humour, excitement or cynicism. Insider trading on stock-market exchanges that amounts to stealing unearned wealth, failing to pay personal debts, producing lewd and sick items for the corruption of children, brawling upon sports arenas instead of playing games with gallantry — all these practices have become commonplace in Western modern communities. They should be a subject for shame, even social contempt. Yet, under some specious policy for personal 'rights', such sleaziness continues unchecked. Life loses a large amount of continuity and dignity in precisely those public areas where a stricter imposition of taboos could not harm inner freedom for the mind and soul and could even benefit their health. A distinction between private fault and public offence is not hypocritical but necessary.

A remissive yet non-permissive culture would do much to relax those systems of 'self-denial' and 'self-control' on which so-called open societies have depended, but which are now observably crumbling in all English-speaking communities. Guilt-based moral and legal systems only tend to create fear and obsession in already sensitive people while presenting but a feeble deterrent to those criminals who have not fully accepted such social taboos during their educative years.

Unlike those cultures founded upon the Judeo-Christian ethic, those inspired by Buddhism, Hinduism and Tao-Confucianism are not overwhelmingly dominated by moral imperatives. Nor are they particularly concerned to inspire long-term guilt. Shameworthy behaviour, on the other hand, is fully deplored, as is dishonourable and uncompassionate conduct towards others. Punishments in Eastern cultures traditionally have been inspired by the simple principle of cause and effect. Disturbances in the social order, such as wilful damage to persons and the surrounding world, have both social and physical as well as spiritual (or karmic) consequences. Accordingly, individual life in Eastern cultures has not been 'cheap' as the popular Western canard has it; it has been treated as one tiny twig of a great social tree. If this twig is seen to be diseased, it is better to cut it off. Hence, stringent punishment for serious crime, including the use of the death penalty, has never been regarded in the East with the quibblings and sentimental revulsion of Western thought. Recourse to mercy has indeed been available, but for the unrelentingly violent person only equal severity in return has seemed just and appropriate. Retribution for extreme wrongdoing once not only removed the wrongdoer; it also atoned for the shame felt by his or her community. In the West, retribution has been lately equated in a maudlin fashion with vengeance. Thus for the first time in millennia there are confused doubts whether the State as representative of the communal order has the 'right' to terminate life at all.

The implications of these reflections for proper law enforcement are clear. Punishment should indeed fit the crime in every case where extenuating circumstances based upon obvious mental derangement or mistaken intent fail to apply. This means a restoration of a prompt, humanely conducted death penalty in rare extreme cases of cruel and premeditated capital crime where there is *no doubt whatever* as to the culprit or his or her intent. The ethical law of cause and social effect should apply without legal chicanery. There should be less emphasis on fantasies about the 'rehabilitation' of many offenders where the prospect of their reform is based upon little but sentiment and hope. Normative statistical arguments about the effects of punishment cannot apply conveniently to specific individuals and they are irrelevant to the question of just retribution.

If such a view seems harsh, it is because so many social theorists have no conception of the spiritual damage wrought by a relativist social code which lacks the courage of its convictions beyond a feeling that death or permanent confinement are nasty things that are better not implemented (but that we inconsistently inflict by the hecatomb during wars and social upheaval anyway).

Education

From once being a process of rote learning and physically enforced indoctrination, the education of the young has lately advanced so far into the permissive Helping Mode that children have become lost for lack of consistent adult direction. Formal schooling should offer a simple microcosm of the social rules and skills for which the young are being prepared. Teachers should forsake 'therapeutic' aims and adjourn to their proper business of instructing children in knowledge of the world around them and also in those intellectual devices by which the processes of the world are approached and harnessed. When a whole society again shows openly that greed, violence and depravity are to be discouraged without exception, there will be little need to teach the 'ought' imperative or for the obsessive anxieties it fosters. 'Have I done wrong?' is a question no child should often need to ask. In a sane society, the very construction of life around him or her should make the answer all too clear. The chief problem with ethical systems in schools is that they are frequently contradictory and self-defeating. Freedom can be confused with licence or prejudice; what applies in one case does not apply in another. The child is often perpetually unclear as to the sort of boundaries to behaviour his or her future community will require. Yet, within quite firm outer boundaries, an educational institution can still encourage a measure of joy, spontaneity, inner freedom and creativity.

Schools and educational institutions that make bold claims to 'form character' should be regarded with some suspicion. A society with firm, consistent rules for the behaviour of its citizens should have no trouble *socially* structuring the conduct of children without constantly invading their inner consciousness. Contrary to what many developmental psychologists have taught, to substitute the guilty 'you ought' for the shameworthy 'you must', hardly confers the sort of freedom that a society with pretensions to democracy habitually adores. Much of what we believe to be 'conscience' in fact is often part of an ossified guilt system, which has very little relationship to our higher spiritual nature. Ideally those working towards enlightenment practise virtue and avoid reprehensible behaviour because they realise that their spiritual nature requires no less. Meanwhile for those who are sceptical of any such higher nature (and this includes the bulk of Western humanity) it is better to have community sanctions based upon the penalty of outwardly imposed shame than to condition people cruelly into a sense of chronic unworthiness.

The family

Since the human creature is in need of intimate nurture for a prolonged period, family life and parenthood must remain of central importance in any remissive culture. As R. D. Laing pointed out, the most enduring and exquisite of all psychological cruelties can be wrought by misguided parents and relatives. Most chronic neuroses still begin in the home. Hence parents should understand three basic principles before bringing life into the world:

1. They are not the owners of their offspring, but caring stewards of future spiritual beings who ultimately must be left in charge of their own destiny.
2. The manipulation of children by instilling some perverted guilt about parental feelings, needs and convictions is an abomination. Children are not ultimately responsible for their parents' emotional happiness and comfort. Parenting cannot occur in reverse. Any generosity of offspring towards elders should be spontaneous rather than demanded.
3. Children must not be treated as a means of extending the life of the parental ego beyond the grave. Ideally the only legacy relatives should leave behind them is a loving and grateful memory. If offspring are merely to replicate the desires of their parents, humanity could never develop according to those universal imperatives of which it is a part.

The chief soul-function of the family is to provide primary models for child identification. If a mother is wise, consistent and kind, she will not require guilt-evocation and emotional blackmail to hold her children's love. If a father is firm and affectionately supportive he will not need excessive authoritarian postures or bullying rationalisations to support his decisions.

In the meantime some realistic attention should be given to the size of families on an increasingly crowded planet. Enforced sterilisation of couples by the State is not only deeply repugnant — it does not work, as the assassination of Mrs Indira Gandhi by resentful fundamentalist fanatics made clear. Even so, procreation for procreation's sake without regard to the psychological, physical or economic capacity of parents must no longer be viewed as a respectable option. Deeper understanding should rightly see parents as co-partners with divinity by not only bearing children, but rearing them with discrimination and good sense. Any two imbeciles can produce a child but it is that same child who is the suffering legatee of their folly. Meanwhile a 'ceiling' upon the number of children born to each family might be required in every society where the national trend toward a near steady-state birthrate is not already apparent. Human dignity is not quantitative but *qualitative*. A plethora of jostling human creatures hardly makes for the spiritual progress of individuals. Over-large families battling at subsistence levels mostly have little time to devote to higher human development.

Less religion and more spirituality?

After two millennia formal Christianity arguably faces its greatest crisis since the conversion of Constantine. Most Protestant creeds have become an anachronism. The original justification for their foundation — the corruption and the overweening pretensions of the medieval Great Church from which they once rebelled — has now receded into history. Much of the extreme Biblical fundamentalism practised by many Protestant sects has become the haven of bigots or fools. The more moderate major Protestant denominations have lately become so entangled in secular causes that they are losing both their congregations and any sense of spiritual mission. Great souls still flourish in all congregations but Protestantism as a larger movement no longer has anywhere to go. Catholicism too has become dangerously secularised since the Second Vatican Council, while its one-time strengths — its healing sacramental system, its old liturgy and its godly minor cults — have beome so eroded that part of what Pope Pius X condemned as 'modernism' before World War I has become the norm. Meanwhile the

obsession of the Catholic hierarchy with sex and procreation has continued without pause, making many of the angry faithful wonder if the
Church is more preoccupied with the liturgy of the phallus than with
the Living Christ. Only parts of Eastern Orthodoxy have endeavoured
to hold fast to the mystic Lord of the higher paths. Alas, Orthodoxy
has been socially weakened over the centuries by the incursions of
Islam and Communism into the old Byzantine heartlands.

It is therefore more necessary than ever before for courageous Christians to retrace their steps back to Apostolic times, asking along the
way whether the Church had not partly mislaid its original purpose,
even by the end of the 2nd century AD. The two most execrated of
early heresies — those of the Gnostic groups and Arianism — had as
large a following as the main Church body before they were harshly
suppressed by Catholic authorities with the support of imperial power.
Are Christians so sure that history has treated either of these impressive deviant movements with honesty and truth? Where did the contribution of the Holy Spirit end and that of human expediency and
intolerance begin?

Regardless of the answers to such questions, the greatest flaw of all
three major monotheistic religions has been their credal imperialism
and their recurring stance of 'our way and no other'. Entire civilisations, for both better and worse, have been wiped out or absorbed by
Christian and Islamic missionary evangelism. Both are linked with
Judaism to Yahweh of Sinai who has been indeed a jealous god. In the
face of such jealousy it is only human for many rebels to adopt the
posture of the tortured Job and protest that none of us can be true to
less than the divine spark each bears within. Any man or woman
deprived of hope has the right to choose even his or her own abyss. In
that respect the old gods were kinder, for they shared and understood
human frailty.

In the meantime only something of a 'scorched earth' policy can
sustain what is left of the Great Church for the third millennium.
Whether followed by church leaders or not, there are simplifications
likely to assist its survival. First, religious groups should move out of
the territory of social policy, which they have increasingly occupied
since the Middle Ages. The fiction of attainable 'social justice' based
on the fallacious Aristotelian abstraction of 'natural law' should be
abandoned. People may assuredly be directed to the Ten Commandments in their original, straightforward understanding. But clerical
attitudes related to the socio-economic order should be chiefly concerned with the *individually* disadvantaged and afflicted. Sociology posing

as theology should be condemned as fraudulent. Religion should be regarded as properly bound up with worship, ritual, fraternal affection, service of the afflicted and, above all, the enhancement of higher human consciousness. Ecclesiastics should not meddle with economic and political processes. The outmoded operations of canon law concerning personal relationships should be curtailed: contraception and birth regulation, for example, should be a civil issue for married folk, not for popes or theologians.

Finally, the smug aphorism 'God chastises his own' suggests a caricatured Judeo-Christian ethic which dimly recognises that the guilt culture it has inspired often punishes the already scrupulous rather than effectively reforming the sinner. It is difficult to imagine the real Christ of the Gospels approving of such a grotesque idea. A conscience based mostly upon guilt must also be based to some extent upon anxiety and low self-esteem — certainly not upon honour or affection. While suffering is an inevitable part of the evolving human condition, none but a witless Deity indeed would add gratuitously to its burden. Even if the orthodox doctrine of the Redemption, that Jesus suffered for our sins, is true, the Church-inspired conclusion that those who believe in Christ must either engineer or immerse themselves in some special misery simply does not follow. If it did, then Nietzsche's savage taunt against Christianity as a religion fit only for slaves would have a point.

TOWARDS ULTIMATE SUBJECTIVITY

The present enthronement of what is loosely termed 'Science' in Western nations is as inappropriate for the psychological and spiritual needs of a compulsive, addicted culture as are Sir Peter Medawar's robustly urged 'massive applications of technology'. The *central* task of humankind should be a broadening and deepening of its own connection with the cosmic experience of which it is a part. Our virtually compulsive convention of 'hands-on' scientific endeavour, however practical and useful, permits no way of weighing, valuing or even evading something as basic as consciousness itself. Science constantly *objectifies* and, in doing so, runs convenient but essentially false divisions through the seamless fabric of the universe. Particle physicists and cosmologists, on the other hand, know only too well the frustrations of an enquiry in which basic matter and energy seem to continually shrink away from being caught in our observers' net. As Werner Heisenberg has pointed out, we have no cognitive-sensory means to apprehend nature *in itself*. What we see, measure and harness is merely filtered

through the attachments and limitations of our own cerebral equipment. As long as intellectuals can regularly remind themselves of this
fact, obsessive arrogance in scientific and technical endeavour can be
avoided.

Mystics of all faiths agree that 'objectivity' is an ever-receding mirage.
Despite the wonderful uses of applied science, there can ultimately be
only that Total Subjectivity which underlies and informs all things.
Ultimate Subjective Reality lies hidden beyond the egoic space–time
slot in which we pass our lives. The divine purpose of this vast egoic
time-trap is surely the Mystery of Mysteries upon which poets and
philosophers have exhausted their speculative vocabularies. As one of
the most eminent of astronomers has remarked in common with many
colleagues: 'The universe is not only more astonishing than we imagine, it is more astonishing than we *can* imagine.'

Put in conventional theological terms, God can never be known
objectively by the mind. He/She/It can only be *experienced*. While all
of us are supported by the same Total Subjectivity, our separate experiences of it cannot be normed, measured or intellectually verified. If
only we could accept this humbly and busy ourselves with our own
experiential enlightenment, most of the problems of our planet would
be solved. These problems originally proceeded from our own inner
conflicts. As Lao Tzu taught long ago, there can be no such thing as
an *independent external* problem. Fundamentally there never has been
such a problem because the very concepts of 'inner' and 'outer' have
no ultimate meaning. The conflicts we have known for so many centuries are nothing more than powerfully materialised egoic hallucina-
tions — tangible projections of our own divided natures. Hence, we
must try to become scientists working upon our own souls — virtual
technologists of experience itself.

TOWARDS A SCIENCE OF SELF

If such propositions seem doubtful, there are numerous personal experiments and techniques which should be able to convince most people
that they are more than the sum of their thought processes. As a
simple exercise, take a watch and decide firmly that you will watch its
second hand for a period of thirty seconds, allowing no other thought,
consideration or object of attention to disturb your focus. As time
elapses you will find that the effort is exceedingly difficult because
thoughts, impressions and flashes of both internal and external cognition will keep intruding themselves. Yet what does become apparent is
that there is some entity which *wills* us to keep concentrating upon the

second hand, while our thought-life takes on an impetus of its own. Concepts race around like independent squirrels trying to breach our single-minded state of attention — but this state is our true Ground.

Most of the higher principles of meditation and contemplation taught by mystical Christianity, Zen and Higher Yoga are merely sophisticated elaborations of this simple experimental approach. Here we seek to *disidentify* with our thought contents until we come to a clear realisation that there is Something within us which is fully conscious, willing and subjectively knowing, but which is not part of the intellectualising process. We merely *have* our thoughts, or in the majority of distracted instances, our thoughts tend to have *us*. Yet this fundamental act of disidentifying, of stepping back from thought, if it could be practised long enough, brings us back to the Basic Ground of consciousness. All the divisions and boundaries between us and the world might then begin to become transparent. This can often be a disturbing experience for the person normally locked into the egoic mode, and the obsessive-compulsive personality is more terrified than most. So the resistances provided by thoughts, reservations, questions, speculations and quibbles resume and we remain too full of uneasy doubt to proceed any further. A simple exercise that could well be practised daily should run somewhat like this:

Sickness and ill health has afflicted me, but I am not my sickness; I merely *have* a sickness. Thoughts teem through my head every day, but I am not my thoughts; I merely *have* my thoughts. I am not really anxious; I merely *have* anxiety. I am not compelled; I merely *have* a compulsion. I *have* a body but *that* which lies at the core of my being is not my body.

In this way, a measure of detachment from human ills is possible; and they can be remedied much more rapidly by the natural processes of mental and physical healing. This occurs because of our regular acts of disidentification with our problems. The process of obsessive identification with such problems is what reinforces and exacerbates them. In some cases an inability to disidentify from a problem creates a problem in itself. Alternatively prayer — if it is absorbed and humble enough — can achieve the same process of disidentification with the life of the ego. For the ego can never be holy — or know wholeness — because of what it constantly excludes.

Seen from the analytical viewpoint of the ego-mind, such recommendations will seem to encourage an indifference to the practical world. It is all too easy to mistake an effort at wise detachment for apathy. But if we reflect upon so many centuries of passionate intellectual meddling, on the part of those who are too ego-involved, with the problems of the people of this world, such a recommendation makes for good healthy sense. The Buddha taught that only the detached person can serve real justice and give practical compassion. Careful consideration of our bloody history suggests that he was right. The greatest misfortune of Christianity occurred when it turned aside, during the time of the early Fathers and after the conversion of Constantine, from the aim of pursuing spiritual love and enlightenment to become too immersed in reforming the moral and civil order. Probably Western civilisation would be the poorer in terms of great art, learning and social service had the Church not held to this course. Yet in so far as such socio-moral absorption distracted the main body of Christians from Jesus' invitation to partake of the Christ-spirit of which he was the living bearer, it became the basis of obsessions that created a barrier to the very spiritual freedom which he promised. In this way Christians became history's first clearly recognisable group of over-achievers. The distorted idea of having made a covenant with God to 'save' the world of time, matter and mundane affairs all but crushed the delicate insight that the kingdom of Heaven is Now. The only real Second Coming could be within the heart of each human being.

We cannot return to the time of the ancient gods, but we can grasp the fact that, for the great mass of contemporary humanity, spiritual reality can still only be sensed and adored under emblematic forms. 'Polytheism' and 'pantheism' therefore are only swear words hurled at nonconformists by the rigidly orthodox. The Everlasting Formless God wears many masks. It is not really blasphemous to personify or even revere these masks as pagans did and still do. Any uplifting spiritual force which is given palpable life and embodied meaning is better than those cold secular abstractions under which we struggle in the post-Christian age: as long as we do not mistake mythic forms for the ineffable Divine Essence that such forms conceal and yet partly reveal. William Blake, the visionary poet often dismissed by people with no imagination as a madman, caught the thrust of this notion when he wrote ecstatically:

What, it will be questioned 'when the Sun rises, do you not see a round disc of fire, somewhat like a guinea?' (I reply) Oh no, no, I see an Innumerable Company of the Heavenly Host crying 'Holy, holy is the Lord God Almighty'. I question not my corporeal or vegetative eye any more than I would question a window concerning my sight. But I look thro' it, and not with it.[4]

The circle of argument is closed. Obsessive-compulsive people partly represent individual parodies of modern Western culture itself. If they could only shed, from time to time, the endless layers of intellectual conditioning that hold them captive, they might become again astonished children in the garden of God — the sort of children whom Jesus fondly referred to as belonging to the Kingdom of Heaven. Unless we embrace the glory and pain of existence without rationalisation in terms of its *own* present manifestations, there can be no cure for our living except our dying. For those who can again glimpse the primal and the ultimate Light, death is only a punctuation point before attaining that peace which surpasses all intellectual understanding. When Christ bade us love our neighbour as ourselves, the rendering of that seemingly impossible demand probably was not fully understood, even by many of his first hearers. If we could realise that, in the profoundest sense, our neighbour *is* ourself — the only Indivisible Self that there can be — then everything in the universe could be ours.

NOTES

Following comments in the text I have tried to heed my own strictures concerning the custom of obsessively detailed notation. I have cited the origin of quotations only where convention requires and left the reader to follow such indications for wider reading as seems helpful. This is a book as much polemical as scholarly, and takes liberties accordingly.

Prologue

The literature of obsessive-compulsive disorders is extensive and this chapter represents in itself a distillation of thirty years' experience in clinically dealing with the disorder. In approaching this syndrome, as in the case of many others, one finds too many contending views, with a sensible eclecticism as the common casualty. Despite its fashionable bias toward organic explanations, *The Boy Who Could Not Stop Washing* by Judith Rapoport, Fontana/Collins, 1990, offers one of the most accessible discussions of obsessive-compulsive disorders for a lay person. A broader, more detailed view is obtained from the symposium *Obsessional States*, edited by H. R. Beech, Methuen/Harper & Row, 1974.

Novels, of course, abound with various studies of obsession, Raskolnikov in *Crime and Punishment*, Heathcliff and Cathy in *Wuthering Heights* and Captain Ahab in *Moby Dick* being only three famous examples. These figures, however, are rather larger than real life.

[1]   Bronislav Malinowski, *Sex and Repression in Savage Society*, Routledge, London, 1934, p. 77.

2   Carl Jung, *Psychological Reflections* (ed. J. Jacobi), Bollingen/Pantheon Books, New York, 1953.

3   The reference to C. G. Jung's comment that the 'gods have become diseases' can be expanded as follows: 'The gods have become diseases; Zeus no longer rules Olympus but rather the solar plexus and curious specimens for the doctor's consulting room.' C. G. Jung, *Collected Works*, Routledge & Kegan Paul, London, 1959, vol. 13, p. 54.

Chapter 1: The time of the gods

1   Cited by Joseph Campbell, *The Masks of God*, Viking Press, vol. 2, New York or Secker & Warburg, London, p. 84.

2   Ibid. p. 88.

3   Cited by William McQuitty, *The Wisdom of the Ancient Egyptians*, Sheldon Press, London, 1978, p. 84.

4   From the notes, L. W. King, *A History of Babylon*, Chatto & Windus, London, 1919, p. 172.

5   Plato, *The Apologia* (trans. Jowett), vol. 7 in *The Great Books Series*, Encyclopaedia Britannica, 1952.

6   Plato, *The Phaedo* (trans. Jowett), vol. 7 in *The Great Books Series*, Encyclopaedia Britannica, 1952.

7   Cited by Dean Inge, *The Philosophy of Plotinus*, vol. 1, Longmans Green, London, 1948, p. 199.

8   This defence made by Porphyry to answer Christian critics appears to have an uncertain source. However, it is virtually a looser paraphrase of the statement from Porphyry's teacher Plotinus in *The Enneads* (trans. McKenna), Faber, London, 1956, Book IV, paras. 3, 11.

Chapter 2: Christianity and perfectionism

Scripture quotations cited in this chapter and in Chapter 7 derive from *The Jerusalem Bible*, Darton, Longman & Todd, London, 1968.

1   Cited by Morton Hunt, *The Natural History of Love*, Alfred Knopf, New York, 1959, p. 96 (from early Latin sources).

2   Jerome, Ibid. p. 115.

3   Robin Lane Fox, *Pagans and Christians*, Viking/Penguin, London, 1986, p. 34.

4   Carl Jung, *Psychological Reflections — A Jung Anthology*, (Ed. J. Jacobi) Bollingen/Pantheon Books, New York, 1949, p. 311.

5   Ibid., p. 310.

6   John Calvin, *Institutes of the Christian Religion*, (trans. Beveridge) vol. 2, James Clarke Ltd, London, 1949, Chapter 5, para. 19.

7   Richard Hooker, *Of the Laws of Ecclesiastical Polity*, Everyman Dent, London, 1907, p. 107.
8   Cited in René Fulop-Miller, *Leaders, Dreamers and Rebels*, (trans. E. and C. Paul), Harrap & Co., London, 1935, p. 39.

Chapter 3: The worship of abstraction
1   Louis de Saint-Just, *Oeuvres Completes*, cited in René Fulop-Miller, op. cit., p. 166.
2   Thomas Jefferson, *American Historical Documents 1000–1904*, P. F. Collier & Son, New York, 1938, p. 150.
3   Isaac Newton, *Opticks; or a Treatise on. . .Light*, Dover Press, New York, 1952, pp. 399–400.
4   John Stuart Mill, *Autobiography*, Oxford World Classics, Oxford, p. 92.
5   Nietzsche, from a letter to Richard Wagner. Precise source not cited, but the same sentiment is scattered liberally throughout Nietzsche's *Beyond Good and Evil* in *The Philosophy of Nietzsche*, Modern Library, New York, 1927.
6   Karl Marx, *Das Kapital*, vol. 1, Modern Library, New York, 1932, p. 648.

Chapter 4: The rise and decline of intimacy
1   Philippe Ariés, *Centuries of Childhood* (trans. R. Baldick), Alfred Knopf, New York, 1962, p. 403.
2   Lloyd de Mause (ed.), *The History of Childhood*, Souvenir Press Ltd, London, 1976, Chapter 1.
3   Edward Shorter, *The Making of the Modern Family*, Collins, London, 1976.
4   V. and M. Goertzel, *Cradles of Eminence*, Little, Brown & Co., Boston, 1962.
5   Denis de Rougement, *Passion and Society*, Faber, London, 1956.
6   Jonathan Gathorne-Hardy, *Love, Sex, Marriage and Divorce*, Jonathan Cape, London, 1981.

Chapter 5: Salvation through structures
1   William Broad and Nicolas Wade, *Betrayers of the Truth: Fraud and Deceit in the Halls of Science*, Touchstone/Simon & Schuster, New York, 1983, pp. 130–1.

Chapter 6: Counterfeits of life
1   Neil Postman, *Amusing Ourselves to Death*, Heinemann, London, 1986 (Quote by author, from blurb).
2   Ibid. p. 159.

3   Ibid. p. 163.
4   Michael Shallis, *The Silicon Idol*, Oxford University Press, Oxford, 1985, p. 154.
5   George Steiner, *In Bluebeard's Castle*, Faber, London, 1971, p. 90.
6   Confucius, cited by David Fame, *The Secret Power of Music*, Turnstone Press, Northamptonshire, 1984, p. 34.
7   William James, *The Will to Believe and Other Essays in Popular Philosophy*, Longmans Green, New York, 1911, p. 256.
8   Philip Rieff, *The Triumph of the Therapeutic*, Harper & Row, New York, 1966, pp. 57–9.
9   Michael Jenike, *New England Journal of Medicine*, 24 August 1989.
10   Prof. Robert Spillane, interview in the *Australian*, 26 March 1987.

Chapter 7: Beyond obsession
1   Ken Wilber, *Eye to Eye*, Anchor/Doubleday, New York, 1983.
2   Ibid., p. 251.
3   W. A. Mozart, cited by Bruno Walter, *New York Times*, Feb. 1956 (from *Collected Letters*).
4   William Blake, from *Notebooks 1810*. Cited by Michael Davis, *William Blake — A New Kind of Man*, Paul Elek, London, 1977, p. 133.

BIBLIOGRAPHICAL NOTES

The citation of good general background histories of Western civilisation would appear unnecessary as these are too numerous to need listing. However, I am greatly indebted to the work of René Fulop-Miller, *Leaders, Dreamers and Rebels*, (translated by E. and C. Paul from the German) G. G. Harrap and Co., London, 1935. Fulop-Miller's skilful survey of the numerous would-be redemptive mass-movements of history and their obsessively messianic movers seems to me unsurpassed by any subsequent book on the subject. For a genetic-biological approach to the rise and geographical dispersal of races, religions and political systems, C. D. Darlington, *The Evolution of Man and Society*, Simon and Schuster, New York, 1969, is indispensable. Similarly, Barrington Moore Jr in his *Social Origins of Dictatorship and Democracy*, Penguin, London, 1967, is valuable, despite an evident socialist bias, in permitting the reader to see how recent and fragile our present popular notions of political and social orthodoxy really are.

Since religions and mythic beliefs are also inextricably interwoven with obsessive-compulsive individual and social attachments, two major works might be consulted. The first is Mircea Eliade, *A History of Religious Ideas*, 3 vols (translated from the French by Trask, Hiltebeitel and Apostolos-Cappadona) University of Chicago Press, 1978, 1982 and 1985. This represents the lifework of the courageous and original Romanian-born scholar; the second is Joseph Campbell's *The Masks of God*, 4 vols, 1962 to 1968, Viking Press, New York, or Secker and Warburg, London (especially vols 2 and 3).

For a useful compendium of the views of great physicists on the relationship between science, humankind and the universe it is well worth examining *Quantum Questions*, edited by Ken Wilber, Shambala Publications, Boulder, Colorado, 1984. Therein the educated non-specialist reader will find an anthology of primary sources from such towering figures in the physical sciences as Heisenberg, Schrödinger, Einstein, De Broglie, Jeans, Planck, Pauli and Eddington. These should go a long way to dispel the journalistic fallacy that 'good' science (and scientists) must necessarily lean toward materialism and reductionism.

Finally, there are eighteen essays edited by David C. Lindberg and Ronald F. Numbers entitled *God and Nature: Historical Essays on the Encounter between Christianity and Science*, University of California Press, 1986. These show the unmistakable linkage between fundamentalist Christianity and fundamentalist/empiricist science and the thought processes and emotional style common to people in both camps.

Supplementary note. Since I wrote Chapter 4, The Rise and Decline of Intimacy, there has been a conservative counterattack against the widely accepted belief among social historians that the enclosed nuclear family is *not* normative throughout human history, but is largely a by-product of the Industrial Revolution. Dr Peter Laslett of Cambridge argues, with statistical backing, that the small enclosed family has *always* been with us, in some form. This view has been borrowed loosely by popularisers such as Ferdinand Mount to defend 'the family', as orthodox Christians still prefer to define it, against alleged 'Marxist' propaganda. I am certainly no Marxist. But I adhere to the well-documented mainstream view that the urban family (as we now know it) is a product of relatively recent influences from Puritan-Victorian and capitalist industrial sources.

INDEX